Appalach　**...ain Club**

River Guide

NEW HAMPSHIRE
VERMONT

Third Edition

APPALACHIAN MOUNTAIN CLUB
BOSTON

Contents

Preface

This edition of the *AMC River Guide: New Hampshire/Vermont* is the first since the heavy industrial pollution of the rivers ended. Paper mills either have closed or cleaned up their act, and many other industries that depended on the rivers for power and waste discharge have moved away. As a result, the rivers are significantly cleaner.

We sought in this revision to identify other human-impact changes to the rivers. Occasionally, dams wash out or a new bridge is built across a river. We have tried to provide current information about these changes, as well as access points. We did not focus on periodic, natural events in the rivers, such as beaver dams, blow-downs, and the like.

The mountainous terrain in these two states is outstanding whitewater country. You can find challenging runs on almost any river falling out of the White Mountains and Green Mountains. Plan your whitewater paddling trip in the spring, during the snowmelt runoff. Also, be sure to scout all your whitewater runs first.

The Northern Forest Canoe Trail passes through Vermont's Northeast Kingdom and northern New Hampshire. You can follow this watery pathway all the way from Old Forge, New York, to Fort Kent, Maine—more than 600 miles. Further details can be found within this volume.

Enjoy New England's mountain scenery and rivers. Spread the word that these rivers are clean and fun, and be safe while you're out there.

John Fiske

Acknowledgments

Thanks to all who helped revise this guide: Greg Lowell, Marcel Polak, Fred Pearson, John Wolfe, Sherwood Libby, Fred Westerburg, Peter Herman, Robin Edward Trudel, Adair Mulligan, Bill Schomberg, Ken Hasting, Nat Tripp, Faith Knapp, Vermont Paddlers Club, Skip Morris, and Roioli Schweicker.

Introduction

Every drop of water that falls in New Hampshire eventually flows southward to the Atlantic Ocean. Water from the north-western part of the state flows west to the Connecticut River. The northeastern part of the state drains eastward into the Androscoggin and Saco rivers and through Maine to the ocean. All of the south-central part of New Hampshire drains south with the Merrimack River. Only a small bit of the coastal-area rivers reach the ocean entirely through New Hampshire. Runoff on the highest mountain in the state, Mount Washington, may flow in three different ways: to the Saco, via the Ammonoosuc to the Connecticut, or via the Peabody River to the Androscoggin.

The drainage pattern in Vermont is more complicated. Surprisingly, the water to the eastern side of the Green Mountains does not all flow east to the Connecticut. Four rivers from the Champlain Watershed have pirated large drainage areas north to the Saint Lawrence River. In addition, the north-ern boundary of Vermont is arbitrary and was not drawn along a watershed, so another portion along the international boundary also drains north, into the Saint Francis River and on to the Saint Lawrence. Finally, a small area southwest of the Green Mountains flows to the Hudson River in New York.

The rivers in this book are arranged by watersheds, from north to south and west to east.

Safety

Although this book was prepared with care, no guidebook should be used on blind faith. It is a very helpful companion, along with a map, to have when you run a river, but it will not prevent every problem.

This book will not protect you from yourself. Managing a boat in current requires a degree of skill that depends on the nature of the river. Maneuvering with style and finesse is considerably different from just paddling hard. Sometimes paddling hard works, but the faster the current, the less effective it is. Be realistic about your abilities and do not underestimate the power and difficulty of a river. The Safety Code of American Whitewater is included in the appendix; it contains many good suggestions for safe boating.

This book will also not protect you from unexpected rapids or obstacles. Many permanent changes in rivers have taken place within the last few decades, and they often have occurred when dams were washed out. New England still has many old dams that could collapse. There is always the possibility of encountering temporary or seasonal obstructions. Snowmobile bridges and ice-dam nets have become noteworthy hazards on some small quickwater streams: they are low and often awash. They usually block a river even more effectively than a fallen tree.

Lastly, this book will not protect you from sudden changes in water level. A moderate spring or autumn rainfall will significantly affect a river with a large, mountainous watershed. In a matter of hours the river can rise several feet and become more difficult and hazardous. Unanticipated releases from dams can have the same effect.

Boating, as an activity, involves certain risks that can be minimized with the proper training, forethought, caution, and equipment.

Be Considerate of Landowners

Many put-ins, take-outs, and portages are open for public use. Others require that you cross private property. You will note that many landowners whose property borders popular canoeing rivers have posted their property against trespass. Paddlers can prevent additional closings by being thoughtful. Always ask permission of landowners and don't cross a property line without permission, don't damage vegetation, park cars out of the way so they don't block roads, pick up litter. Make your portage expeditiously and leave; don't hang around picnicking or making a disturbance.

Don't expect local residents to be responsible for rescuing you and your canoe or kayak. Dumping boats and getting them pinned on whitewater rivers happens to the best of us, and paddlers should prepare before launching by having suitable equipment, clothing, and a large enough group. Access to put-ins and take-outs is the right of a private landowner, and only the privilege of the user. Access is becoming limited on some rivers, so it is increasingly important to maintain good relations with property owners.

River Stewardship

Paddlers can get active in efforts to ensure that boat acces will be available in the future. Part of doing so involves accepting the resonsibilty of thinking of rivers as complex ecosystems serving the needs of many. Nothing guarantees that put-ins and take-outs that exist today will be around tomorrow. Paddlers should be aware of the issues that surround rivers. Water quality, wildlife habitat, driking water, dams, recreation, and land ownership all affect rivers and the paddling experience.

Fortunately many resources are available to paddlers interested in having a role in river stewardship. Local watershed coucils and river groups, conservation commissions, nonprofit recreation groups such as the Appalachian Mountain Club (www.outdoors.org), the American Canoe Association (www.acanet.org), and American Whitewater (www.americanwhitewater.org), and national river conservation groups like American Rivers (www. amrivers.org) are excellent resources for information on rivers and how to become a steward. By knowing all the facts about river issues, paddlers can be better advocates in protecting the rivers they love.

Using the River Guide

Organization

Each chapter begins with a list of the rivers described. The tributaries of each river are listed below it. The principal river is described first, then its tributaries in descending (downstream) order.

Format for River Descriptions

Each description starts with general information about the river as a whole. Longer rivers are then broken into sections that are of reasonable length for a paddling trip, mentioning unrunnable sections to be omitted while paddling that river. These sections are introduced by a boldfaced heading and, in most cases, a table that summarizes significant information about that segment. This table includes what kind of water the paddler can expect, the recommended water level for paddling that section and the season or conditions when that level is most likely to occur, what kind of scenery the river passes through, what maps to refer to, directions and distances for portages, and total distances to be covered, in miles. A new addition to the description is the date on which this information was verified by a volunteer river checker. It is recommended that you scout drops and other obstacles before running the section.

The tables codify the information that is usually required to plan trips rapidly. In the descriptive text that follows the tables, cumulative distances from the section's starting point are placed within parentheses.

Table Format

Starting Point–Ending Point	Total Miles
Description:	(Difficulty of the river in this segment)
Date checked:	(Last date that information was verified as being corect)
Navigable:	(Recommended water levels and seasons)
Scenery:	(What you will see from the boat)
Maps:	(U.S. Geological Survey quadrangles and other maps)
Portages:	(Where to, when to, and how far to carry)

Terminology: Difficulty of River

The following terms appear opposite the "Description" heading in the summary table and are used to describe the difficulty of the water to be paddled:

Lake The segment being described flows through a lake, or it is necessary to paddle across a lake to reach the beginning of a river.

Flatwater There is little or no current, and the river's surface is smooth and unbroken. Paddling upstream is easy.

Quickwater The river moves fast. Its surface is nearly smooth at high water levels, but is likely to be choppy at medium water levels and shallow at low water levels.

Marsh/swamp Vegetation often obstructs the river. Paddling may be slower than the distance alone would indicate.

Class Difficulty of rapids in a segment is rated according to American Whitewater classifications: I, II, III, or IV. See the appendix for a description of these classifications.

When two or more terms appear together opposite the "Description" heading in the summary table, the paddler should expect to encounter all of these conditions in that segment of river. When one of these terms describes water conditions throughout most of the segment, it appears in boldface type.

Judging the difficulty of rapids is subjective. It depends on the type of boat, on how well paddlers read the river, and on how skillfully they maneuver their boats.

The difficulty of rapids changes with the water level. A given stretch of rapids may become easier or harder to paddle when there is more water in the river. Water level affects different parts of the same river differently. As a general rule, more water washes out a river with a low gradient and small rocks, but it generates larger waves and more turbulence in a river that drops steeply through large rocks.

As water level rises, current picks up. Be aware of this. If the river is high and the air and water are cold, increase the rating by at least one—and possibly two—classes.

On small rivers, fallen trees present a greater hazard to paddlers than do rapids, especially since their location cannot be documented in advance. Barbed wire fences frequently cross rivers in rural areas and are hard to spot. Be alert and have your boat under control at all times.

Terminology: Water Levels

The following terms appear opposite the "Navigable" heading in the summary tables. They describe the water level recommended for paddling a particular segment. The dates and conditions most likely to produce the recommended water level follow in parentheses.

Low water There is a clearly defined shoreline below the bank. Small rocky rivers will be uncanoeable, but flatter stretches and rapids in large rivers will be navigable.

Medium water The river extends to the bank, and soft vegetation along the shore may be underwater. Marshy areas may be wet. Larger whitewater rivers, depending on the type of rapids, will be navigable at this water level, and dodging rocks will be the major entertainment.

High water The river is near the top of its defined bank, and alders along the shore may be underwater. This is an acceptable water level for small whitewater rivers.

Very high water Large trees or clumps of smaller ones have their roots in the water. Reaching shore may be difficult or impossible. This water level is recommended only for experts who are familiar with the particular river and its problems.

Flood The river overflows its banks and makes pillows on large trees. This stage is dangerous for everybody.

Levels lower than those recommended do not necessarily mean that the river is not runnable; a river for which high water is recommended may be traveled in medium water, but it is likely to be scratchy, and paddlers may have to wade down some sections.

Terminology: Scenery

The following terms are used in the tables to describe the territory through which the river flows:

Wild Long sections of semiwilderness, with no more than a few isolated camps and occasional road access. Dirt roads may parallel the river within sight or sound but only for short distances, and they do not noticeably alter the atmosphere of the trip. These roads may in fact be closed to the public or altogether impassable.

Forested Banks on both sides of the river look densely wooded, but there are good dirt and asphalt roads that follow along the river or are not far from it. These roads may frequently approach or cross the river. There may be farms and houses nearby, but not many of them are visible from the water.

Rural Farms are visible from the river, and some fields may extend down to the water.

Towns Small, isolated towns border the river. Aside from their effects on water quality, these towns have little impact on the trip.

Settled There are many houses or small buildings within sight or sound of the river.

Urban Multistoried buildings are visible. The shorelines are frequently unattractive.

Maps

Each chart includes pertinent topographic maps in 7.5-minute series unless followed by "15" to indicate that they are in 15-minute series.

Topographic maps may be ordered from map dealers or from the USGS itself at its website: www.ask.usgs.gov, by mail from: Map Distribution, USGS Map Sales, Box 25286, Federal Center, Bldg. 810, Boulder, CO 80225, or by phone at: 888-ASK-USGS (275-8747).

The Canada Map Office no longer distributes maps directly to the public. You can order Canadian National Topographical Survey (CNTS) maps through a map dealer; look in the Yellow Pages under "Maps."

DeLorme has expanded its Atlas & Gazetteer series to include many states around the country, including New Hampshire and Vermont. Contact DeLorme at www.delorme.com, or 207-846-7000.

Portages

The portages in each chart are unavoidable carries, like those at dams, waterfalls, and difficult sections usually not runnable because of insufficient water. In addition, some rapids are listed as portages if they are significantly more difficult than the rating for that segment of the river. Unlisted portages included lift-overs to pass fallen trees and low, temporary bridges. There may be additional carries around rapids that you do not wish to run. Portages that appear within parentheses are at the end of the river segment being described; only those who plan to paddle farther downriver must complete these portages.

Abbreviations

The following abbreviations are used in the summary tables:

ft	foot, feet
mi	mile, miles
yd	yard, yards
L	left
R	right
e	either
USGS	United States Geological Survey
CNTS	Canadian National Topographical Survey

Example: How to Read a Summary Table

Smithville➤ Brownville	3.75 mi
Description:	Class I–II
Date checked:	2000
Navigable:	High water (April to early May)
Scenery:	Forested
Map:	USGS Waitsfield
Portages:	1.5 mi L dam 15 yd
	2.0 mi L two ledges 100 yd

Smithville➤ Brownville The starting point for this imaginary segment is Smithville. The end point is Brownville.

3.75 mi The total distance to be covered is 3.75 miles.

Description: Class I–II Paddlers will encounter Class I and II whitewater on this segment. Most of the segment is Class II.

Date checked: 2000 The description was accurate in 2000.

Navigable: High water (April to early May) The river is

runnable at high water levels, which are most likely to occur during April and the first part of May.

Scenery: Forested Paddlers will pass between wooded banks, but access roads may exist in the woods, close to the river.

Map: USGS Waitsfield The topographic map for this segment is the U.S. Geological Survey Waitsfield 7.5-minute quadrangle.

Portages: **1.5 mi L dam 15 yd**
                  2.0 mi L two ledges 100 yd

Paddlers will have to carry their boats for about 15 yards around a dam about 13.5 miles from Smithville. The best route for the portage is on the left as you face downstream. There is another portage in 0.5 mile, 2.0 miles from the starting point at Smithville. The best route here is also on the left, and paddlers will have to carry their boats about 100 yards to avoid two ledges. The last portage is not the take-out point for the end of this section, however. If it were, it would appear in parentheses to indicate that only those wanting to continue downriver must complete that portage.

Security

Regrettably, crime has reached canoeing rivers. At put-ins for some popular rivers, close to 100 percent of the parked cars are burglarized. To discourage this, do not leave money, cameras, or other valuables in cars. The first place thieves look is in your bag of dry clothes; leave your wallet at home and take only the cash and cards that you will need; carry them in a waterproof folder in your pocket. If this is not possible (for example, on an extended trip), pay to park your car at a gas station or at a house.

Time

It's impossible to estimate time realistically for a paddling trip. Too many factors influence how long it will take. The water height affects the speed of the current. The boater may pursue paddling as an athletic endeavor or may prefer to float silently with the current, observing. A small, well-qualified party may scout nothing, while an instruction trip may scout everything.

Paddlers may spend time bailing out canoes, taking pictures, or negotiating blowdowns.

On a large river with the current and wind favorably behind, the miles whiz by. A paddler may take hours to travel a single mile on a small stream blocked with alder thickets and fallen trees. The same mile will require far less time when it is free of obstructions. It is good practice to select alternate end points for a trip, especially on an unfamiliar river.

River Levels in New England

The water-level information given in the summary tables for individual river levels include approximate dates, which are subject to wide variation from year to year. Some of the factors that influence water levels are discussed here.

Snow depth, temperature, rainfall, and transpiration are four seasonal factors that affect river levels. The farther south you get in New England, the less important the first two become, since snow is usually less deep and occasionally nonexistent. As the snow cover disappears, temperature becomes less important, although runoff is greater and swifter when the ground is frozen.

Once the leaves are out, surface runoff decreases substantially, because the plants use a great deal of water. Conversely, the fall foliage season invariably signals a rise in water levels. Significant rainfall in autumn is also more likely than it is in summer.

Terrain also must be considered. A river flowing from steep-sided hills and mountains will quickly collect the runoff from rainfall and melting snow. On the other hand, lakes, swamps, and gently rolling hills buffer the spring runoff, and the result is an extended canoeing season in spite of the weather. Knowledge of New England's topography will be as helpful to you as familiarity with its weather.

You also must take into account the nature of the river itself. If a river is flat, weather matters little as far as paddling is concerned. If the river is steep and full of rapids, then heavy snow, warm temperatures, and moderate rainfall may all be necessary to keep it runnable. Also, you must consider the size of the river. A large river will generally peak and ebb more gradually, so it will have a much longer season than a small stream.

Many of New England's rivers have just enough quickwater and easy rapids to make high or medium water necessary for good passage. In early March, rivers all over central and southern New England become runnable. Farther north, access to the water in early spring is hindered, first by snow and later by mud. Furthermore, ice shelves along the banks are a hazard in rapids and an inconvenience elsewhere.

If you wish to run rapids in early March, Connecticut is best. By late March the season for good Class II and Class III rapids is fading in that state, and you will probably be limited to some of the larger rivers. By May the rivers of northern New England which are fed by melting snow deposits in the high mountains are usually at optimal levels. Sometimes they are passable through Memorial Day, but there have been years when the season is over in late April.

Many of New England's rivers have gauges set up by the U.S. Geological Survey. Many USGS gauges have Internet links (see page xx for more information). This book contains occasional references to these gauges and other water level indicators, but comprehensive and detailed information about their use is not included.

River levels can vary tremendously from season to season, and unusually heavy rainfall can make any river passable at any time. If you do enough canoeing and kayaking, you will probably meet someone who will defend winter boating and will claim that the paddling season includes any sunny day when the temperature is above freezing.

Over a period of several years, a person who runs a lot of rivers develops a sense of river levels. Those who fish the ocean acquire an instinct for the tides, those who live off the land can almost smell the weather, and so it is with river people. After a while they get to know when a river runs and when it does not.

Water Releases

With many of New England's rivers passable for only a few weeks in the spring or after an unusually heavy rainfall, releases of water from dams can extend the paddling season in some localities. There are many dams on large New England rivers, but unless there are rapids below them, as is the case with the examples given, effects of releases may not be very noticeable.

The first type of release comes from dams used in connection with power generation. On the Pemigewasset River (Merrimack Watershed), a dam that supplies peaking power usually provides ample water for fine Class II boating weekdays throughout the season.

The second type of release is one scheduled solely for the benefit of paddlers. These are arranged by whitewater clubs, the Appalachian Mountain Club (AMC) among them. They take place on weekends during the spring, summer, and fall, and the dates can be obtained from the AMC (www.outdoors.org). The West River (Upper Connecticut Watershed) is one example.

The third type of release is the annual drawdown of lakes that are used primarily for summer recreation. These releases generally take place in the middle of fall and greatly augment the natural flow for that time of year. A drawdown often takes several weeks to complete. Rivers on which drawdowns provide ample water include the Mascoma River (Upper Connecticut Watershed), the Winnipesaukee River (Merrimack Watershed), and the Pine River and the West Branch (Saco Watershed). In New Hampshire many drawdowns are controlled by the Water Resources Board (603-271-3406), and late in the summer you can obtain a schedule from that agency.

Water releases also can provide an augmented flow on several other rivers in the area covered by this book.

Rentals

There are many places to rent canoes and kayaks in New England, and they are easy to find. Begin your search in the Yellow Pages under "Canoes." Check the Internet, also, by beginning a search with the name of the river you want to run.

Rivers Omitted from This Guide

Paddlers who would like to run a river that is not included in this guide and who are willing to report their findings may send a self-addressed stamped envelope to the AMC River Guide

Committee (5 Joy St., Boston, MA 02108) to receive whatever information is available for that river.

Northern Forest Canoe Trail

The Northern Forest Canoe Trail is a 740-mile waterway from Old Forge, New York to Fort Kent, Maine. The trail follows Native American travel routes, and now serves to encourage canoe/kayak travel in the Northern Forest regions of New York, Vermont, New Hampshire, and Maine.

Below is an outline of the route, from west to east. This is not sufficient information to make the trek (just enough to get you interested), but you can get detailed information from:

Northern Forest Canoe Trail
P.O. Box 572
Waitsfield, VT 05673
802-496-2285
www.northernforestcanoetrail.org

New York

Beginning at Old Forge, ascend the Moose River via the Fulton Lake Chain and portage to the Raquette River. Descend the Raquette and portage to the Saranec River. Descend the Saranec to Lake Champlain.

Vermont

Cross Lake Champlain and ascend the Missisquoi River to the North Branch of the Missisquoi River. Ascend the North Branch of the Missisquoi River to above Mansonville, Quebec. Portage to Lake Memphremagog. Paddle down Lake Memphremagog to Newport, Vermont. Portage to the Clyde River. Ascend the Clyde River and portage to the Nulhegan River. Descend the Nulhegan River to the Connecticut River.

New Hampshire

Descend the Connecticut River to the Upper Ammanoosuc River. Ascend the Upper Ammanoosuc River and portage to the Androscoggin River. Ascend the Androscoggin River to Lake Umbagog.

Maine

Portage the Rapid River to the Richardson, Mooselookmeguntic, and Rangeley Lakes. Portage to the South Branch of the Dead River. Descend the Dead River to Spencer Stream. Ascend Spencer Stream to Little Spencer Stream. Ascend Little Spencer Stream to Whipple Pond and portage to the Moose River. Descend the Moose River to the Penobscot River. Descend the Penobscot River to Chesuncook Lake. Cross Chesuncook Lake to Umbazooksus Lake and portage to the Allagash River. Descend the Allagash (Wilderness Waterway) to the St. John River. Descend the St. John River to the mouth of the Fish River at Fort Kent.

USGS Gauges in New Hampshire and Vermont

The U.S. Geological Survey maintains gauges in many locations throughout the region. Many of these gauges transmit data that is posted on the Web at: http://bowdnhbow.er.usgs.gov/rt-cgi/gen_tbl_pg. The list below is provided for interest only.

On many rivers you will find hand-painted gauges—on bridge abutments, for example. These gauges are meaningless except if: you know and are familiar with the river in many water levels or you were the one who painted the gauge in the first place. Never substitute a gauge reading for your own common-sense river-reading judgment, particularly when you may not be familiar with the river.

It is the belief of the editors that gauges are of secondary value to river runners, and this river guide only inconsistently mentions them.

Androscoggin River Basin

Diamond River near Wentworth, NH

Androscoggin River at Errol, NH

Androscoggin River near Gorham, NH

Saco River Basin

Saco River near Conway, NH

Bearcamp River near Tamworth, NH

Piscataqua River Basin

Salmon Falls River at Milton, NH

Oyster River near Durham, NH

Lamprey River near Newmarket, NH

Exeter River near Brentwood, NH

Merrimack River Basin

East Branch of the Pemigewasset River at Lincoln, NH

Pemigewasset River at Woodstock, NH

Baker River near Rumney, NH

Pemigewasset River at Plymouth, NH

Smith River near Bristol, NH

Poorfarm Brook near Gilford, NH

Shannon Brook near Moultonboro, NH

Lake Winnipesaukee at Weirs Beach, NH

Winnipesaukee River at Tilton, NH

Merrimack River at Franklin, NH

Contoocook River at Peterborough, NH

Nubanusit Brook near Peterborough, NH

Contoocook River near Henniker, NH

Contoocook River at West Hopkinton, NH

Warner River at Davisville, NH

Blackwater River near Webster, NH

Piscataquog River near Weare, NH

Piscataquog River near Goffstown, NH

Merrimack River near Goffs Falls, NH

Souhegan River at Merrimack, NH

Beaver Brook at North Pelham, NH

Spicket River at North Salem, NH

Spicket River near Methuen, MA

Connecticut River Basin

Connecticut River near Pittsburg, NH

Mohawk River near Colebrook, NH

Connecticut River at North Stratford, NH

Upper Ammonoosuc River near Groveton, NH

Connecticut River near Dalton, NH

East Branch of the Passumpsic River near East Haven,VT

Moose River at Victory, VT

Pope Brook near North Danville, VT

Sleepers River near St. Johnsbury, VT

Passumpsic River at Passumpsic, VT

Ammonoosuc River at Bethlehem, NH

Connecticut River at Wells River, VT

Wells River at Wells River, VT

East Orange Branch at East Orange, VT

Ompompanoosuc River at Union, VT

Ayers Brook at Randolph, VT

White River at West Hartford, VT

Connecticut River at West Lebanon, NH

Mascoma River at West Canaan, NH

Mascoma River at Mascoma, NH

Ottauquechee River near West Bridgewater, VT

Ottauquechee River at North Hartland, VT

Sugar River at West Claremont, NH

Black River at North Springfield, VT

Williams River near Rockingham, VT

Connecticut River at North Walpole, NH

West River near Townsend, VT

Ashuelot River below Surry Dam, Keene, NH

Otter Brook below Otter Dam, Keene, NH

Ashuelot River at West Swanzey, NH

Ashuelot River at Hinsdale, NH

Hudson River Basin

Walloomsac River near North Bennington, VT

St. Lawrence River Basin

Poultney River below Fair Haven, VT

Otter Creek at Center Rutland, VT

Otter Creek at Middlebury, VT

New Haven River near Middlebury, VT

Little Otter Creek at Ferrisburg, VT

Laplatte River at Shelburne Falls, VT

Englesby Brook at Burlington, VT

Dog River at Northfield Falls, VT

Mad River near Moretown, VT

Little River near Waterbury, VT

Winooski River near Essex Junction, VT

Lamoille River at Johnson, VT

Lamoille River at East Georgia, VT

Missisquoi River near North Troy, VT

Missisquoi River near East Berkshire, VT

Missisquoi River at Swanton, VT

Lake Champlain at Burlington, VT

Black River at Coventry, VT

Clyde River at Newport, VT

Suggested Rivers with Flatwater and Quickwater Canoeing

State(s)	Miles	Portages	Lake	Flatwater	Quickwater	Class I rapids	Short, easy class II rapids	Passable, at all levels	Scratchy sections in lower water
VT	34.25	4[1]	●		●	●			●
VT	27.75	1		●	●				●
VT	21.5	3		●	●		●		●
VT	32.25			●	●			●	
VT	38.25	2		●	●		●	●	
VT	9.25			●				●	
NH	42.25	3		●	●				●
NH	31		●	●	●		●		●
NH	12	1		●		●			●
NH	10.25			●	●			●	
NH, ME	49.5	1		●	●		●	●	

Suggested Rivers with Easy Rapids

[1] includes one Class II rapid

State(s)	Miles	Portage(s)	Short, intermittent rapids	Several miles of continuous rapids	Mostly continuous rapids	Flatwater	Quickwater	Class I	Class II	Class III rapids
VT, NY	30.5	1	●				●	●	●	●	
NH, VT	33.25	1	●				●	●		●	
NH	4				●	●			●	1
NH	5.25				●				●	
NH	2.75				●				●	1
NH	9.75				●		●		●	
VT	10.5			●			●		●	2
VT	25.5			●			●		●	
NH	6.75	2			●				●	
NH	19		●				●		●	
NH	11.75	2[1]	●			●	●		●	1
NH	22.5			●			●		●	3
ME	20.75	1		●		●	●		●	1
NH	13					●	●		●	1

Suggested Whitewater Runs
of Class III Difficulty

[1] Londonderry Rapids

[2] includes two Class III–IV rapids

	State	Miles	Portage(s)	Difficult Class IV rapids	Water releases in summer or fall
....	NH	2.75			
....	NH	8.25	1	2	
....	NH	5.5	1	1	•
....	NH	4.75			
....	VT	7	1^2	1^1	
....	NH	3.5			
....	NH	3.75	3^2	2	

Suggested Whitewater Runs
of Class IV Difficulty

[1] gauge reading of 8.0 or higher

[2] gauge reading over 1 foot at Kancamagus Highway

	State	Miles	Portages	Covered boats only
......	NH	4.5		
......	NH	3		•
......	NH	4		•
......	NH	3.25		
......	VT	3.5		•
......	NH	3		•[1]
......	NH	12		
......	NH	6	1	•[2]
......	NH	3		
......	NH	3.75		
......	NH	2.5		
......	NH	4		•

Chapter 1
Memphremagog Watershed

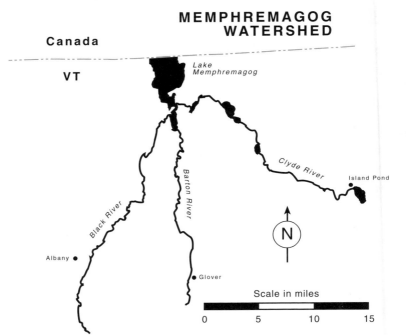

MEMPHREMAGOG WATERSHED

Canada

VT

Lake Memphremagog

Clyde River

Island Pond

Barton River

Black River

Albany

N

Glover

Scale in miles

0   5   10   15

A small area in the extreme northeast central part of Vermont drains north through Lake Memphremagog and the Magog River in Quebec to the Saint Francis River and from there to the Saint Lawrence River at Lake Saint Peter. The three rivers described here flow northward through extensive sections of quickwater and easy rapids, broken intermittently by steep ledges. The rural Vermont seen from the banks is pleasant and the towns small. The quickwater parts can often be run late in the season and after summer rains.

All water in Vermont eventually flows into five drainage basins. Three of these basins flow into rivers; the other two empty into Lakes Champlain and Memphremagog. Together, these two lakes drain more than half the land area of Vermont, their watersheds reaching from Island Pond in the Northeast Kingdom to the headwaters of the Mettawee River in Bennington County.

Black River VT

This more northerly of the two Black rivers in Vermont rises in Craftsbury and trickles south to meet the outlet of Eligo Pond, where it reverses course and flows north and northeast to Lake Memphremagog.

Dams, waterfalls, and ledges divide it into three distinct sections. The middle, from Irasburg to Coventry, can be run only in high water, since it is wide, with rocky rapids. The upper and lower parts can be run almost any time. Although not far from the road, the banks are forested and unsettled, and wildlife is abundant.

Eligo Pond ➤ Albany   12.0 mi

From the bridge a mile north of Eligo Pond, the first 1.5 miles to the second bridge are very winding and overgrown. The 2.0 miles to the next bridge are also tortuous. From the third bridge to Albany the paddling improves, as does the size of the river, which is fed by many brooks. Fallen trees can be a problem.

Albany ➤ Irasburg   11.5 mi

Description:	Flatwater, quickwater
Date checked:	2001
Navigable:	Almost any time (wet summer)
Scenery:	Forested, rural
Maps:	USGS Hardwick 15, Irasburg 15

Put in at the northern (downstream) bridge in Albany. Bushes overhang the narrow, deep brook from both sides as it meanders, crosses under VT 14 (5.5 miles), circles to the left of the valley past a log crib, and runs under three farm bridges and a number of snowmobile bridges to another VT 14/58 bridge, which is a good place to take out.

Irasburg Portage   1.5 mi

In 0.25 mile there is another possible access on the left above the Black River Sawmill Dam. Ledges continue below the mill, as the river crosses twice under the dirt road alongside and approaches VT 58.

Irasburg ➤ Coventry (VT 14 bridge)   4.0 mi

Description: Class I–II
Date checked: 2001
Navigable: High water (early May)
Scenery: Rural, forested
Maps: USGS Irasburg 15

Put in from a dirt road on the right bank below the last ledge where the river swings away from VT 58. A mile downstream is an interesting covered bridge. The Class II rapids are continuous and pleasant, and the river is wide and shallow. Take out at the next VT 14 bridge.

VT 14 bridge ➤ Coventry   3.0 mi

The river flows smoothly through farm country and runs under a covered bridge to an iron bridge with an eight-foot waterfall below it, which can be portaged on the right. Several minor ledges and riffles speed the river around a big loop to the north. At the base of the loop is another eight-foot waterfall in a gorge just above Coventry. Riffles continue 0.25 mile as the valley opens out.

Coventry ➤ Lake Memphremagog   7.5 mi

Description: Flatwater, quickwater
Date checked: 2001
Navigable: Spring, summer, fall
Scenery: Forested
Maps: USGS Memphremagog 15

The river is shallow in low water near a small park off US 5, but it deepens rapidly. For the first few miles, the river is smaller and more obstructed by trees. An alternate start is possible at several places downstream, including the bridges at US 5 (0.75 mile) or at a side road (1.25 miles). Much of the remaining distance is deadwater, as the river meanders through the Black River Wildlife Management Area. The dark-colored water shows how the river got its name. Past a final bridge (6.5 miles) the river wanders through a low-lying delta and eventually emerges from a long neck of land into the South Arm of Lake Memphremagog. Deep in a cove 0.5 mile to the left is a launching ramp, which is accessible from a side road.

Barton River VT

The Barton River flows north into Lake Memphremagog. The valley through which it flows is one of the main routes to Canada, and it is followed all the way by a railroad and part of the way by major highways, including I-91.

Glover ➤ Orleans	9.25 mi
Description:	Quickwater, Class I–II
Date checked:	2001
Navigable:	High water (spring)
Scenery:	Rural, towns
Maps:	USGS Lydonville 15, Memphremagog 15
Portages:	4.0 mi L waterfall 0.25–0.5 mi
	8.75 mi dam in Orleans

Begin on VT 16 at the first bridge north of Glover. The river there is small but navigable. The first 2.25 miles to the VT 16 bridge are Class I.

Barton is located on a broad floodplain, and the river is flat. Two and a half miles north of Barton there is a section of Class III-IV rapids that requires scouting. Stop just before the US 5 bridge (3.75 miles). **Caution!** Under no circumstances go under the second railroad bridge (4.0 miles) at the end of the rapid, because there is an eight-foot drop. Portage part or all of this rapid on the left along US 5 and put in at the next bridge.

A half-mile below the second US 5 bridge (4.25 miles) there is a low, private bridge that may block the stream in high water. In the next 0.5 mile to the third US 5 bridge there are several Class II–III drops for which scouting is recommended. The last 3.75 miles of winding river to the first bridge in Orleans are Class I.

A take-out is recommended at the first bridge (8.5 miles), but if you are continuing through town, there is a dam. There is a bridge across the river where the Willoughby River enters on the right (9.25 miles).

Orleans ➤ Newport   12.5 mi

Description:	Lake, flatwater, Class I
Date checked:	2001
Navigable:	Passable at most water levels
Scenery:	Forested
Maps:	USGS Memphremagog 15

From the bridge at the confluence of the Barton and Willoughby rivers just north of Orleans, there are no obstructions to Lake Memphremagog. The river meanders across a broad floodplain between low mills and in 10.0 miles reaches South Bay. From there it is 2.5 miles to the US 5 bridge (12.5 miles) in Newport.

Clyde River vt

The Clyde River flows roughly northwest from Island Pond to Newport on Lake Memphremagog. It offers three runnable sections: the first two meander through farmland and small towns, the third is a Class II run that flows away from the road between beautiful cedar-lined banks.

Island Pond ➤ Pensioner Pond   15.0 mi

Description:	Flatwater, quickwater
Date checked:	2001
Navigable:	High or medium water (spring or after heavy rains)
Scenery:	Forested, rural, town
Maps:	USGS Island Pond, Memphremagog 15

In this first section there are lovely marshes, cedar swamps, and farmland. Trees droop their branches, and occasionally their trunks, as well, into the river. Good boat control is required, and in low water this section may not be passable.

The first 2.5 miles beginning at Island Pond are very obstructed with snowmobile bridges, fallen trees, rotten logs, and debris. There is a short Class II rapid.

Put in (2.5 miles) near the VT 105/114 junction. A hundred yards or so northeast along VT 105/114 there are places to pull off the road, and the river is just beyond some bushes. You can also put in just northwest of the same junction, on VT 105.

In 0.5 mile the river goes through a culvert on a side road from which there is good access. Soon you enter a marsh where there is little current and many side channels. There are good views of the small hills surrounding the river, but there is very little solid shoreline to the VT 105 bridge.

Past the VT 105 bridge (7.5 miles) the river flows first through a cedar swamp, where there is likely to be a snowmobile bridge to lift over, and then it goes through farmland to the next bridge on a side road in East Charleston (8.5 miles). There is more swamp and farmland, and another bridge, in the remaining 6.0 miles to Pensioner Pond (14.5 miles).

It is 0.5 mile across Pensioner Pond to a fishing access 15.0 miles at the far end on the right. It cannot be seen from a distance but is to the right of the obvious sandy beach.

Pensioner Pond ➤ West Charlestown   2.5 mi

In the gorge beyond the VT 105 bridge there is an old dam. Less than a mile farther, at the far end of Lubber Lake, there is a second dam, which diverts water to a power station. Below the power station the river drops over ledges.

West Charlestown ➤ Salem Pond   3.25 mi

Description:	Pond, quickwater, Class I–II
Date checked:	2001
Navigable:	Medium water (spring or after rain)
Scenery:	Forested, rural
Maps:	USGS Memphremagog 15

Start at the covered bridge in West Charleston. The Class II rapids diminish over the first 0.5 mile, but the river runs swiftly all the way to Little Salem Pond. A channel on the right passes the shallow area in the center. Access is at a bridge over the outlet from Little Salem Pond into the thoroughfare.

Salem Pond ➤ Clyde Pond   6.5 mi
Description: Pond, Class I–II
Date checked: 2001
Navigable: High to medium water (May)
Scenery: Forested, wild
Maps: USGS Memphremagog 15

The thoroughfare below the bridge leads in 0.10 mile from Little Salem Pond into Salem Pond, with a further 1.75-mile stretch across the pond. There is no public access at the far end.

Except for the VT 105 bridge 3.0 miles down the rapids, the river stays away from the road and habitations. Its steep banks are covered with evergreens, so the river is often in shadow. Class II rapids start almost immediately and continue most of the way, the most difficult section being in the vicinity of the bridge. Clyde Pond is down another 2.75 miles of rapids. The outlet is a mile down on the northwest side, where there is a dam and a road.

Clyde Pond ➤ Lake Memphremagog   2.0 mi

Many paddlers will probably elect to end the trip at the Clyde Pond outlet, in view of the carries and steep running involved in the last 2.0 miles to Newport. With some care and finesse, however, it is possible to negotiate this section. Take out near the end of the dam. Carry past the house on the right, cross the road, and continue down a dirt road 0.75 mile. If there is sufficient water, you may be able to put in at the bridge between the two powerhouses and shorten this carry. Otherwise put in again at the bridge below the lower powerhouse for the final mile to Lake Memphremagog at Newport.

Chapter 2
Champlain Watershed

CHAMPLAIN WATERSHED

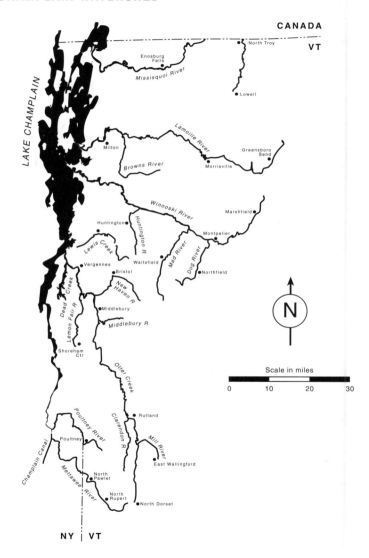

The rivers of the Champlain Watershed are longer and bigger than the distance of 25 miles from the main ridge of the Green Mountains would lead one to expect. Four of them have successfully pirated water from the east side of the range, making them some of the largest rivers in the area. The large watershed makes many miles of river runnable even in times of low water. Upper reaches and tributaries offer whitewater during the spring runoff.

Missisquoi River VT, PQ

The Missisquoi River flows westward across the top of Vermont, with a loop into Quebec, to Lake Champlain. Its course is through a beautiful valley, with views of hills and mountains. The Missisquoi was an important route to the Native Americans, since most of the drop is in the falls, making it easier to paddle than the Lamoille.

Many of the drops have now been harnessed for power. Roads are convenient but not unduly noticeable from the river. The entire length can be run in low water.

North Troy ➤ East Richford	16.0 mi
Description:	Flatwater, quickwater
Date checked:	2002
Navigable:	Passable at most water levels
Scenery:	Rural
Maps:	USGS Irasburg 15, Jay Peak 15
	CNTS Memphremagog 31 H/1, Sutton 31 H/2
Campsite:	6.0 mi R campground

This loop of the Missisquoi circles through Quebec as it passes through the main ridge of the Green Mountains. It is an enjoyable and popular paddle. Fallen trees may be a problem.

Locals advise launching in Highwater, Quebec. Report to Canadian Customs at the border on VT 105A before launching your canoe below the dam at North Troy. The river meanders leisurely and extensively to Highwater, Quebec (5.75 miles), where there is a campground on the right shore. Below that point the river is occasionally in sight of the road as it passes through farming country. Land on the left at the bridge in East Richford to report to U.S. Customs.

East Richford ➤ Enosburg Falls	19.0 mi
Description:	Flatwater, quickwater, Class I–II
Date checked:	2001
Navigable:	High or medium water (spring)
	Low water, some wading required
	above Richford
Scenery:	Forested, rural, towns
Maps:	USGS Jay Peak 15, Enosburg Falls 15
Portages:	5.25 mi L Class III rapids in Richford—
	take out above factory
	14.0 mi L old dam in Samsonville
	(18.5 mi L dam at Enosburg Falls 0.5 mi)

The river here consists mostly of pleasant riffles around islands, and much of it is close to the road. Two sections of Class II and III rapids, one in Richford and the other 2.25 miles below East Berkshire, should be avoided by inexperienced paddlers.

In the 5.25 miles to Richford there are riffles that may require some wading in low water. Below a railroad bridge (4.5 miles) the river approaches Richford.

Rapids begin just below a factory (5.25 miles) on the left, and just above another bridge the river becomes confined within retaining walls where it drops over ledges near an old dam site. The most difficult ledge, a Class III pitch, is below the bridge.

From Richford (6.0 miles) the river is mostly quickwater to the washed-out dam at Samsonville (14.0 miles). Line the top half of the rapids on the left, and run the rest. There is 0.25 mile of Class II ledges below.

Between Samsonville and Enosburg Falls the river is mostly smoothwater. The best way around the dam at Enosburg Falls is to take out on the left under the first bridge (18.5 miles). Walk up to the road along the river and follow it downstream past the second bridge about 0.25 mile to a field with a gate. Go through the gate and down to the river (19.0 miles) to put in.

Enosburg Falls ➤ Highgate Falls   18.5 mi

Description:	Flatwater, quickwater, Class I–II
Date checked:	2001
Navigable:	Passable at most water levels
Scenery:	Forested, rural
Maps:	USGS Enosburg Falls 15, Highgate Center
	10.5 mi L dam at Sheldon Springs 0.5 mi
	17.0 mi R ledge in Spring Rapid
	(18.25 mi L dam at Highgate Falls 0.25 mi)

Although largely quickwater, this section contains several sets of rapids. Below Sheldon Springs much of it is wild and away from the road.

From below the dam at Enosburg Falls there are 5.5 miles of quickwater to the North Sheldon bridge. Just around the bend, about 200 yards below the dam, there are 0.3 miles of ledgy rapids with lots of nasty rocks, not runnable or even linable with a loaded canoe at low water.

There is an easy half-mile portage around all this. Take out on the left at the "Danger Dam" sign, just above the bridge. Walk 30 yards to the road, cross the bridge and keep going straight on Saint Albans Street for 0.4 mile. At the far corner of a small, square brick building on the left there is a vehicle barrier, but an open gate for pedestrians and portagers. Turn left here, walk 20 yards across the parking lot and put in where a small creek enters the river.

At Sheldon Springs (10.5 miles) take out on the left above the bridge and carry down the road past the mill on the right. Continue along the road to a crossroads and turn right. At a point 150 yards beyond a gully, leave the road, follow the edge of the woods for 150 yards, and enter the woods at the birches below the transformer station, heading down to the river (11.0 miles) below the impassable cascade.

Water releases can now be made available for expert paddlers through Boise Cascade, owners of the hydropower dam. For more information, call Ray Gonda at 802-862-6164.

Below Sheldon Springs there is quickwater for 3.75 miles through woods to East Highgate (14.25 miles). Ledges start when the bridge is in sight. The abutments of an old dam are just below that bridge, and ledges of approximately Class II continue for 0.5 mile below it.

After East Highgate the river leaves the road again and flows through lovely woods. After a few miles there is a ledge that can be run, but just below it is another, 5-feet high (17.0 miles) that can be portaged on the right, but it is most easily lined on the left. This section is called Sheldon Springs Rapid because of an old mineral spring on the hill above.

In another mile the dam at Highgate Falls (18.25 miles) stands just above the old bridge. Carry on the left for 0.25 mile to reach the river again (18.5 miles).

Highgate Falls ➤ Lake Champlain   14.0 mi

Description:	Flatwater, quickwater
Date checked:	2001
Navigable:	Passable at all water levels
Scenery:	Forested, rural, town
Maps:	USGS Highgate Center, East Alburg
Portage:	6.5 mi R dam at Swanton

There are no difficulties in this section except at a dam at Swanton, and the river is mostly away from the road. Naturalists will enjoy the last 5.25 miles through the Missisquoi National Wildlife Refuge.

From Highgate Falls to Swanton there are 6.5 miles of slow current, and in that distance you pass under I-89, US 7 (3.5 miles), and an abandoned, covered railroad bridge (4.25 miles).

Below Swanton (6.5 miles) the river is flat. In 2.25 miles you enter the Missisquoi National Wildlife Refuge at the entrance to Dead Creek (8.75 miles), which branches off to the right and leads in 2.5 miles to Lake Champlain. The mouth of the Missisquoi has a number of islands in its delta. Once you reach Lake Champlain (14.0 miles), you can take out at a marina to the southwest, or you can paddle to the southeast and take out at Highgate Springs (6.25 miles).

Lamoille River ᴠᴛ

The Lamoille River rises in Horse Pond north of Greensboro Bend and flows for more than eighty miles westward across northern Vermont to Lake Champlain, entering the latter north of Burlington. It was discovered by Samuel de Champlain in 1609 and put on his map as "La Mouette," the French word for gull. Either Champlain or a later engraver evidently forgot to cross his t's for it eventually became "lamoille," a meaningless but melodious name.

The river once originated a mile father north at Long Pond, which prior to June 6, 1810, was a mile and a half long and a half-mile wide. On that day about sixty people went to the pond to open an outlet to the north so that the mills on the Barton River would receive an additional supply of water. A small channel was excavated, and the water started running.

The northern barrier of the pond consisted entirely of quicksand, except for an encrustment of clay next to the water. The quicksand was washed out, and the unsupported clay broke away. The whole pond discharged to the north within fifteen minutes. The deluge advanced like a 60-foot wall of water, sweeping along livestock, barns, houses, and mills for a distance of 10 miles. A rock, estimated to weigh 100 tons, was moved half a mile. Nothing remains of the pond but its bottom, a meadow and swampy area off VT 16 called Runaway Pond, which is now in the southern headwaters of the Barton River.

Greensboro Pond ➤ Hardwick		8.5 mi
Description:	Quickwater, Class I–III	
Date checked:	2001	
Navigable:	High water (April to early May)	
Scenery:	Forested, rural, towns	
Maps:	USGS Hardwick 15	
Portage:	4.0 mi L ledges in East Hardwick	

A readable gauge is now located under the bridge at the take-out, along Wolcott Street, VT 15. The gauge is on granite on the right and is visible from the street. It runs from 3 feet and up. Three and a half feet is runnable, 4–4.5 feet is a Class III exciting run.

The town of Hardwick, after several serious ice jams, has installed granite pillars to hold back the ice. These tire booms are removed as soon as the ice is gone. They are located just above a motel, at approximately mile 8.0.

Begin 7.0 miles below the outlet of Horse Pond in Greensboro Bend at the iron bridge just off VT 16. The river at that point is about 20 feet across and quiet, but it is fast, and in the 4.0 miles to East Hardwick the difficulty reaches Class III. This is a nice section that has a few sharp bends to make it interesting. Close to the road about halfway down there is a pitch that must be run on the left side because of a 4-foot drop. With caution it can be done easily.

Upon entering East Hardwick there is stillwater and the roar of some beautiful ledge falls that can be portaged on the left, a short carry between some houses, across a road, and down a large path to the river. There is a bridge (4.0 miles) going over the beginning of the falls.

The trip from East Hardwick is a beautiful 4.5 mile Class I–III run with some stillwater breathers. There are some ledges and rocks in this section that make the rapids exciting. At Hardwick, open canoes without proper flotation have to run on the right all the way to the second bridge (8.5 miles), where the gauge is located and where there is a good parking area for take-out.

Hardwick ➤ Jackson Bridge   1.5 mi

The river soon flows into Hardwick Lake, a long slim body of water largely in the valley of Alder Creek, a tributary to the north. The dam is at the southwest end, above the bridge. One can start in Hardwick off VT 12B on Alder Creek at the north end of Hardwick Lake and enjoy a pleasant 2.0-mile paddle down this scenic lake. Access to Hardwick Lake is also possible on Alder Creek, 2 miles north on VT 12B.

Jackson Bridge ➤ Pottersville   5.0 mi
Description: Quickwater, Class I
Date checked: 2001
Navigable: Medium water (wet summers)

Scenery:	Rural, forested
Maps:	USGS Hardwick 15
Portage:	(4.5 mi L dam in Pottersville 150 yd)

The river starts again at Jackson Bridge (VT 15) at the dam at the foot of the lake. The Lamoille is still small here and flows swiftly through woods and farmland. At high water the rocks will be mostly covered, and at low water there will be more rock dodging.

The most notable landmark is the covered railroad bridge (3.5 miles) with a small park to the right. This is the first ice boom location (see Greensboro Pond ➤ Harwick). Beyond the VT 15 bridge (4.0 miles) there is a short rapid to the backwater from the dam. Take out on the left above the dam, where a heavy-duty vehicle may be driven.

Pottersville ➤ Wolcott   1.25 mi

The ledges below the dam, which can be run by the right boat at the right water level, gradually decrease in difficulty over the next 0.25 mile. Another steep drop at a washed-out dam lies above and below the VT 15 bridge (0.75 mile). There is yet another ledge behind the store in Wolcott just below the bridge. All of these obstacles should be portaged individually on the left, or the whole distance can be portaged by car.

Wolcott ➤ Morrisville   10.25 mi

Description:	Flatwater, quickwater, Class I
Date checked:	2001
Navigable:	Medium water (wet summers)
Scenery:	Rural, forested, towns
Maps:	USGS Hardwick 15, Hyde Park 15
Portage:	(10.25 mi L dam in Morrisville 325 yd)

To put in, ask for and obtain permission to cross private property in Wolcott. A mile below town on the right bank there is a barn with an octagonal cupola. The river flows under many small farm bridges and some railroad bridges. The VT 15A bridge (7.75 miles) offers good access. Below it the current gradually slows as the river approaches the power dam below the next bridge, VT 100. Take out as close to the red building at the left end of the dam as safety permits. Carry down the road, past the end of the bridge, 250 yards to the transformer station, then make a sharp reverse turn to the right. Proceed 75 yards to the river and beautiful Lake Lamoille.

Morrisville ➤ Johnson	9.75 mi
Description:	Lake, quickwater, Class I
Date checked:	2001
Navigable:	Passable at most water levels
Scenery:	Forested, rural
Maps:	USGS Hyde Park 15
Portage:	1.25 mi L Cady's Falls Dam 100 yd
	9.25 mi L Dog's Head and Sloping Falls 350 yd

Put in below the dam at Morrisville at the mouth of Potash Brook. At first there is a pleasant paddle on Lake Lamoille, the backwater from Cady's Falls Dam (1.25 miles). Carry around the dam on the left for 100 yards to the main road. Follow the road across the bridge, turn left, and follow a road to an open field where a put-in is possible. This makes for an easy carry around the dam and ledges.

After Cady's Falls Dam (1.25 miles) there is a pleasant, 8.0-mile paddle through meadows to Dog's Head Falls, a dangerous spot that can be recognized easily by a gravel pit on the right bank. Take out on the left and carry 350 yards around both Dog's Head and Sloping Falls, two sharp drops that are separated by a pool. **Caution!** A lot of mishaps have occurred at Sloping Falls. Avoid it.

One quarter-mile below the two falls you reach the Johnson bridge (9.75 miles).

Johnson ➤ Fairfax Falls	24.5 mi
Description:	Quickwater, Class I
Date checked:	2001
Navigable:	Passable at most water levels
Scenery:	Rural, towns
Maps:	USGS Hyde Park 15, Jeffersonville, Gilson Mountain

Portage:	2.75 mi L ledge below VT 15 (may be runnable)
	3.25 mi Ithiel Falls (may be runnable)
	(24.25 mi L dam at Fairfax Falls 0.25 mi)

This is a pleasant paddle through delightful Vermont countryside. The Long Trail crosses the VT 15 bridge; just beyond there the river cuts through the Green Mountains. Farther on there are splendid views looking back to the east toward Vermont's highest mountains.

Put in 0.25 mile above the Johnson bridge on the west side of the river. Immediately below it, the Gihon River enters on the right. About 0.25 mile below the VT 15 bridge (2.5 miles) there is a ledge constriction with a 100-yard rapid going through it. This pitch can cause trouble at low water, and it can be up to Class IV in high water. About 0.5 mile farther is Ithiel Falls, which is also about 100 yards long and up to Class IV in high water. Both rapids should be scouted before running for the first time. Ithiel Falls was blasted out after the 1927 flood backed up water into Johnson Village.

Immediately below Ithiel Falls there are huge and beautiful granite islands, which make intricate channels that require alert paddling. The best channel is to the left. A road follows this whole stretch along the northern bank.

The river passes the VT 108 (11.5 miles) and the VT 15 bridges (12.0 miles) in Jeffersonville. Then it meanders through farmland for 12.25 miles to the bridge at Fairfax Falls (24.25 miles). Take out on the left at the bridge and portage around the dam to the river below (24.5 miles).

Fairfax Falls ➤ Milton		9.75 mi
Description:	Lake, quickwater, Class I–III	
Date checked:	2001	
Navigable:	Passable at all water levels	
Scenery:	Rural	
Maps:	USGS Gilson Mountain, Milton	
Portage:	9.25 mi R first dam in Milton	
	9.5 mi L second dam in Milton	

The upper part of this section is an interesting series of rapids away from the road, and the remainder is flatwater through Arrowhead Mountain Lake.

Quickwater extends past the VT 104 bridge at Fairfax (1.5 miles) to a set of rapids that begins as the river bends to the left (3.0 miles). These rapids range from Class I to Class III, and they extend nearly continuously for 2.5 miles.

At the beginning of these rapids, rocks appear in the streambed and increase in density over the next 0.25 mile with a corresponding increase in the velocity of the flow. The main current at this section is Class I, follows the right bank about 100 yards and leads into Two Islands Rapids.

Two channels begin in another 100 yards. Very large rocks at the right bank signal a 2-foot and 3-foot drop, which are best run with care through the right channel. Two Islands Rapids are Class III in medium water, and at high water the whole set of rapids is more difficult because the rocks create big eddies.

Class I rapids (lots of waves during medium water flows) continue to another 3.75-mile set of rapids that culminates at Five Chutes, a ledge that extends across the river. Use caution in high water. Take out above the gauging station on the right to scout. Lots of unpredictable eddies and holes form toward river left. In another 0.5 mile you reach the East Georgia bridge (6.0 miles).

Arrowhead Mountain Lake is 3.25 miles long and shaped like a monkey wrench. Paddle west and then south to Milton (9.25 miles).

Milton ➤ Lake Champlain		8.25 mi
Description:	Flatwater, quickwater, Class I	
Date checked:	2001	
Navigable:	Passable at all water levels	
Scenery:	Forested, rural, town	
Maps:	USGS Milton, Georgia Plains, Fort Ethan Allen	
Portage:	2.75 mi L Peterson Dam	

Begin at the Milton hydroelectric station. Ask for and obtain permission to access the river on location and notify the dam operator before running below the tailrace. It is 1.0 mile to the I-89 bridge where the backwater of Peterson Dam begins. The remaining 1.75 miles is very isolated and scenic. Be careful in approaching the dam, and take out on the left bank past the last large ledge outcrop. It is best to portage along the power station access road to the town road unless you wish to run the 100 yards of rapids immediately below the dam.

The remaining 5.25 miles lead past West Milton (3.25 miles) and the US 2 bridge (6.25 miles), and through a wildlife refuge to Lake Champlain (8.25 miles). There is a large island at the mouth of the river, and to take out you can paddle north for 1.0 mile to Sand Bar State Park (9.25 miles) on US 2.

Browns River vt

Because the upper Browns drains the steep western flank of Mount Mansfield (4393 ft), flash flooding is not uncommon on this section of the river. Runoff on the lower reaches is buffered by bottom lands between Underhill and Westford, extending the season there.

Underhill State Park Road ➤ Underhill Flats		4.4 mi
Description:	Class I, II	
Date checked:	2001	
Navigable:	High water (March–April)	
Scenery:	Forested, rural	
Map:	USGS Underhill	

Put in at a side road bridge off the Underhill State Park Road, 0.6 mile from Pleasant Valley Road. Continuous small but technical Class II rapids moderate to Class I–II as you approach Underhill Center. Downed trees in the current require vigilance. In medium water, the small park off Stevensville Rd. in Underhill Center is an alternate put-in (1.3 miles).

Class II rapids in Underhill Center give way to mainly Class I (with the possibility of livestock fences and/or trees across the river) en route to Underhill Flats. Take out at the Browns River School ball field on the right.

Underhill Flats ➤ Old Pump Road (Jericho) 3.2 mi

Description:	Quickwater, Class II
Date checked:	2001
Navigable:	High water (March–early May)
Scenery:	Rural
Map:	USGS Underhill
Portages:	2.7 mi L Cilley Hill Rd. Dam

Quickwater/Class I predominate as the river passes beneath VT 15 (0.7 mile) and Raceway Road (1.4 miles), where access is possible. Some unsightly logging and farm equipment here spoils the view. A large oxbow meander precedes the Cilley Hill Road dam, which must be portaged (2.7 miles). A put-in between the dam and bridge is possible at river left, in a short Class II rapid. More quickwater and a Class II ledge bring you to the take-out above the Old Pump Rd. bridge, on the left. **Caution!** Immediately below this bridge the river enters a Class IV gorge with no practical egress for 0.6 mile.

Old Pump Road ➤ Old Mill 0.6 mi

Description:	Class IV
Date checked:	2001
Navigable:	Medium water (late April–early May)
Scenery:	Dramatic gorge
Map:	USGS Underhill
Portages:	0.6 mi R Old Mill Dam/Cascade

Continuous Class IV whitewater suitable only for advanced to expert paddlers finally moderates as the Old Mill building comes into view. The gradient averages 100 feet/mile. Be sure to take out well above the Class VI spillway of the dam, on the right.

Jericho ➤ Westford 11.6 mi

Description:	Quickwater, Class I–II
Date checked:	2001
Navigable:	High and medium water (spring and late fall)
Scenery:	Rural
Map:	USGS Underhill, Essex Center

Put in on the Lee River at the Plains Road bridge crossing (0.3 mile south of VT 15 in Jericho) which promptly joins the Browns River. Meandering quickwater predominates all the way to Westford, with some wading necessary in low water. Access points include bridges on VT 15 at Naylor Road (1.4 miles), VT 128 (3.2 miles), and Pettingill Road (6.6 miles). Take out in Westford above the VT 128 bridge on river right.

Westford ➤ Lamoille River	5.1 mi
Description:	Quickwater, Class II–III
Date checked:	2001
Navigable:	Medium water (April–May)
Scenery:	Rural
Map:	USGS Essex Center, Milton
Portages:	0.3 mi L Westford Dam

If there is ample water to negotiate the first Class II ledge below the put-in on VT 128, then the rest of the run should be passable as well. The Westford Dam is washing out, and has been run successfully on the right side at medium water. The first ledge is at 1.0 mi, where the river diverges from Huntley Road.

In very high water (i.e. when farm fields above Westford are flooded) the ledges section of the Browns River should be avoided, as the current is extremely swift and any eddies that might exist are in the trees. The next access is the VT 128 bridge (3.7 miles). Watch for fences across the river in the next 0.9 mile to a side-road bridge (4.6 miles). Quickwater continues to the Lamoille River confluence, where most will paddle down the Lamoille another 4.0 miles to Arrowhead Mountain Lake.

Winooski River VT

The Winooski River rises in Cabot and flows westward through the Green Mountains to Lake Champlain near Burlington. Although the course circles some of the largest cities in Vermont, the banks are largely pastoral. Lovely mountain views are obtained in the middle portion. It offers 78.25 miles of paddling.

Marshfield ➤ Montpelier	24.0 mi
Description:	Flatwater, quickwater, Class II–III

Date checked:	2001
Navigable:	High water (early spring)
Scenery:	Rural, towns
Maps:	USGS Plainfield 15, Barre 15, Montpelier 15
Portage:	1.0 mi dam in Marshfield
	9.5 mi dam in Plainfield
	18 mi dam below East Montpelier, three dams in Montpelier

In this section the river is very small, and it can be run only in high water. The 8.5 miles from Marshfield to Plainfield range in difficulty from quickwater to Class II. Most of the lower part consists of short sections between dams. The rapids below the Green Mountain Power Station above the town of Marshfield are Class II-III, and they require very high water. The US 2 bridge (1.0 mile) is just below the dam in Marshfield.

Access at the Twinfield Elementary School below the dam is followed by 0.5 mile of Class II water. Then the river meanders for several miles of mixed flatwater and small rapids to Twinfield High School, where access is available at a bridge. From the high school to the Onion River Campground, there is some Class II water. Since access is difficult near the building at the dam in Plainfield (9.5 miles), take out well above it.

Below the Plainfield Dam (9.5 miles) is 0.5 mile of Class III rapids. Then the river meanders with a good current and easy rapids past East Montpelier (16.5 miles) to a dam (18.0 miles), which is a good place to end a trip on the upper river. Access is on the left bank off US 2.

In the next 6.0 miles there are three dams. Above the first one there are Class III rapids. Below it, Class II rapids diminish to flatwater above a small dam that can be portaged on either side. You reach the third dam in the center of Montpelier after passing under four bridges.

Montpelier ➤ Jonesville	22.75 mi
Description:	Flatwater, quickwater, Class I–II
Date checked:	2001
Navigable:	Passable at all water levels

Scenery:	Rural, towns
Maps:	USGS Montpelier 15, Waterbury, Richmond
Portage:	6.0 mi L dam in Middlesex 100 yd
	16.25 mi L Bolton Falls Dam 0.5 mi

Below Montpelier the river can be run all year. The section described here has much more quickwater with occasional rapids. The two dams are in scenic natural gorges, and the run is very attractive.

Access is at the Montpelier High School on the south bank just below the last bridge. About 0.75 mile downstream from the high school, the Winsooki goes under I-89 where the Dog River comes in from the left. There is another bridge 1.75 miles farther downstream. The river continues with a slow current for another 3.0 miles to the bridge in Middlesex. Here the river divides. Take the left channel, from which a portage can be made around the dam (6.0 miles).

A chute followed by a large pool lies 0.5 mile below the dam. With sufficient water this may cause unprepared open boats some difficulty. There is quickwater for the next 0.5 mile to the mouth of the Mad River (7.0 miles) on the left just above the US 2 bridge. Below this is 0.5 mile of Class II rapids (Junkyard Rapids), where the first drop just around a corner is the most difficult. Next the Winooski flows through a gorge with high cliffs on both sides, and 3.5 miles of slow current bring you to the first bridge (11.0 miles) in Waterbury. Just after the third Waterbury bridge, the Little River (14.0 miles) enters on the right from Waterbury Reservoir.

Below the Little River in 2.25 miles is Bolton Falls Dam (6.25 miles). **Caution!** This disused dam is in a natural gorge, and it is very dangerous to approach. Rapids start about 0.5 mile above the dam where the river swings to the right. Take out on the left at the southernmost part of the bend and carry across the field to the railroad and the road. Take the first cart path to the right to reach the pool below the falls.

A short distance below the dam there is 0.25 mile of Class II rapids above the railroad trestle (17.0 miles). This can be a boat-eater in higher water. The next 5.75 miles to Jonesville are quickwater. The Huntington River comes in on the left just below the bridge (22.75 miles).

Jonesville ➤ Essex Junction	15.5 mi
Description:	Flatwater, quickwater
Date checked:	2001
Navigable:	Passable at all water levels
Scenery:	Rural
Maps:	USGS Richmond, Essex Junction
Portage:	15.5 mi dam in Essex Junction 250 yd

The river now leaves the mountains and follows a broad, smooth course through farmland. It is an easy paddle.

There are 3.5 miles of easy current to the Bridge Street bridge at Richmond where there is good access, and another 2.5 miles past I-89 to the US 2 bridge (6.0 miles). Then you pass a railroad bridge (8.0 miles), the bridge at North Williston (11.0 miles), and another railroad bridge (13.25 miles) before reaching the power dam (15.5 miles) at Essex Junction. Portage on either side. The right side, although longer, is mostly on a road.

Essex Junction ➤ Lake Champlain	16.0 mi
Description:	Flatwater, quickwater
Date checked:	2001
Navigable:	Passable at all water levels
Scenery:	Forested, urban
Maps:	USGS Essex Junction, Burlington, Fort Ethan Allen, Colchester Point
Portage:	5.75 mi L dam at Winooski Gorge
	6.75 mi dam at Winooski

Most of the runnable part of this run is flatwater, but there are two difficult carries. Winooski Gorge is most easily enjoyed from the bank. In low water it is possible to visit the gorge by paddling down to it from a new access at the recreation area in Essex, then returning back upstream to take out.

After 0.5 mile of Class I rapids there are 4.75 miles of quickwater to Winooski Gorge, which begins behind Lime Kiln Bridge (5.25 miles). A railroad bridge 0.5 mile farther on precedes a dam. Take out on the left and carry up a steep bank and down the far side to the left beyond some cliffs. Below this first dam there is almost 1.0 mile of quickwater to the ledges above the next dam, but since there is no easy take-out above them, it is recommended that you portage both dams at one time by taking out at the launching ramp in Essex on the right bank and following the highway to Winooski. By car this portage is about 1.5 miles long.

In Winooski there is access to the river below the dam. The river meanders for 6.5 miles to the VT 127 bridge (13.25 miles), and in another 2.75 miles it empties into Lake Champlain (16.0 miles). At the mouth of the river there are cottages and a beautiful view across the lake toward the Adirondacks.

Dog River vt

This river is followed from its source in Roxbury to the Winooski River by a railroad and a main highway. Its most serious hazards are fallen trees and wire fences strung across it.

The best time to run this river is after a rainstorm in the spring, before the middle of May.

Northfield ➤ Montpelier	10.25 mi
Description:	Quickwater, Class I–II
Date checked:	2001
Navigable:	High water (April)
Scenery:	Rural, towns
Maps:	USGS Barre 15, Montpelier 15
Portage:	1.25 mi L pitch by first covered bridge 100 yd
	1.75 mi dam at Northfield Falls
	3.5 mi L pitch past railroad bridge
	4.25 mi old wooden dam at Riverton

Put in just below the dam at Namtang Mill. There is about 0.5 mile of quickwater to a ledge obstruction just upstream of the concrete bridge on VT 12, from which the ledge can be seen. At the correct water level this ledge can be run with scouting.

Quickwater continues past the first covered bridge to a 6-foot pitch (1.25 miles) that requires a short carry on the left. Take out again in 0.25 mile at the next covered bridge and carry along the road past the dam in Northfield Falls.

Below the falls (1.75 miles), the river is smooth for 1.0 mile to a high railroad bridge, past which there is a minor obstruction that can be run easily on the far left. This is followed closely by two small ledge drops that can be run at the proper water level. Scouting is recommended.

Just past the next railroad bridge (3.5 miles) there is an 8-foot pitch that requires a short portage on the left. In 0.25 mile there are two more ledge drops that can be run at the right water level. They too should be scouted. The remaining 0.25 mile to Riverton is smooth.

The old wooden dam in Riverton (4.25 miles), which can be seen from the VT 12 bridge in Riverton, must be carried because of obstructing timbers. The next 3.5 miles are smoothwater to a short Class II rapid. The first section can be run on either side; the second section is best on the far right. The remaining 2.5 miles to the Winooski River (10.25 miles) are smooth, with the exception of four minor ledge constrictions, each of which can be run straight through.

Mad River VT

The Mad River flows northward on the east side of the Green Mountains from Granville Notch to the Winooski River below Middlesex. It offers scenic spring whitewater runs of varying degrees of difficulty.

Warren ➤ Irasville	3.75 mi
Description:	Class I–II
Date checked:	2001
Navigable:	High water (April to early May)
Scenery:	Forested
Maps:	USGS Waitsfield
Portage:	1.5 mi L ledge 15 yd
	2.0 mi L two ledges 100 yd

Put in from VT 100 0.8 mile south of the turn to the Sugarbush ski area, where the river is close to the road. Most of the distance is easy rapids, but in the first 1.25 miles to the next VT 100 bridge there are three small ledges, all of which can be run but should be scouted.

The first of the three difficult ledges is marked by a section of rock sticking up in the middle of the river, with a chute to each side. Both chutes have a sharp drop with a considerable hydraulic at the bottom; the one on the right is undercut at the bottom. The river takes a sharp right turn at this point.

The second and third ledges are immediately above and below a small bridge on a side road (2.0 miles). Both may be portaged by a carry of 100 yards circling the house on the left, or they can be run at the right water level.

Below the ledges the river flows easily to the next VT 100 bridge.

Irasville ➤ Waitsfield Picnic Area	3.75 mi
Description:	Class I–II
Date checked:	2001
Navigable:	High water (April to early May)
Scenery:	Forested, towns
Maps:	USGS Waitsfield

Begin near the Vermont highway garage 1.75 miles south of Waitsfield. The rapids are pleasant and easy, with no particular problems. The old dam in Waitsfield is gone; the covered bridge is passed at 1.75 miles. The picnic area 2.0 miles north (downstream) of town provides easy access.

Waitsfield Picnic Area ➤ Moretown	4.75 mi
Description:	Quickwater, Class I–II
Date checked:	2001
Navigable:	High water (April to early May)
Scenery:	Forested, towns
Maps:	USGS Waitsfield, Waterbury
Portage:	4.75 mi R gorge

This section is appreciably easier than the ones above. The only difficulty is a Class II drop shortly after the start where the river abuts VT 100, then swings ninety degrees to the right and drops past a ledgy outcrop. Various routes can be taken through this pitch. It is best to scout it the first time it is run. The remaining distance is mostly quickwater.

Take out from a side road on the right 0.25 mile above the VT 100B bridge. Both the landing and the carry-up at the bridge are difficult.

Moretown 0.5 mi

The gorge directly beneath the bridge can be run in a heavy-water boat; it is Class II-IV. Take out on the right from the pool below, since there is another gorge with a dam just below.

Moretown ➤ Power dam 4.75 mi
Description: Flatwater, quickwater, Class I–II
Date checked: 2001
Navigable: High water (April to early May)
Scenery: Forested, rural
Maps: USGS Waterbury
Portage: 2.25 mi gauging station—lift over (4.75 mi high dam R 200 yd)

Put in from a side road below the lumberyard. All the rapids are easy. The river passes the main highway again in 0.5 mile. The low wooden dam below the bridge on a side road usually can be run. However, in high water, when the dam is covered, a strong reversal is created and it should be avoided. Soon the river opens out into the pond, which extends nearly a mile from the dam, with several take-out options on the left.

Power dam ➤ Winooski River 2.0 mi
Description: Quickwater, Class I,II
Date checked: 2000
Navigable: Spring, late May, after a good rain in summer
Scenery: Rural
Portages: Horseshoe Falls 15 yd

This section of the Mad is more challenging than the previous section. It can be run at a variety of water levels. The put-in is reached by Hathaway Road, left off VT 100B South. At the turnoff on the right, follow the path to the bottom of Moretown Dam. The Mad starts shallow then constricts to a deep-running channel with lots of deep-running eddy lines. There is a series of ledge drops which could vary from Class III to Class IV depending on the water level. All drops on this section should be scouted from the right bank. As you reach the VT 100B bridge, the action picks up with a series of shallow Class II wavy rapids.

As the river widens and flattens out you want to make your way to the left shore to portage a horseshoe-shaped waterfall. **Caution!** After the waterfall there is a small narrow gorge with a ledge drop at its entrance. Scout this as you portage the falls. As the channel opens up there is a short section of small ledges. As you pass under the Lovers Lane bridge and round the bend, the river opens up and splits. Stay right. The last rapid, a short ledge drop with a pool at the bottom, is ahead. The river then flattens out, and you are at the confluence with the Winooski River. The take-out is on the Winooski at the US 2 bridge, on the left, up a steep bank. Watch out for poison oak and ivy. Make sure to park off the side of the road and respect private property; ask for and obtain permission before crossing property lines.

Huntington River VT

The Huntington River is a southern tributary of the Winooski River. It flows through woods and farmland west of Camel's Hump and consists mostly of Class I–II rapids. For the first 10.0 miles the gradient averages 20 feet per mile, but it becomes steeper after that.

The river can be run for most of its length at high water in April. At very high water it may be run from as far south as Hanksville. At just below flood stage, it becomes a fairly big-water run with mostly large waves and a few notable holes, but without many visible rocks.

Hanksville ➤ Huntington Gorge		10.5 mi
Description:	Class I–II	
Date checked:	2001	
Navigable:	High water (April)	
Scenery:	Forested, rural, towns	
Maps:	USGS Huntington	

Put in at the bridge that crosses the river east of the paved road in Hanksville. Just below there is a 4-foot drop that can only be run at certain water levels, and it should be scouted. There may be fallen trees and wire fences in the 4.0 miles to Huntington Center. A bridge (3.0 miles) on the paved road south of Huntington Center also makes a good put-in.

In medium water, begin at the bridge 3.5 miles farther north in Huntington (6.5 miles), east from the center of town. Farther downstream the road to Richmond crosses twice (8.75 and 9.25 miles).

Caution! A rock wall on the right where the river bends left (10.5 miles) marks the approach to Huntington Gorge, a treacherous cleft where swimmers have drowned. There are many take-out spots on the left along the road, but be sure to ask for and obtain permission before carrying canoes or kayaks, or parking on the roadside strip. Although most of the road is marked "No Parking," many of the homeowners on Dugway Road (parallel to the river above the gorge) have parking spaces and if asked may grant permission for a car or two to park for shuttle purposes. There are spectacular views of the falls in the gorge from below.

(A half-mile below this gorge is a lower gorge, which is also impassable because of a series of waterfalls. The river is potentially runnable for another 1.5 miles below the lower gorge, but it is hard to reach).

Lewis Creek vt

Lewis Creek offers interesting paddling in attractive, rough country during the spring runoff in late March and early April. The flow varies widely with temperature, recent rain, and sunshine. If the water is right, the trip can start at the bridge on the Hinesburg-Monkton Ridge Road, or even higher up. The upper part is mostly quickwater until just before a short fall above a covered bridge south of Prindle Corners. The fall should be portaged.

Prindle Corners ➤ North Ferrisburg		6.0 mi
Description:	Class I–II	
Date checked:	2001	
Navigable:	High water (April)	
Scenery:	Forested, towns	
Maps:	USGS Hinesburg, Mount Philo	
Portage:	3.0 mi dam 30 yd	
	(6.0 mi L waterfalls 0.25 mi)	

The usual starting point is at the covered bridge south of Prindle Corners, about 2.5 miles south of Hinesburg. Easy rapids are encountered until the deadwater above the Scott Pond Dam, where a short carry must be made. This bit makes a lively Class II run through rugged country. Below the dam a ledge kicks up waves. There is a good take-out 0.5 mile below, and there is another covered bridge.

After another mile there is a 4-foot ledge that should be looked over. Class I and II rapids continue on to North Ferrisburg. Shortly below a ledge by a mill site there is a waterfall. Take out on the left as soon as a house comes into view on the left bank. This point should be inspected for the best take-out before starting the trip.

North Ferrisburg ➤ Greenbush Road		2.5 mi
Description:	Quickwater, Class I	
Date checked:	2001	
Navigable:	Medium water	
Scenery:	Forested, rural	
Maps:	USGS Mount Philo, Monkton	
Portage:	1.5 mi ledge under bridge—difficult	

At medium water a skillful party that wants to continue may portage the falls on the right. In this case, scout the ledge beneath the bridge in advance and make sure you can deal with it. Easy rapids continue to the US 7 bridge. Below this bridge lies an old bridge followed by another ledge. In fairly low water the ledge can be lined easily. Rapids continue halfway to the next bridge.

Greenbush Road ➤ Lake Champlain		3.5 mi
Description:	Flatwater	
Date checked:	2001	
Navigable:	Spring, summer, fall	
Scenery:	Forested, rural	
Maps:	USGS Port Henry	

At high water there may still be a current, but at low water the river is slow enough to paddle upstream. Beyond the farms the marshy area widens out and is home to many birds and some beaver activity. A launching ramp provides access 0.25 mile before the lake.

Otter Creek vт

Otter Creek flows north from Dorset and drains a broad valley between the Green Mountains and the Taconic Range. North of Rutland it runs somewhat westward and empties into Lake Champlain near Vergennes. At high water it provides an easy trip of just over 100 miles, but much of it can be run in medium or low water, so it is suitable for summer trips. Otter Creek is highly recommended for its pleasant paddling and its scenic views of the Green Mountains, the Taconics, and the Adirondacks in New York.

There are several dams on this river, and at many of them the current is strong right up to the edge. Take out well above all dams, especially in high water.

North Dorset ➤ Wallingford	17.75 mi
Description:	Quickwater, Class I
Date checked:	2001
Navigable:	High water needed above South Wallingford (early spring)
	Medium water (late spring)
Scenery:	Forested, rural, towns
Maps:	USGS Wallingford 15
Portage:	11.5 mi R Class III ledges 0.5 mi
	17.25 mi Class II rapids and rock dam

High water is necessary in the upper part where the river is very narrow. Below South Wallingford at least medium water is necessary, and in that part the river may be obstructed by an occasional fallen tree. This whole section is mostly quickwater, except for the rapids in South Wallingford and Wallingford.

Begin in North Dorset 0.75 mile north of the Emerald Lake dam by putting in from a farm road on the east side of US 7. From there to Danby it is 5.75 miles. Beaver dams and lodges are numerous. There are plenty of brushy impediments but no rapids.

Below the Mount Tabor road in Danby (5.75 miles) there are riffles over a gravel bottom. The rapids at South Wallingford (11.5 miles) are Class III for 0.5 mile and can be portaged easily on the right along the railroad tracks.

Below South Wallingford quickwater continues to Wallingford, where there are four bridges. The first one is US 7 (16.25 miles). Class II rapids start below the second bridge, VT 140 (17.25 miles), and continue past a rock dam and under the third bridge to the fourth, where there is a ledge partially blocking the left-hand span.

Wallingford ➤ Rutland   13.0 mi

Description:	Quickwater
Date checked:	2001
Navigable:	High or medium water (spring)
Scenery:	Rural
Maps:	USGS Wallingford 15, Rutland

The winding river is still small here. There are roads on both sides of the valley, but they are hardly noticeable because of the trees that border the river.

This quickwater run has an occasional fallen tree. Begin at the fourth (last) bridge in Wallingford. In 2.75 miles the Mill River enters on the right. This is the fourth and southernmost river that cuts through the Green Mountains, and it greatly augments the flow in Otter Creek.

There is a bridge (5.0 miles) near Clarendon and another (9.75 miles) near North Clarendon. Take out at the River Street bridge (13.0 miles) in Rutland, a short distance above the first dam in that city.

Rutland ➤ Proctor   8.25 mi

Description:	Flatwater, quickwater, Class II
Date checked:	2001
Navigable:	Passable at all water levels
Scenery:	Rural, towns
Maps:	USGS West Rutland, Proctor
Portage:	0.25 mi e dam in Rutland 100–400 yd
	1 mi e dam in Center Rutland—difficult
	(7.75 mi R dam in Proctor 0.5 mi)

The 6.5 miles of flatwater in this section are set off from the rest of the river by high dams requiring long portages. Below Rutland the river is larger, and it can be run all summer.

A quarter-mile below the River Street bridge, which is the first bridge in Rutland, there is a low dam that is hard to see from the river. It can be portaged on either side, and it is followed by 0.5 mile of Class II rapids. The current remains strong up to the dam in Center Rutland. Take out at the double bridge (1.0 mile). The carry up the steep bank and through the factory yards is difficult on either side.

In Center Rutland, put in at the US 4 bridge (1.25 miles) below the dam, and pass the mouth of the Clarendon River (1.5 miles) on the left. From there the river flows slowly between wooded banks. Pass a railroad bridge (6.25 miles) and take out at the next bridge (7.75 miles) to portage the dam in Proctor. Carry on the right down the hill on the highway, take the first left past the sewage treatment plant, and follow the dirt tracks down to the river (8.25 miles).

Proctor ➤ Middlebury	35.75 mi
Description:	Flatwater, quickwater
Date checked:	2001
Navigable:	Passable at all water levels
Scenery:	Rural
Maps:	USGS Proctor, Brandon, Sudbury, Cornwall, Middlebury
Portage:	(35.75 mi L dam in Middlebury 0.25 mi)

This is a beautiful paddle through farming country and under covered bridges. There are some mountain views. The river meanders through a broad valley with clear water and a sandy bottom.

In Proctor, put in at the east bank at the bottom of the hill by taking the first left past the sewage treatment plant. This trip is popular, and there are many bridges that offer access to the river. They include: the bridge in Florence (6.25 miles) 0.5 mile north of a railroad bridge; two bridges southwest of Brandon, Dean Bridge (13.0 miles) and Sanderson Bridge (14.5 miles); the VT 73 bridge west of Brandon (18.25 miles); the bridge at Leicester Junction (21.5 miles); and Threemile Bridge (32.25 miles). The latter, located next to the mouth of the Middlebury River, is the recommended take-out. It can be reached most easily from US 7 in East Middlebury by following Creek Road just to the north of the Middlebury River.

If you are continuing on to Middlebury, take out well above the VT 30/74 bridge (35.75 miles), because the dam is only about 100 feet downstream from the bridge.

Middlebury ➤ Weybridge   6.0 mi

Description:	Flatwater, quickwater, Class II–III
Date checked:	2001
Navigable:	Passable at all water levels
Scenery:	Forested, urban
Maps:	USGS Middlebury
Portage:	1.0 mi L second dam in Middlebury 100 yd
	3.0 mi R Beldens Dam 0.25 mi
	4.75 mi L Huntington Falls Dam 0.25 mi
	6.0 mi L dam at Weybridge 100 yd

Three of these dams—all except Beldens Dam—are below bridges and should be portaged on the left. The banks consist of cliffs, ledges, and evergreen growth. There are rapids below the dams, and the most difficult ones are below Beldens, where there is a gorge. Below Beldens Dam after 0.75 mile, the New Haven River (3.75 miles) enters on the right.

Weybridge ➤ Lake Champlain   19.75 mi

Description:	Flatwater, quickwater
Date checked:	2001
Navigable:	Passable at all water levels
Scenery:	Forested, rural
Maps:	USGS Middlebury, Port Henry 15
Portage:	12.0 mi R dam in Vergennes 0.5+ miles

This section is mostly away from roads, but there are some buildings along the banks. The mouth of the river is very attractive, with views across the lake toward the Adirondacks. Below Vergennes the river is large enough for big boats, and there are many motorboats.

Put in from the end of the island below the dam at Weybridge, or 0.5 mile downstream on the left if you wish to avoid the faster water. The current is moderate past the mouth of the

Lemon Fair River (3.5 miles) to Vergennes (12.0 miles), where the take-out above the dam is difficult at high water. Carry on the right bank down a road.

Four miles below Vergennes, Dead Creek (16.0 miles) enters on the left. The best take-out is at the Fort Cassin Fishing Access, 0.5 mile before the mouth of the river at Lake Champlain (19.75 miles).

Mill River VT

This is a small, rural, Class II–III stream southwest of Rutland. In the spring it provides 4-6 miles of intermittent whitewater paddling beginning at East Wallingford off VT 103. See the USGS Wallingford 15 and Rutland maps.

From East Wallingford, follow the road and put in at any convenient point south of town. The best take-out is at a roadside picnic area on VT 103 north of Cuttingsville. You can paddle farther, but the road pulls away from the stream, and there are no really good places to take out. If you do continue past the picnic area take out as soon as you see the suspension bridge where the Long Trail crosses Clarendon Gorge. This gorge is definitely impassable for open boats and perhaps for closed boats as well.

Tinmouth Channel VT

South of Rutland, Tinmouth Channel flows northward through the township of Tinmouth and into Clarendon, where it becomes the Clarendon River. It empties into Otter Creek just west of Rutland. There are two runnable sections.

The first is a 5.0-mile section on Tinmouth Channel, which is crossed by VT 140. It can be paddled in the spring, but it is overgrown by brush.

The second section is separated from the first by a steep and unrunnable area.

Tinmouth Channel ➤ Tinmouth		5.25 mi
Description:	Swamp	
Date checked:	2001	
Navigable:	High to medium water	

Scenery:	Rural
Maps:	USGS Middletown Springs

An athletic paddler can put in at the Lawrence Road bridge south of VT 140 and fight through the swamp alders and beaver dams down to a bridge north of town. A less-committed person can put in at the north-of-town bridge, paddle south as far as desired, and return. Below this bridge the river soon starts its precipitous drop.

Clarendon River VT

This is the northern (downstream) continuation of Tinmouth Channel. Most of its course is small and plunges steeply downhill, but the last few miles to Otter Creek can be paddled.

From the confluence with Ira Brook it is 4.75 miles to Otter Brook. This stretch starts as a fat Class II run. Watch for a low bridge around the first corner. Gradually the water slows down as it flows across the valley to the junction with Otter Creek just below Center Rutland. Take out at the US 4 bridge 0.25 mile before the confluence, or continue down Otter Creek for 4.0 miles to Proctor. See USGS West Rutland.

Middlebury River VT

The Middlebury River rises in Middlebury Gap and flows into Otter Creek above Middlebury.

US 7 bridge ➤ Otter Creek	5.25 mi
Description:	Flatwater, quickwater, Class I
Date checked:	2001
Navigable:	Medium water (May)
Scenery:	Rural
Maps:	USGS East Middlebury, Cornwall

Put in at a picnic area near the US 7 bridge south of the junction with VT 125. The river winds through fields and dances over some riffles, passing under two bridges on side roads. There is good access to Otter Creek at a former bridge site, reached by following the side road that leads to the picnic area.

New Haven River VT

The New Haven River rises in Lincoln Gap and flows west to Otter Creek. The upper part is scattered with unrunnable waterfalls, so the river normally is not run until just above Bristol. A frequent starting point is on Baldwin Creek.

Baldwin Creek/Beaver Brook ➤ Bristol	4.0 mi
Description:	Class I–IV
Date checked:	2001
Navigable:	High water (late April to early May)
Scenery:	Forested, towns
Maps:	USGS Bristol

Put in at the junction of Beaver Brook and Baldwin Creek. For 2.0 miles Baldwin Creek flows over easy rapids. The New Haven River enters from the left in the middle of a Class III rapid and soon passes under the VT 116 bridge. At the Baldwin Creek confluence, the river doubles in size.

There are steady Class II and Class III rapids for the next 1.5 miles to Bristol. Here, standing above and running under a green steel bridge, is a heavy, boulder-strewn Class IV or V rapid, although a passage on the extreme right exists. This section is the hardest, with sustained technical rapids. This should always be scouted as it varies considerably with the water level. Class III-IV rapids continue through the village as the river makes a sweeping curve to the left and passes under an iron bridge. Take out here; there is convenient parking at the bridge.

Bristol ➤ New Haven Mills	4.5 mi
Description:	Class I–III
Date checked:	2001
Navigable:	High water (late April)
	Medium water (early May)
Scenery:	Forested, rural
Maps:	USGS Bristol, South Mountain

Below the second iron bridge in Bristol the river descends in a series of rapids that decrease in difficulty. The heaviest rapids are immediately below the bridge, and you can put in a little farther down the road along the west bank. The rocks generally are small, with the river dropping over boulder bars that can generate waves in high water. Watch for fallen trees. After a mile the rapids moderate somewhat as they run past a bridge (2.75 miles) and nearly into New Haven Mills.

Where a white steeple becomes visible on the right, the river turns left, dropping steeply through an old mill site, which can be scouted from the bridge below. A slight pool at the bridge offers a respite before the second half of the rapids, which starts immediately below.

New Haven Mills ➤ Pair of bridges	5.25 mi
Description:	Flatwater, quickwater, Class I–II
Date checked:	2001
Navigable:	Medium water (mid-May or wet summers)
Scenery:	Rural
Maps:	USGS South Mountain, Middlebury
Portage:	(5.25 mi L falls at Dog Team Tavern)

Below the short drop at New Haven Mills, the rapids moderate considerably; much of the distance is winding quickwater, with only an occasional rock patch or riffle. Watch fallen trees. You pass a bridge (4.0 miles), and you should take out at the next pair of bridges, since there is a small waterfall around the corner to the right.

Dog Team Tavern (pair of bridges) ➤ Otter Creek   1.0 mi

The falls can be run, and it is easy to carry back up and run them over and over. Carry up the dry rock ledges at river left, not across the private lawns at river right. The falls and the ledges at the Dog Team are a convenient park-and-play spot.

The gradient moderates as it approaches the confluence with Otter Creek. There is no take-out at the confluence. Paddle down Otter Creek to the vicinity of Huntington Falls Dam for the next access.

Lemon Fair River VT

The Lemon Fair River rises in the southeast corner of Orwell and flows north to join Otter Creek just a few miles below Weybridge. The runnable part is composed of winding channels in a flat bottomland with splendid views of nearby hills and mountains.

According to a local story, the name of the river is derived from the remark of an early traveler who had lost his horse from miring in mud or quicksand as he crossed the stream. He referred to this episode as a "lamentable affair." Another legend is that the name is an anglicized version of "Les Monts Verts."

Richville Pond   5.0 mi

The dam at Shoreham Center makes a pond of the Lemon Fair for 5.0 miles or so, offering pleasant flatwater paddling. There is a fishing access by the bridge that crosses the center of town.

Shoreham Center ➤ VT 74 bridge   7.0 mi

Description:	Quickwater, Class I—IV
Date checked:	2001
Navigable:	Medium water (late April)
Scenery:	Rural
Maps:	USGS Orwell, Bridport

Put in 0.5 mile or so below the dam, where the river comes close to the road. A shallow riffle is followed by a clay rapid and finally a 3-foot rock dam. Another rapid leads into a gorge with sheer walls and over a little, washed-out dam on a 2-foot ledge. Where the gorge opens out there is a set of transverse ledges with water running in all directions, and there is another ledge above a side-road bridge (4.0 miles). The gorge should be scouted in advance.

Rapids continue for another 0.25 mile below the bridge, followed by quickwater to a rock dam a few feet high at an old abutment. The river meanders on past occasional fallen trees to the VT 74 bridge.

VT 74 ➤ Otter Creek		11.5 mi
Description:	Flatwater, quickwater	
Date checked:	2001	
Navigable:	High to medium water (April and May)	
Scenery:	Rural	
Maps:	USGS Bridport, Cornwall, Middletown, Port Henry 15	

The river flows through farmland drained by ditches along both sides. There are aquatic birds and animals in abundance. It flows under VT 125 (5.25 miles) and two bridges on back roads before reaching VT 23 (11.5 miles) at the confluence with Otter Creek.

Dead Creek VT

Dead Creek is a marshland stream that rises in Bridgeport and flows north to join Otter Creek 4.0 miles below Vergennes. It is as flat as a stream can be. The navigable portion extends for about 10.0 miles and, with adjacent land area amounting to 2,814 acres, is known as the Dead Creek Wildlife Management Area (WMA). The WMA headquarters is on VT 17, 1.0 mile west of Addison. It is the largest state-owned waterfowl area in Vermont and is especially recommended for all those who wish to combine bird watching and paddling.

There are so many sloughs and potholes that it is a little difficult to follow the main channel, especially in late summer, when the weeds and rushes are at full height. There are, however, many relatively large expanses of water. The combination makes a wonderful place for waterfowl, including ducks, bitterns, herons, gallinules, various shore birds, and others. Over two hundred species of birds have been sighted here. For further information, contact: Vermont Department of Fish and Wildlife, 111 West Street, Essex Junction, VT 05452 (802-878-1564), or Dead Creek WMA Refuge Office (802-759-2398).

Paddlers using the Dead Creek WMA during the spring months (April to June) are asked to be careful not to disturb the birds nesting along the waterways.

Dead Creek ➤ Otter Creek 10.0 mi

Description:	Flatwater, marsh
Date checked:	2001
Navigable:	Spring, summer, fall
Scenery:	Wildlife management area
Maps:	USGS Port Henry 15

Dead Creek is not a flowing stream throughout the year. The level of Lake Champlain directly influences water levels within Dead Creek, as do periods of runoff resulting from flooding during the remainder of the year. The main marsh has been improved by dikes to permit flooding 1,000 acres of cattail marsh. These dikes divide the area into three major parts.

South Section 2.0 mi

Access to the south section, as well as to the middle, is at the Brilyea West and East dams, reached by a road running south from VT 17, just west of the bridge. Access to the East Branch is easy from the road running west from VT 22A, 0.75 mile south of Addison.

Middle Section 4.0 mi

This section runs upstream from Stone Bridge Dam to Brilyea West Dam 1.0 mile south of VT 17. The easiest approach is at the bridge on VT 17, but approach is also possible at Stone Bridge Dam or from the Farrell access road that leaves the country road 2.75 miles south of Panton, a few feet south of the Panton-Addison line. A permit is required to paddle this section's waterfowl refuge portion, which extends from VT 17 south to the Brilyea West Dam.

North Section 4.0 mi

You can visit this section as a side trip from Otter Creek or you can start at the mouth of Dead Creek from the bridge on the Vergennes-Basin Harbor road. The bridge on the Vergennes-Panton road, several miles farther upstream, offers access as well. Normally one can ascend the creek only 1.0 mile south of this road, since the growth of reeds and rushes is very heavy in the 0.5 mile north of the dike (Stone Bridge Dam) that follows the line of the road running west from the East Panton School. There is a road to the dike from the road corner marked 125 on the USGS map. For reaching this corner, a better road is one from the Vergennes-Panton road directly south across the Holcombe Slang.

Poultney River VT, NY

The Poultney River rises in Tinmouth, Vermont, and flows west to Poultney, where it turns north and becomes the boundary between Vermont and New York for the rest of its circuitous route to the East Bay of Lake Champlain. The upper reaches through the Taconic Range are too rough to run, but from Poultney down there is much easy paddling interspersed with difficult or impossible ledges. Much of this section may be run in the summer, although the rapids may have to be carried.

Hampton, NY ➤ US 4 bridge		9.5 mi
Description:	Quickwater, Class I	
Date checked:	2001	
Navigable:	High to medium water	
Scenery:	Forested, rural	
Maps:	USGS Poultney, Thorn Hill	
Difficulties:	Three low ledges	

Put in at the old slate mill, below the dam and gorge. The water is greenish and fairly clear. The stream is shallow and rocky in medium water, with the usual overhanging trees and occasional blockages. Animal tracks abound on the banks.

Below the NY 22A bridge (4.0 miles) there are three ledges: the first is 3 feet high, the others only half that. All can be run, lined, or lifted over. It is probably best to stay to the right.

Immediately below the bridge there is a high ledge that is practically impossible to run.

US 4 bridge ➤ Carver Falls Dam	4.5 mi

This is a ledge-lover's paradise, perhaps better suited to fishing and swimming than to paddling. The ledges are of various heights, and some are difficult or impossible to run. They are interspersed with easier rapids, although jagged blacks in runnable rapids may tend to damage the boat. Before embarking be sure to inspect the ledge immediately underneath the railroad bridge that can be seen below from the US 4 bridge.

Just above the West Street bridge the Castleton River enters on the right. The Castleton adds considerably to the flow in summer months if the Lake Bomoseen hydroelectric plant is operating.

Below the West Street bridge (1.0 mile) the ledges become relatively more runnable, although the river runs into a deep gorge that makes portages difficult. Over the last mile the rapids moderate and run over a shallow spot, by an old abutment, to flowage from the Carver Falls dam. Take out on the far left.

The Carver Falls Cave is found by following the portage trail down the left bank into the gorge. The cave is at the head of the second little stream coming in from the left, which is a 0.5-mile walk.

Carver Falls ➤ Lake Champlain	12.0 mi
Description:	0.25 mi of Class II rapids in gorge at start, flatwater, quickwater
Date checked:	2001
Navigable:	Spring, summer, fall (dam controlled)
Scenery:	Rural
Maps:	USGS Thorn Hill, Benson, Whitehall

During the summer this section may be difficult if the Carver Falls Station is not operating, because no water is then allowed to flow downstream. Check with the Production Department at Central Vermont Public Service (802-747-5207).

Carver Falls is accessible by car from the New York side only. From Fair Haven, Vermont, take West Street 2.0 miles to a bridge over the Poultney River. Take the first road on the right, in 0.25 mile, and another right at the sign for the dam.

The gorge below the dam is impressive, but the rapids are short. If you choose to avoid them, an old woods road goes down to the river at the lower end of the gorge. It starts between the tool sheds behind the engineer's house. It is not passable for cars, but boats may be carried down.

The water is somewhat opaque, but the banks are high, rocky in some places, and the area is known for its wildflowers. The current slows very gradually. Below a side-road bridge (3.5 miles) a four-wheel-drive road follows imperceptibly along the right bank. The bridge at the Elbow (12.0 miles) provides good access. You can also continue to the confluence with Wood Creek, 0.5 mile farther downstream, and bear right into Lake Champlain or bear left and paddle a mile up the creek to Whitehall, New York.

Mettawee River VT

The river rises on the west slope of Dorset Mountain and passes, as a small brook, under VT 30, where it might be possible to start at high water.

North Rupert ➤ North Pawlet		9.0 mi
Description:	Class I–II	
Date checked:	1983	
Navigable:	Medium water	
Scenery:	Rural	

Put in at the VT 30 bridge 1.0 mile north of North Rupert. The stream is about 15 feet wide and runs through pastureland. Downed trees and old barbed wire fences are the worst problems; the current and rocks are easy. In Pawlet, Flower Brook joins the river and doubles its size. This section runs through attractive, high, wooded banks. After a mile the river returns to pastureland and after another 2.0 miles reaches a steel bridge. The bridge is on a road that is the first left off VT 30 north of Pawlet. Another 1.0 mile may be run to the next bridge at VT 153. **Caution!** The river drops 25 feet through a narrow cleft just beyond.

North Pawlet ➤ New York State barge canal   about 35 mi.

Most of this distance is quickwater through farmland, but there are many waterfalls and ledges. The first is Button Falls, 2.0 miles downstream of the previous take-out.

Chapter 3
Hudson Watershed

HUDSON
WATERSHED

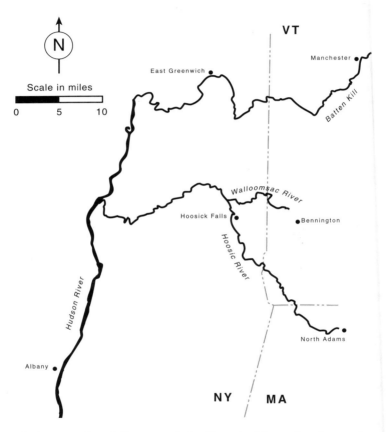

Rainwater that falls west of the Taconic Mountains in southern Vermont flows into the Hudson River in the Hoosic, or the more attractive Walloomsac and Batten Kill Rivers. The Hoosic crosses the most southwestern corner of Vermont, while the Walloomsac and Batten Kill rise in Vermont and offer pleasant paddling.

Batten Kill <small>VT, NY</small>

The Batten Kill is a beautiful, clear stream that flows west across southern Vermont, from the Green Mountains to the Hudson River. The water is also enjoyable for swimming. It has a moderate current with riffles, and there are only two places, which are fairly close together and in the first section, where a less skillful paddler might wish to line or carry.

Manchester ➤ Arlington	10.5 mi
Description:	Flatwater, quickwater, Class I–II
Date checked:	2001
Navigable:	High or medium water (spring and normal summers)
Scenery:	Rural
Maps:	USGS Equinox 15

To put in, take the road east of the monument on US 7 in Manchester, and follow it for 0.75 mile to a bridge. At the beginning the river is small and shallow. If there is enough water to run the rapid below the bridge, the river is runnable, but some fallen trees will have to be lined or lifted over.

It is 2.75 miles to the first bridge; below that the Batten Kill is generally slower and deeper. There is flatwater, along with a few riffles. The river flows through farming country, much of which is posted. Ask for and obtain permission before crossing property lines. There is good access to the river on the right bank just downstream of the US 7A bridge (8.0 miles).

Just below the mouth of Roaring Branch, a large stream which enters on the left, there is strong, fast current, with Class II rapids in high water. The river swings left and is divided into two channels by a large rock. If you wish to line or carry this spot, do so on the right.

Easy rapids continue past the VT 313 bridge (9.75 miles), which also provides good parking upstream on the left. The river takes a sharp turn to the right 0.5 mile below, where there is a pool followed by a washed-out dam that can be scouted from the right bank if desired. Shortly beyond is the Rochester bridge (10.5 miles), located off VT 313 just west of Arlington.

Arlington ➤ East Greenwich   20.0 mi

Description:	Quickwater, Class I
Date checked:	2001
Navigable:	Passable, at most water levels
Scenery:	Forested, rural towns
Maps:	USGS Equinox 15, Shushan, Salem, Cossayuna

The river here is a little wider, and it runs quickly and steadily, giving a fast ride through easy riffles. Except when it is very dry, it can be run all summer, and there are occasional deep pools for swimming. The stretch is also very popular for float trips on rubber rafts, inner tubes, air mattresses, logs, and anything else that will float.

Bridges cross the river every couple of miles, from any one of which there is access to the river.

In 3.0 miles you pass the mouth of the Green River near West Arlington, and 4.5 miles farther is the NY 313 bridge (7.5 miles). To improve the fishing on the Batten Kill, the state of New York has built several rock cribs and a low, sometimes runnable weir. The latter extends across the river above the County 61 bridge (8.75 miles), which is the first NY 313 bridge.

After several miles the river swings north, passes Shushan (13.75 miles), goes under four railroad bridges and NY 22 (17.75 miles), and then heads right again. Go under another railroad bridge near East Greenwich, and take out on the right above the dam (20.0 miles).

Hoosic River MA, VT, NY

The Hoosic River rises in Lanesboro, Massachusetts, flows north to North Adams, where it turns west to Williamstown, and then takes off northwesterly across a corner of Vermont into New York, where it again turns north to make a big loop to meet the Hudson River near Mechanicsville. The flood-control works in Adams and North Adams have reduced the threat of flooding and have also eliminated the paddling in Adams and North

Adams, as the river drops between high retaining walls. Boating is not only illegal there, it is suicidal.

The upper sections are passable only in high water, but below North Adams much of it can be done later in the year. (See the *AMC River Guide Massachusetts/Connecticut/Rhode Island* for information on the section above North Adams.)

North Adams, MA ➤ North Pownal, VT		15.0 mi
Description:	Quickwater, Class I, II	
Date checked:	1998	
Navigable:	Medium water	
Scenery:	Swamp, forested, towns	
Maps:	North Adams, Williams, Williamstown, MA; Pownal, North Pownal, VT	
Portage:	11.25 mi R dam in North Pownal 0.25 mi	

Put in below the last dam at the west end of North Adams, just west of the Protection Road bridge. The most convenient place is the old sewage treatment plant on the north side.

Most of the distance is smooth, with only occasional rapids of moderate difficulty and stretches of quieter water between them. Pass two bridges close together in a little more than a mile; then at 3.0 miles the bridge that carries the Appalachian Trail; at 4.5 miles the US 7 bridge at Williamstown; at 6.25 miles the Massachusetts/Vermont state line; and at 9.0 miles the bridge at Pownal.

The dam at North Pownal is confined between cliffs and walls, so it should be scouted in advance. You can carry up the road on either side; neither is easy. By the time you can see the factory chimney from the river, you may be past the best take-out.

North Pownal ➤ Hoosick Falls	15.0 mi

This is a pleasant run through farming country, with high hills on either side of the valley. There are a few easy riffles. On approaching Hoosick Falls, take out on the left just before the railroad bridge. **Caution!** Under no circumstances go below the railroad bridge, because the steep rapid beneath it is followed by rapids confined by two concrete retaining walls, which lead into impassable cataracts below. There is no convenient place to put in below these falls, and the power dam 1.0 mile below involves another carry, so it is better to portage by car 2.0 miles to Hoosick Junction.

Walloomsac River VT, NY

The Walloomsac flows west from Bennington to the Hoosic River. It provides a delightful paddle through beautiful and historic terrain. The river riffles over gravel beds and around fallen trees, sometimes near the road or railroad, sometimes in more remote areas. It is best run in the spring, because some stretches may be too shallow in the summer.

Bennington ➤ Walloomsac Village	8.75 mi
Description:	Flatwater, Class I
Date checked:	2001
Navigable:	High or medium water (spring or after moderate rain)
Scenery:	Rural, towns
Maps:	USGS Bennington, Hoosick Falls
Portages:	1.25 mi dam at Paper Mill Village— carry on island
	2.25 mi L dam 30 yd

Begin a couple of miles west of Bennington off VT 67A by following Silk Road across the covered bridge. Put in where the road comes close to the river opposite a white house.

Winding over riffles and passing under the covered bridge, the stream becomes flat as it reaches the first dam at Paper Mill Village in 1.25 miles. The dam is under the second covered bridge. The stream divides here. Take out before the iron bridge and carry on the left, crossing Murphy Road, following a path.

There is some Class II water for a short distance below the first dam (1.25 miles). The next dam, 1.0 mile farther, is slightly above the Henry Bridge and is not easily spotted. A white colonial house on the left across an open field is a good landmark. Carry on the left. After about 2.25 miles more of pleasant riffles, the hamlet of Sodom is reached. Here there is a tiny dam or obstruction entirely across the river. This may be readily run at high water, but it may have to be carried at lower water levels.

About 4 miles below Sodom (4.5 miles) is another dam. The riffles are almost continuous in the last 0.5 mile, and the dam (8.75 miles) appears suddenly around a bend to the right. A tall smokestack is very conspicuous, however; observe caution as soon as it comes into view. Boats may be taken out on the left and carried uphill through a farm field to the road.

It is possible to relaunch well below the dam and rapids, but there is only about 1 mile to the next dam (10.0 miles); look for a tall brick chimney. Getting out is difficult. Carrying around the dam is even harder. There is no good take-out point below here, unless you continue down the Hoosic below the mouth of the Walloomsac (11.75 miles).

Chapter 4
Upper Connecticut Watershed

UPPER CONNECTICUT WATERSHED

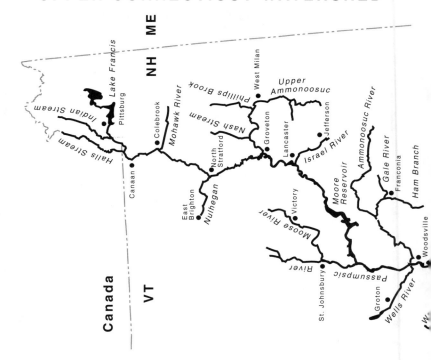

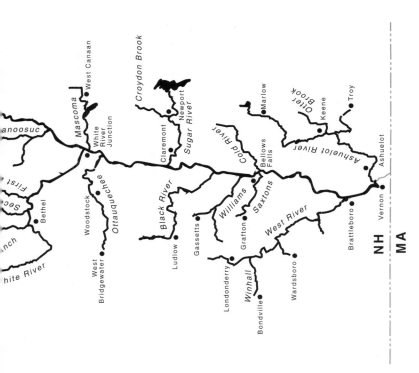

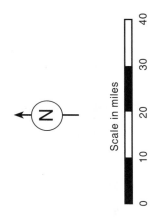

Scale in miles

0   10   20   30   40

The hilly and mountainous terrain of the Upper Connecticut water-shed causes rainfall and snowmelt to run off fairly quickly—quickwater and rapids dominate the region. Most of these rivers collect drainage from a small area and are not large. While there are some very nice flatwater sections, they tend to be broken up by quickwater and rapids, so that long summer trips are generally impossible.

The Connecticut River always has sufficient water for passage, but much of it consists of long thin lakes behind high dams.

There are water releases on several of the rivers. Refer to the information in the text for details, and plan to call to get the water-release schedules.

Connecticut River NH, VT

The Connecticut is New England's longest river. Like many other New England rivers it is most attractive near its source; farther downstream it passes through large towns and cities. Paddling on the lower river is popular, however, and it can be done in summer low water.

From the upper end of First Connecticut Lake, the river offers about 400 miles of varied lake and river paddling, with few unrunnable sections but with fifteen dams that require carries of different lengths.

The Connecticut River Watershed Council, 125 Ferry Rd., Easthampton, MA 01027, publishes a guidebook, *The Complete Boating Guide to the Connecticut River*, with maps showing the fishing, sailing, boating, and water-sports areas. Connecticut River Joint Commissions publishes a free pamphlet, "Boating on the Connecticut River in New Hampshire and Vermont." Download it from www.crjc.org/recreation.htm, or send $.55 postage to CRJC, P.O. Box 1182, Charlestown, NH 03603. AMC's *Exploring the Connecticut River from Source to Sea*, by Michael Tougias, examines the history and natural history of the Connecticut River (www.outdoors.org).

The Connecticut Lakes
Maps: USGS Second Lake 15, Indian Stream 15

From its source at Fourth Lake, the Connecticut is a tiny trout brook to Third Lake. From Third Lake to Second Lake, it is still too small and steep to paddle, and from Second to First Lake, paddling is not advised. Some paddlers do run this stretch, but great care should be taken because there is a tremendous drop halfway down which must be carried. This drop is about 0.5 mile below the Second Lake dam and about 50 yards below a left turn on the river. Although both Second and Third Lakes offer pleasant paddling, fishing, swimming, and other water sports, paddlers who wish to run the river will probably start at the head of First Lake. A side road leading from US 3 to Metallak Point offers easy access to that end of the lake. There is a launching area at the foot of the lake near the dam. Below First Lake the stream becomes runnable for the first time, but since the level of First Lake is controlled by a dam, water is likely to be insufficient unless some is being released to generate power. Releases are posted daily at the dam. Call the Flo Fone for flow forecasts (888-356-3663).

Below the dam the river is very rough and steep for 1.0 mile, then easier rapids follow for 0.5 mile to the entrance of Perry Stream to the right. These easy rapids continue another 1.0 mile to Lake Francis, but under some water conditions this entire stretch can offer hard rapids, and the last 150 yards should be examined in advance. Lake Francis is an artificial lake over what was formerly a less-attractive stretch of river that flowed through farmland. Below the Lake Francis dam there is rapid water to the bridge and dam at Pittsburg, where you must take out. **Caution!** Take out above the dam; there is an impassable gorge for 1.5 miles below to a covered bridge. It is possible to line down this gorge in low water, but if a car is available, carrying will be much easier, and you must carry at medium or high water.

Pittsburg ➤ West Stewartstown/Canaan	9.25 mi
Description:	Quickwater, Class I–II
Date checked:	2001
Navigable:	Passable at most water levels
Scenery:	Forested, rural, towns
Maps:	USGS Indian Stream 15, Averill 15, Dixville 15

Portage: 9.0 mi R Canaan Dam 0.5 mi
2.0 mi R Indian Stream
Campsites: 28.5 mi L Countryside Campgrounds

The river throughout even the uppermost parts is bucolic, not wild; an outing on this section can be very pleasant.

Begin at the covered bridge on Bacon Road just off US 3 and 0.9 mile south of Pittsburg. There is also a small parking area here that cannot be seen from the main highway.

Starting immediately under the bridge, there are 150 yards of Class II rapids in high water. Then in the next 2.0 miles the Connecticut has intermittent Class I+ rapids. The highway, US 3, follows the river, almost constantly within sight on the right. An attractive, forested area rises on the left. Two miles beyond Indian Stream (2.5 miles), which enters on the right, US 3 (4.5 miles) passes over the river, and below this point there are 350 yards of Class II rips. The boundary marker between New Hampshire and Vermont is 0.5 mile farther and south of this point.

In another 2.25 miles, Halls Stream (7.5 miles) enters on the right, and shortly after passing under a bridge with houses visible on each bank, you reach Beecher Falls (8.0 miles). The falls are a short Class II rapid that may be run at any point, although passage on the extreme left or right is probably drier and safer.

Canaan Dam lies 1.0 mile below Beecher Falls, and the easiest portage is on the Vermont side. In high water, more-experienced boaters who are willing to do some scrambling on the right bank can put in again almost immediately below the dam. This river should be taken to the right of the islands after the dam, but the going is scratchy in high water and probably impassable in low. A longer portage of 0.5 mile on the right is the more conventional route around the dam.

After a level stretch there is a short, solid Class III drop before the NH/VT 114 bridge at West Stewartstown/Canaan (9.5 miles).

West Stewartstown/Canaan ➤
North Stratford/Bloomfield   24.5 mi

Description:	Quickwater, Class I–II
Date checked:	2001
Navigable:	Spring, summer, fall
Scenery:	Rural
Maps:	USGS Averill 15

For the 10.0 miles from West Stewartstown/Canaan to Colebrook, the river is mostly smooth and relatively shallow, except for a 100-yard Class I–II rapid 0.5 mile below the bridge. The river meanders through level pastureland, which borders both sides. Dairy cattle graze along the banks for most of this section, reason enough to bring along fresh water if you plan to camp. At Colebrook the river passes below Monadnock Mountain, which rises steeply on the Vermont side.

Below Colebrook (10.25 miles) the river is quick for 3.0 miles; then it develops small rips for another 2 miles. It is mostly smooth for 4.0 miles below the Columbia covered bridge to a campground on the left (19.25 miles). The river should be taken on the right through small riffles.

Two-and-a-half miles below Countryside Campgrounds are the remains of Lyman Falls Dam (22.0 miles). The river has several islands on the left, and close to the right bank there is a log crib. The dam is immediately below; the abutment is not very visible, and paddlers are often washed over this dam by mistake. Keep to the right on a wide, sweeping turn.

Caution! The remains of Lyman Dam should be scouted, but for moderately skilled whitewater paddlers it probably provides the most sport on the Connecticut to this point. In high water the best run over the old dam is directly below the log crib that lies 75 yards upstream. The small curler below the dam can provide some very interesting spots for paddlers to play and surf. In higher water it should be approached cautiously, but the curler should not present a problem to a strong Class II boater. Even so, it is probably best not to engage in too much play at this point unless you are prepared for a swim. The dam is in the process of washing out, and conditions change after every storm, so scout carefully.

There are riffles for the next 2.75 miles to North Stratford/Bloomfield (24.5 miles).

North Stratford ➤ Guildhall   25.0 mi

Description:	Flatwater, quickwater
Date checked:	2001
Navigable:	Spring, summer, fall
Scenery:	Forested, rural
Maps:	USGS Averill 15, Guildhall 15

The river meanders, placid and wide, from here to the breached dam at Guildhall. It is 5.0 miles to North Stratford, opposite where Paul Stream comes in on the Vermont side, and another 6.0 miles to the historic metal truss bridge at Stratford. It is then 11.0 miles on a flat river plain with fine views of the mountains to the confluence with the Upper Ammonoosuc River at Groveton. Only 3.0 miles farther is the breached dam at the bridge at Guildhall. Portage on the Vermont shore. There is hazardous rebar protruding from the remains of the dam.

Guildhall ➤ Gilman   23.0 mi

Description:	Flatwater, quickwater
Date checked:	2001
Navigable:	Spring, summer, fall
Scenery:	Forested, rural
Maps:	USGS Guildhall 15, Whitefield 15
Portage:	(23.0 mi L Gilman Dam)

The placid water continues for the next 23.0 miles to the dam at Gilman. It is 10.0 miles to Lancaster, another 7.0 miles of winding river to the covered bridge at South Lancaster, and another 3.0 miles to the next bridge at South Lunenburg. About 0.25 mile below the railroad bridge is a Class II rapid. From there it is only 3.0 miles more to the dam and bridge at Gilman. Take out on the New Hampshire side at the end of the boom above the dam.

Gilman ➤ East Ryegate 30.0 mi

Description:	Flatwater, quickwater, Class I
Date checked:	2001
Navigable:	Spring, summer, fall
Scenery:	Forested, rural, towns
Maps:	USGS Whitefield 15, Littletown 15, St. Johnsbury 15, Woodsville 15
Portages:	11.25 mi R Moore Dam 0.5 mi
	18.75 mi L Comerford Dam 0.5 mi
	25.5 mi L McIndoe Falls Dam 200 yd
	30.0 mi L East Ryegate Dam 100 ft–300 yd

The beautiful Fifteen-Mile Falls section of the river formerly began at Gilman. These fine rapids, the best on the river, are now completely inundated by the Moore Reservoir and the Comerford Reservoir, although when the former is low there is still 0.25–0.5 mile or more of fastwater with rocks and boulders. PG&E National Energy Group, which operates these two dams and the McIndoe Falls Dam, has provided a number of boat-launching and picnic areas on the reservoirs, but no overnight camping is allowed at these points. The paddler can put in at Gilman on the Vermont side just below the bridge. From here to Moore Dam it is 12.0 miles. This stretch is mostly lake travel on the reservoir, although when the water level is low there may be 0.5 mile or more of easy rapids. Take care, however, if the water volume is great, since the waves can be high. Once you reach the reservoir the going is very pleasant, but a headwind can make progress a strenuous affair. It is best to start this section early in the morning before the wind rises. There are three boat-launching and picnic areas on the south shore of the reservoir and one on the north bank in Waterford near the dam. The carry at the Moore Dam is on the Vermont side, about 0.5 mile long and well marked by signs. The bank at the put-in is somewhat unstable, so take care. There is a visitor center at Moore Dam.

Since the backwater from the Comerford Dam reaches practically to the Moore Dam, the 7.0 miles between the two are almost all lake paddling. There is a boat-launching and picnic area just below the VT 18 bridge on the New Hampshire side and another on the Vermont side not far from the dam. The carry at the Comerford Dam is on the New Hampshire side, about 0.5 mile long and marked by signs.

The 7.0 miles from the Comerford Dam to the McIndoe Falls Dam can be very interesting. If the Comerford Dam is discharging water, the current will be swift and paddling easy. There are, though, some large boulders about 1.0 mile below the dam which present a hazard to navigation. In another mile, the Passumpsic River enters on the right and the river turns to a southerly course. The next 5.0 miles are through a narrow, wooded valley, with high hills on either side most of the way. The portage at the McIndoe Falls Dam, on the New Hampshire side, is easy, about 200 yards long, and well marked.

The narrow, wooded valley continues for the next 4.0 miles to the Ryegate Paper Company's dam at East Ryegate. The 15-foot-high dam should be approached with caution, since water often spills over the top. It is just below a left bend in the river and, because the carry is on the New Hampshire side, it is best to approach it along the left bank. Several portage routes are available, varying from a few feet if the current is slow, to several hundred yards if the current is too fast to approach the dam closely. There is car take-out above the dam, and fine, though ledgy, access.

East Ryegate ➤ Hanover	51.0 mi
Description:	Flatwater, quickwater, Class I–II
Date checked:	2001
Navigable:	Spring, summer, fall
Scenery:	Forested, rural, settled, towns
Maps:	USGS Woodsville 15, Mount Cube 15, Mascoma 15, Hanover

This is one of the more interesting and picturesque sections of the river and one on which there is a certain amount of boating, especially in the lower portion. Below the dam at East Ryegate there is some fastwater, and the best channel is usually on the New Hampshire side. It is 4.0 miles to Wells River/Woodsville, where the Ammonoosuc River enters on the left and, 0.25 mile below, the Wells River enters on the right just below the US 302 and railroad bridges. Depending on water levels, this can be rather wild, as the river goes through narrow ledges, and turns sharply west at Woodsville, above the bridges. There is a short but easy rip just below these bridges, then 10.0 miles of shallow, winding river to the bridge at Newbury, where there is a launching ramp on the right bank. It is another mile to South Newbury.

The valley has now become wider, with farmland on the level areas, and mountain views in the background. There is a new boat launch in Haverhill at Bedell Bridge. The current begins to slacken near the red barn on the right at Placey Farm as the river reaches water backed up by the Wilder Dam 37.0 miles below. This section is now known as Wilder Lake and is provided with boat-launching ramps at the dam.

There is little perceptible widening of the river for many miles. It is 6.0 miles to Bradford and the entrance to the Waits River on the right bank. Bradford is easiest to visit by paddling up the Waits River. In another mile the paddler passes under the VT 25 bridge and in 10.0 more miles under the bridge from Fairlee to Orford. Here it was that Samuel Morey tested his steam-propelled vessel in 1792–93. At Orford, New Hampshire, there is a municipal boat-launching area. It is then 6.0 miles to a former bridge abutment still visible in the middle of the river at North Thetford and 2.0 miles more to the bridge at East Thetford. At this point the river is obviously becoming wider. In 5.0 miles you pass the mouth of the Ompompanoosuc River on the right and in another 5.0 miles the bridge at Hanover, below which only 2.0 miles remain to the dam in Wilder. Note that headwinds and pooling of water behind the dam can drastically alter times for doing this section.

Hanover ➤ Bellows Falls   46.0 mi

Description:	Flatwater, quickwater, Class II
Date checked:	2001
Navigable:	Spring, summer, fall
Scenery:	Forested, rural, towns
Maps:	USGS Hanover, North Hartland, Claremon 15, Bellows Falls 15

Portages:　　　　　　2.0 mi L Wilder Dam 0.25 mi
　　　　　　　　　　　　11.0 mi R Hartland Rapids 0.25 mi
　　　　　　　　　　　　(46.0 mi L Bellows Falls 1.0 mi)

It is 2.0 miles down Wilder Lake to the dam, which should be carried on the east, the NH side, where the 0.25-mile portage is well marked by signs. PG&E National Energy Group runs a visitors' center (802-295-3192) at the dam which has exhibits on the fish ladder. To reach it, pull to the VT shore above the dam and walk. Below the dam the water level can vary quite suddenly if the generators are started or stopped. Call the Flo Fone for flow forecasts (888-356-3663). The water is swift but shallow for 2.0 miles to White River Junction and the mouth of the White River on the right. Osprey, bald eagles, ducks, eagles, and beaver have been spotted in this more-isolated section, as well as the Atlantic salmon, which is just barely making a comeback. One mile below the White River confluence, the Mascoma River enters on the New Hampshire side practically at the I-89 bridge. About 4.0 miles below that, at North Hartland, the Ottauquechee River comes in on the Vermont side. It is then only 2.0 miles to the difficult and dangerous Sumner Falls, and the two signs that read Danger—Falls Ahead should be taken very seriously by even the most-experienced boater. Also known as the Hartland Rapids, this area is notorious for sudden changes in wind speed and, more important, water volume. Water releases occur without warning, and this area literally washes through moments after the dam gates have opened. Many anglers and boaters have been caught by surprise. At the actual approach of the rapid, the river narrows, and a wooded bank on the right juts out, cutting off any view of the rapids below, although you should hear the roar of the water by this point. **Caution!** These rapids should not be attempted at any water level. Portage on the right, on a marked path that is 0.25 mile long, ending at the picnic area at the foot of the rapid. At low water expert paddlers might run these rapids, but they should check in at the Wilder Dam beforehand to check the release schedule. Below the dam are many play areas for boaters to practice surfing and other techniques; again, paddlers should be aware of changes in water level.

At this time the entire river flows through two channels. The channel nearer the west bank, about 15 feet wide, has a drop too abrupt for loaded canoes. The other channel, near the center of the river, is 30 feet wide but narrows to only 7 feet at the bottom of the initial pitch, where some large rocks must be avoided. Once through this pitch, you can ride the haystacks for 75 yards until a 180-degree right turn brings the boat into the western chute with only choppy water to the bottom of the rapid.

Below the rapids it is 8.0 miles to the covered bridge at Windsor and then another 5.0 miles to the NH 103 bridge at Ascutney. Just below the bridge the Sugar River enters on the left, and Wilgus State Park offers camping areas on the Vermont shore. This whole stretch of the river passes through fine hills, with Mount Ascutney dominating the view. Below is an 8-mile stretch of river around the Weathersfield Bow, then the Little Sugar River enters on the left at North Charlestown. There follow 4.0 miles more of easy paddling down to the Cheshire Toll Bridge at Charlestown, just below which the Black River enters on the right. In 7 more miles you pass the mouth of the Williams River on the right, where there is a boat-launching and picnic area. Then after 3.0 miles of deadwater, the dam at Bellows Falls requires a long portage, 0.5–0.75 miles, right through the town. Either side of the river can be used, but the easier route is probably on the east bank. Take out on the left and carry on the New Hampshire side to a put-in below the falls. A carry by car is strongly advised, because traffic is heavy and there is no shoulder.

Bellows Falls ➤ Vernon Dam	31.75 mi
Description:	Flatwater, quickwater
Date checked:	2001
Navigable:	Spring, summer, fall
Scenery:	Forested, rural towns
Maps:	USGS Bellows Falls 15, Keene 15, Brattleboro 15
Portage:	(31.75 mi R Vernon Dam 0.25 mi)

There is a visitors' center at the dam. Below the powerhouse at Bellows Falls the paddler passes the mouth of the Saxtons River in 0.5 mile on the right bank, in another 0.25 mile the Cold River on the left bank, and then in 2.0 miles more the bridge at Walpole. There are then 14.0 miles of unobstructed river through open farming country to the NH 9 bridge above Brattleboro. In 1.0 mile the river reaches the NH 119 bridge. From the island with a bridge on either side at Brattleboro, there are 7.0 miles of deadwater to the dam at Vernon, which requires a 0.25-mile carry on the west shore from the log boom above the dam. Signs mark the portage. The Vermont Yankee Nuclear Power Plant is directly adjacent to the dam, and it has an Energy Information Center that can be visited during normal working hours.

Vernon Dam ➤ Turners Falls	20.0 mi
Description:	Flatwater, quickwater, Class I–II
Date checked:	2001
Navigable:	Spring, summer, fall
Scenery:	Forested, rural, settled, towns
Maps:	USGS Brattleboro 15, Keene 15, Northfield, Millers Falls, Greenfield
Portage:	20.0 mi R Turners Falls

Below the dam the going is swift and rocky if the water is low. It is only 2.0 miles to the mouth of the Ashuelot River in Hinsdale, and in another 3.5 miles the Connecticut crosses the Massachusetts border. All through here, and for the next 10.0 miles to the gorge at French King, the river flows in open farmland, which offers good camping spots.

In 1.5 miles from the border the river reaches the MA 142 bridge. From there it is 8.5 miles to the gorge, at the upper end of which there is a large rock, which creates turbulence even when the rest of the river is calm. A route close to either shore is preferred at this point. Here the current quickens, and the river turns right, under the French King Bridge at the confluence with the Millers River, and continues heavy to Turners Falls, 4.0 miles away. At high water this section of river can become extremely rough, and under these conditions some paddlers may prefer to take out at the bridge that crosses the Millers River at its mouth. At Turners Falls, take out at the steel bridge 0.25 mile above the dam on the right side.

Indian Stream NH

This is the northernmost runnable stream in New Hampshire; it rises even farther north than the Connecticut River, into which it flows below Pittsburg. The river is formed by several branches joining near the former Depot Camp, an early logging headquarters so remote that it was supplied from the railroad in Malvina, Quebec, Canada.

The only habitations are occasional hunting camps and some farms in the valley adjacent to the Connecticut River. A gravel logging road leads up to the east bank from US 3 beyond Depot Camp, and a branch road connects to Back Lake.

The entire watershed lies within the town of Pittsburg. Although the region was claimed by both the United States and Canada, each exercised only sporadic jurisdiction. In 1836 the settlers formed the Indian Stream Republic. This led to an immediate settlement of the boundary, and brought an end to the dispute and to the republic.

Depot Camp ➤ Connecticut River		17.0 mi
Description:	Flatwater, quickwater, Class I	
Date checked:	2001	
Navigable:	High water (May)	
Scenery:	Forested, rural	
Maps:	USGS Indian Stream 15	

Put in by carrying to the river near Depot Camp or by coming down one of the branches if the water is high enough. There are a few easy rapids, then a long, meandering stretch with weaker current. The road is frequently nearby. The last 2.5 miles to Camp Brook contain more rapids.

Camp Brook is about 0.5 mile north of the Indian Stream and Back Lake roads. The river is close to the road, and there is an old, unusable bridge. South of this point the road does not follow the stream. It is 2.5 miles to the site of the Kim Day Dam (10.5 miles).

Below the old dam site (10.5 miles) there is a ledge at the head of an island, followed by 200 yards of Class II–III rapids, which can be portaged on the left. Then there are about 3 miles of Class I rapids through woods. The last 3.5 miles to the Connecticut River, broad and meandering through fields, are passable in the summer. The US 3 bridge is 0.25 mile above the Connecticut (17.0 miles).

Halls Stream PQ, NH, VT

Halls Stream is one of the northernmost rivers in New Hampshire. The runnable portion of it was once the boundary between Quebec and New Hampshire, but as a result of channel changes the river now meanders back and forth across the border. Most of the river is a pleasant run of easy rapids with a gravel bottom. Fallen trees can cause occasional problems.

Access to the upper river is best from the Canadian side, where gravel roads lead close to it in two places. There is a public road on the New Hampshire side along the lower river, and with four-wheel-drive vehicles it may be possible to reach the upper river via logging roads along Halls Stream or from Indian Stream.

The CNTS Malvina 21 E/3 map is best for the upper river since it shows the Canadian access. The USGS Indian Stream sheet is adequate for the lower river, but it shows only the U.S. side of the border. The CNTS Coaticook 21 E/4 and Averill maps show the last mile, including the take-out.

Malvina Stream, PQ ➤ Tabor Notch, NH	9.0 mi
Description:	Class I–II
Date checked:	2001
Navigable:	High water (April and May)
Scenery:	Forested, rural
Maps:	USGS Indian Stream 15, Averill 15
	CNTS Malvina 21 E/3, Coaticook 21 E/4

The key to Canadian access is the village of Paquette (Saint Venant-de-Hereford), which is located about 10.0 miles north of Beecher Falls on PQ 253. Take the gravel road north out of the village up a long hill. After 5.5 miles, go down a steep hill and turn right. Proceed 0.75 mile to a bridge over Malvina

Stream. Put in here or 1.0 mile downstream at a farm. Remember to ask for and obtain permission before crossing property lines. If the water is too low, Halls Stream is probably too low as well.

Malvina Stream is a gravelly Class I stream about a boat-length wide. Roughly 0.5 mile from the farm the stream passes an old railroad embankment and enters Halls Stream. The latter is mostly Class I, but occasionally there are harder spots. One rocky drop adjacent to the old railroad embankment should be looked over. The banks are mostly wooded.

Five and a half miles from Malvina Stream a large farm on the Canadian shore provides access. It is reached by taking the road east from Paquette for 1.0 mile.

In another 3.0 miles there is a farm (9.0 miles) on the New Hampshire shore and a gravel road adjacent to the river. This is at the foot of Tabor Notch, a deep pass on the New Hampshire side which has no road through it.

Access is also possible elsewhere on the lower river from the Canadian side where PQ 253 comes close to the river.

Tabor Notch, NH ➤ Connecticut River, VT   9.5 mi

Description:	Quickwater, Class I
Date checked:	2001
Navigable:	High water (spring and after moderate rains)
Scenery:	Rural, town
Maps:	USGS Indian Stream 15, Averill 15

To put in on the New Hampshire side, follow the road up the east bank for 7.0 miles to a location adjacent to the river, after which the road ascends for 0.5 mile and enters at a farm.

There are occasional riffles and fallen trees. From time to time there is access on the New Hampshire shore. In 9.0 miles the international boundary runs west from the stream, which from that point flows through Vermont. Another 0.5 mile brings you to the bridge at Beechers Falls and, just below, the Connecticut River (9.5 miles).

Mohawk River NH

The Mohawk rises in Dixville Notch and flows west to the Connecticut River at Colebrook. It is almost continuously rapid, with a decreasing gradient.

Kidderville ➤ Connecticut River		8.0 mi
Description:	Class II–III	
Date checked:	2001	
Navigable:	High water (early May)	
Scenery:	Forested, towns	
Maps:	USGS Dixville 15	

Put in on the Mohawk River in Kidderville from Diamond Pond Road just below the junction of two brooks and a dam. The first mile is almost continuous Class III ledges around blind corners. All are runnable somewhere but may require scouting. Below the NH 26 bridge (1.0 mile) there are only a couple of additional ledges, and then it is riffly Class II going with beautiful evergreen banks all the way to Colebrook and the NH 26 and US 3 bridges (7.0 miles). The confluence with the Connecticut is another easy mile, and the next access is the bridge over the Connecticut 0.5 mile downstream.

Nulhegan River VT

The Nulhegan River and its numerous tributaries drain an extensive area of swamps, wooded hills, and mountains east of Island Pond, in the least-inhabited part of Vermont. The main river rises in Brighton just east of Island Pond and flows through high but swampy country.

Although the river is close to the road and a railroad, little is seen of them. The view is mostly alders, birds, and an occasional distant mountain.

Nulhegan Pond ➤ VT 105 Bridge		5.0 mi
Description:	Quickwater, swamp	
Date checked:	2001	
Navigable:	Medium water	
Scenery:	Wild	
Maps:	USGS Island Pond 15	

Swamp-lovers can put in at the outlet of Nulhegan Pond, or at the inlet at the previous bridge, and paddle through the pond. The river's span is barely a canoe-width, and that is somewhat obstructed. The worst part can be avoided by putting in at a side stream about 1.0 mile down.

VT 105 Bridge ➤ Gorge   3.25 mi

The next 3.0 miles are similar to those above, but the river is larger and offers easier going. If you really want to run the entire river, you could take out on the right above the gorge, to VT 105, or on either side to carry for 0.25 mile (neither side is very good). It may also be possible to run or line the gorge. The railroad crosses at the top of the drop, but the rapids start above it.

Gorge ➤ "Stone Dam"   3.0 mi

The gorge can just be seen from the end of a private road, but access is poor. Remember to ask for and obtain permission before attempting to access here. Easy rapids continue below the gorge and soon become quickwater as they approach the stone dam at the next VT 105 bridge.

"Stone Dam" ➤ East Branch   1.75 mi

There is no dam at the bridge, but Class III–IV rapids start promptly and continue for 1.0 mile with one drop that is often portaged on the right. The rapids ease off to the confluence with the East Branch (no access).

East Branch ➤ Connecticut River   2.5 mi

This section can be run by putting in at the East Branch bridge 0.5 mile above the confluence or at a gate on the logging road on the right bank another mile up the East Branch. The run down the East Branch is Class II. The going is easier on the Nulhegan until the 0.5 mile of rapids that leads to the Connecticut River. Access is at the Nulhegan bridge just above the Connecticut.

Upper Ammonoosuc River NH

The Upper Ammonoosuc River drains the Kilkenny region of the White Mountains, flowing north and then west to the Connecticut River at Groveton. It has no connection with the Ammonoosuc or Wild Ammonoosuc rivers farther south.

West Branch ➤ York Pond Road 2.0 mi

Take the road to the York Pond Fish Hatchery from NH 110. Continue on the road for approximately 5 miles, take a left, and go 0.5 mile to a bridge. This is the West Branch of the Upper Ammonoosuc, a short and frisky run that can only be accomplished in the spring. It is a very small stream, only 20 feet wide, and it drops 40 feet in the first 0.5 mile. Tight eddy turns are possible. The small size of the stream keeps the rating at Class III, and the small size requires alertness and excellent boat control. The first mile drops 100 feet, and a long Class III builds up to a Class IV stretch where the river narrows and drops—watch for rock walls on the sides—which culminates in a difficult 5-foot drop best run right center. The river then approaches the York Pond Road on the right bank, where you can take out for a rest and put in to continue the run. If the West Branch is high, the main river will be very high. This run will be up when the Nash Stream is not.

York Pond Road ➤ West Milan 6.0 mi

Description:	Quickwater, Class II
Date checked:	2000
Navigable:	High water (late April and May)
Scenery:	Forested
Maps:	USGS Percy 15

Put in where the York Pond Road crosses the river. The rapids at the bridge are a good indication of what the rest of the run is like. In high water the river is a wavy Class II; it is rocky at lower levels.

It is 4.0 miles to Higgins Brook where there is a Class III rapid that should be scouted. There is a rock ledge on the left and a short sandbank on the right. The first drop is a ledge around a sharp right turn, followed by a rocky rapid in a right turn.

There are more Class II rapids for 1.25 miles to a side road bridge (5.25 miles). Below this bridge there is 0.75 mile of quickwater and riffles to the mouth of Pond Brook, near the bridge at West Milan (6.0 miles).

West Milan ➤ Groveton	17.25 mi
Description:	Flatwater, quickwater, Class I–II
Date checked:	2000
Navigable:	High or medium water (late April and May)
Scenery:	Rural, towns
Maps:	USGS Percy 15, Guildhall 15

This stretch of the river begins with over 9 miles of smooth-water. The NH 100 bridge is reached in 1.25 miles and Crystal Bridge in another 2.25 miles, with the mouth of Phillips Brook a short distance below. It is 1.5 miles to the Bell Hill Road bridge (5 miles) and another 2.25 miles to the bridge at Percy (7.25 miles). Then there are almost 2 miles of smoothwater, followed by a 1.0-mile Class II boulder patch that is often too low to run. The latter ends at a covered bridge in Stark, one of the most photographed bridges in the state.

Below Stark (10.0 miles) are 4.5 miles of quickwater and riffles to the mouth of Nash Stream, then 0.25 mile of Class II water to the bridge on Emerson Road (14.75 miles). Then it is 2.5 miles to the first dam in Groveton (17.25 miles), which is the usual take-out.

Groveton ➤ Connecticut River	3.75 mi

There were once four dams in the 1.25 miles through Groveton. For 2.5 miles below the town, the river meanders to the Connecticut River.

Phillips Brook NH

Phillips Brook flows into the Upper Ammonoosuc River from the north, 3.75 miles downstream from West Milan. It is smaller than Nash Stream to the west.

Above Paris there are 2.5 miles of winding brook, followed by 3.0 miles of rapids, but the only access is by a private paper company road that is usually closed during the paddling season. Remember to ask for and obtain permission before crossing property lines.

It is a 4.0-mile run from the nearby abandoned settlement of Paris to the Upper Ammonoosuc River. A 50-yard portage around a cascade in Paris is followed by 0.75 mile of shallow Class II–III rapids. Then the brook meanders through swamps and fields with a good current for 0.75 mile to the Bell Hill Road bridge. It is then another 1.5 miles to Crystal Bridge, where you must portage around the spectacular cascade that terminates in a 6-foot-wide, undercut slit beneath the bridge. This is followed by 0.75 mile of Class II–III rapids that run to the Upper Ammonoosuc. See the USGS Percy 15 map.

Nash Stream NH

This small mountain stream, once noted for its log drives, flows south from Nash Bog Pond in Odell to the Upper Ammonoosuc River below Stark. It drains a large, forested area that is undeveloped except around what used to be the pond. Floods in May 1969 washed out the dam at Nash Bog Pond, leaving only a large marsh.

A private road follows the river, but it is usually closed during the paddling season. Remember to ask for and obtain permission before crossing property lines. The river flows for 9.0 miles from the pond to the Upper Ammonoosuc, with an average gradient of 75 feet per mile. It is recommended that the river be scouted carefully before it is run.

Nash Stream has been run for 3.5 miles from Benchmark 1368 to the gate near Benchmark 1061 (USGS Percy 15). There is a mile of quickwater to an old, runnable log dam, then Class IV rapids with multiple channels. Choose the ones where the water drops first. Because of the tight, rocky drops, short closed boats are recommended. Very high water is necessary, but the clarity of the water makes the water level appear lower than it actually is.

Israel River NH

The Israel River originates on the slopes of Mount Jefferson in the Presidential Range. It flows northwest to the Connecticut River near Lancaster. Called Sinoogawnock by the Indians, it was renamed for Israel Glines, a hunter who frequented the area before its settlement.

The upper portion is a pleasant Class I run, while below Riverton there are Class II–III rapids. There are occasional views of the Presidential Range if you look back upstream.

Jefferson ➤ Riverton	6.0 mi
Description:	Quickwater, Class I
Date checked:	2001
Navigable:	High and medium water (May)
Scenery:	Forested, rural
Maps:	USGS Mount Washington 15, Whitefield 15

Put in at the NH 115A bridge 2.5 miles south of Jefferson Village. The river is a small stream flowing through cultivated land with large trees along the banks. There are some Class I rapids and a few fine swimming holes. It is 2.5 miles to a side-road bridge and another 3.5 miles to the US 2 bridge in Riverton.

Riverton ➤ Lancaster	5.0 mi
Description:	Quickwater, Class II—III
Date checked:	2001
Navigable:	High and medium water (May)
Scenery:	Forested, rural, towns
Maps:	USGS Whitefield 15
Portages:	9.5 mi ice-control dam
	11.0 mi dam below Lancaster

Class II rapids start below Riverton, followed by a mile of smooth-water. Beyond the mouth of Otter Brook (3.5 miles) various types of dams and ice nets have been installed to prevent flooding in Lancaster. Be alert for the net of the year. There is also an old dam that is washing out and can probably be run.

Beyond the railroad bridge the rapids become more difficult; the most difficult Class III drops lie beyond a right turn and above the covered bridge (4.75 miles). Rapids continue under the US 2/3 bridge, just below which is a low dam that paddlers usually run. Access is on the right below the dam.

Lancaster ➤ Connecticut River	1.75 mi

Below the dam in Lancaster the rapids slack off, and the river meanders across the flats to the Connecticut. Take-out near the confluence is difficult.

Passumpsic River VT

The Passumpsic River rises from the height-of-land south of Lake Willoughby and flows south into the Connecticut River. The main river forms at the junction of the East and West branches near Lyndonville.

The Passumpsic River suffered in the past from industrial pollution but water quality has improved in recent years. It does have an excess number of dams, but it is an attractive river in a rural area. You can run the Passumpsic when the water is too low to run most other rivers, and you will also find the dams easier to deal with at low water.

Lyndonville ➤ Connecticut River	22.25 mi
Description:	Flatwater, quickwater, some rapids, Class II
Date checked:	2001
Navigable:	Anytime, but low water is best
Scenery:	Forested, rural, towns
Maps:	USGS Burke 15, Lyndonville 15, St. Johnsbury
Portages:	5.25 mi R dam—liftover 10 yd
	6.0 mi R dam 0.25 mi
	7.25 mi R dam—liftover 25 yd
	8.25 mi ledge
	10.25 mi ledge
	13.0 mi island at dam at St. Johnsbury 50 yd

15.0 mi L dam 50 yd
17.0 mi R dam at Passumpsic 100 yd
21.5 mi L dam at Barnet 50 yd

Note: Portage distance given for low water; high or medium water will greatly increase difficulty and change take-out locations.

Put in near the highway garage at the VT 114 bridge north of Lydonville and just below the confluence of the East and West branches. The river meanders down the valley over a sand or gravel bed, with occasional deep pools. In a few places, old cars have been used to stabilize the banks.

The US 5 bridge and the covered bridge immediately below it are passed at 0.75 mile. Then comes the VT 122 bridge (2.5 miles) and US 5 again (4.5 miles). Take out here at a side road on the left to avoid a series of three dams in impressive gorges.

One can put in from a side-road bridge adjacent to US 5 (8.0 miles). On the loop to the left away from the highway there is a 3-foot ledge. Below the US 5 bridge at St. Johnsbury Center, an island can be seen from the road. It had a ledge on each side (10.25 miles); the right may be easier.

When the water is medium or high, take out in the vicinity of the next US 5 bridge, above St. Johnsbury, since the Concord Avenue bridge has no access. The dam immediately below the Concord Avenue bridge can be portaged on the island when the dam is not spilling.

Pleasant Class I rapids run through town past the confluence of the Moose River on the left. The river gradually slows to the backwater of the next dam, which can be dropped on the left.

The river is quickwater to the dam at Passumpsic, which always spills. An easy portage starts under the bridge, then through the power station parking lot. In the next 2.5 miles there are four ledges. The first one, under the railroad bridge within sight of the dam, is the most difficult and can be lined if desired. The others are run easily. The third is immediately below the confluence on the right where Water Andric drops over a scenic waterfall framed by the arch of a railroad bridge. This section of the river is very lovely.

The old Barnet dam is washing out and should be checked. Portage on the left over ledges. The river makes a big S through a scenic gorge with no difficult water and then fans out into the delta at the confluence with the Connecticut.

Passumpsic River (West Branch) vt

The West Branch rises in Westmore below the height-of-land at the south end of Lake Willoughby and flows south to join the East Branch northeast of Lyndonville. It offers a pleasant, easy run.

Calendar Brook ➤ Confluence		3.5 mi
Description:	Quickwater, Class I	
Date checked:	1983	
Navigable:	High water (early May)	
Scenery:	Forested	
Maps:	USGS Burke 15, Lydonville 15	

Put in at the bridge over Calendar Brook. The brook flows immediately into the West Branch. Fallen trees provide the only difficulty.

It is easier to put in at the bridge a mile farther up on Calendar Brook, if desired.

Passumpsic River (East Branch) vt

The East Branch rises in Newark and flows south to join the West Branch northeast of Lyndonville. In high water, you can probably put in somewhat above the section described below.

East Burke ➤ Confluence		4.5 mi
Description:	Class II	
Date checked:	2000	
Navigable:	High water (early May)	
Scenery:	Forested	
Maps:	USGS Burke 15, Lyndonville 15	

Put in immediately below the dam at East Burke to run the easy ledge below, or put in from the road below the ledge. The rapids are continuous Class II with no pools. The gradient eases as the river approaches the confluence.

Take out at the VT 114 bridge 0.25 mile below the West Branch junction.

Moose River VT

The Moose River rises in the sparsely settled area of northeastern Vermont and flows south to the Passumpsic River in St. Johnsbury. Quiet marshes alternate with exciting rapids. Although close, the roads are not obtrusive.

Bridge on dirt road ➤ Bog Brook		3.75 mi
Description:	Quickwater, Class I	
Date checked:	2001	
Navigable:	High water	
Scenery:	Wild	
Maps:	USGS Burke 15	

The Moose River below Gallup Mills flows through some small gorges and over ledges. The description starts at the bridge more than a mile south of Gallup Mills on the dirt road that follows the left bank.

A Class III rapid continues under the bridge. Put in wherever you desire. The intensity decreases rapidly, and the remainder is Class I nearly to the bridge over Bog Brook, which is adjacent to the river on the right.

Bog Brook offers a mile or so of padding through a marsh, but the bridge is too low to paddle under when the water is high enough to paddle the river.

Bog Brook ➤ Snowmobile bridge		2.25 mi
Description:	Flatwater, quickwater	
Date checked:	2001	
Navigable:	Spring, summer, fall	
Scenery:	Marsh	
Maps:	USGS Burke 15	

| **Portage:** | (2.25 mi water drops into Class III–IV gorge) |

The paddle through the marsh is pleasant; the snowmobile trail is visible from the dirt road along the right bank. This is the Victory Bog Wildlife Management Area.

Snowmobile bridge ➤ US 2 Bridge   5.5 mi

Description:	Quickwater, Class I, II, III, IV
Date checked:	2001
Navigable:	High water, medium water (April to early May)
Scenery:	Forested
Maps:	USGS Burke 15, Miles Pond

The first part of the gorge can be Class IV in high water, but after 0.25 mile the difficulty diminishes to and is mostly Class II. There are three difficult ledges not far above the Victory bridge. The first one is out of sight around a blind corner to the left and can be scouted from the road. The next two are more straightforward. All three may be run best to the left.

Below the bridge in Victory (3.5 miles) there is a short difficult section. Then the rapids ease to Class I for a while, and finally almost to flatwater. Take out on a dirt road 0.25 mile down from Victory Brook on the right.

US 2 Bridge ➤ East St. Johnsbury   7.0 mi

Description:	Quickwater, Class I–II
Date checked:	2001
Navigable:	High water
Scenery:	Rural, towns
Maps:	USGS Miles Pond, Concord, VT
Portages:	(7.0 mi gorge)

Rapids start again 0.25 mile below the bridge and continue on past the bridge in Concord (2.25 miles). Then another quiet section starts, almost in medium water, and continues past an abutment (5.0 miles). A few rapids pick up approaching the bridge on a side road in East St. Johnsbury. Take out well above the bridge to avoid a high ledge under the railroad bridge immediately downstream.

East St. Johnsbury ➤ The Mills   3.25 mi
Description: Class II
Date checked: 2001
Navigable: High to medium water
Scenery: Settled, towns
Maps: USGS Concord, VT, St. Johnsbury 15

In East St. Johnsbury there is an impassable drop under the railroad bridge; lining is necessary. The lower section of the river is not so attractive, because the valley is settled and the railroad and highway follow the river. The river from the East St. Johnsbury railroad bridge to 0.5 mile above the railroad bridge in St. Johnsbury is continuous Class II rapids. The section is delightful—there are many locations for practicing eddy turns, ferrying, and other techniques.

Above the mills in St. Johnsbury, all paddlers should pull out except those with covered boats or those who are expert open boaters.

St. Johnsbury ➤ Passumpsic River   1.5 mi

There are several Class IV drops that require scouting and intricate maneuvering. Strong crosscurrents and fairly large haystacks are added obstacles. **Caution!** Beyond the two bridges (railroad and highway) and after the mills, all boats must take out on the right, because there is an impassable drop hidden around the next corner.

Wells River VT

The Wells River flows into the Connecticut opposite Woodsville, New Hampshire. It is paralleled by US 302, which occasionally is visible from the river.

The section described here, the Wells is a small, steep brook, and below it is a series of falls and ledges that most people consider a scenic attraction rather than a paddling possibility.

Groton ➤ Snowmobile bridge   9.5 mi
Description: Flatwater, quickwater, Class I—III
Date checked: 2001

Navigable:	High water (April and May)
Scenery:	Forested, rural, towns
Maps:	USGS Woodsville 15
Portages:	7.0 mi L dam in Boltonville
	7.25 mi L gorge below Boltonville

Put in from a side road 0.33 mile east of the Groton Bridge and just below an old dam. Following 0.5 mile of Class II rapids, the river is mostly slow current with a few riffles as it meanders through pastureland. There are old railroad pilings in South Ryegate which tend to accumulate debris.

Below South Ryegate (4.0 miles) Class II rapids extend for 1.5 miles. After that there is a series of four ledges visible from a side road on the left bank. The last one is past an old abutment. Another drop, obstructed with old granite blocks, starts just below an old US 302 bridge. Then the current slows down, and the river meanders the remaining distance to Boltonville.

Just below the bridge in Boltonville (7.0 miles), there is a 50-foot dam and cascade that must be portaged on the left. Put in below the old power station, now a summer cottage. One quarter-mile of rapids leads to the head of a small gorge, where there is a 4-foot waterfall, best carried on the left. The ledges continue through the gorge, and you should scout then while you portage the falls.

Below the high I-91 bridge (7.75 miles) the river becomes slow and meandering, with a sandy bottom, for 1.75 miles. Take out on the right where the river first approaches US 302 (9.5 miles) at the major snowmobile bridge in the area.

Snowmobile bridge ➤ Connecticut River   2.5 mi

Below the first access to US 302 the Wells River drops over a series of ledges ranging from 3 to 15 feet high. Most are unrunnable. After the ledges the river reaches a small millpond with a dam. There is another mile of ledges to the Connecticut River.

Ammonoosuc River NH

The Ammonoosuc River, one of the largest rivers in New Hampshire north of the White Mountains, flows from the western slopes of Mount Washington to the Connecticut River in Woodsville. It offers some of the finest whitewater paddling in New England. This river is famous for a strong upstream wind, and even in rapids it may be necessary to paddle hard to progress downstream.

Bretton Woods ➤ Twin Mountain	7.0 mi
Scouted only:	See the USGS Mount Washington 15 and Littleton maps.

Begin at the junction with Clinton Brook near the Bretton Woods church. The water is smooth but fast for 3.5 miles to Lower Ammonoosuc Falls, a 30-foot cascade.

The next 3.0 miles after the falls contain several rapids that are normally impassable. The last is 0.5 mile east of Twin Mountain. Then there are moderate Class III rapids to Twin Mountain where there is an especially rocky drop above the US 3 bridge (7.0 miles).

Twin Mountain ➤ Littleton	16.0 mi
Description:	Quickwater, Class II–IV
Date checked:	2001
Navigable:	High water (late April to end of May)
Scenery:	Forested, rural, towns
Maps:	USGS Whitefield 15
Portages:	7.5 mi E Maplewood Dam 100 yd (16.0 mi dam at Littleton)

Put in at the US 3 bridge (or 0.5 mile above town off US 302). Below the bridge there are Class II rapids with small waves at high levels and lots of rocks to dodge at low water levels. It is 3.0 miles to the River Bend Motel, where the road leaves the river and the difficulty of the rapids increases to Class III. At high water levels the boater should hug the shore to avoid the large waves in the center. When the water is lower, fast maneuvering is required.

It is 2.75 miles from the motel to the steel truss Pierce Bridge on US 302 (5.75 miles), which is preceded by a rocky patch that gives trouble at lower water levels. Most of this run is away from the road, but one of the more difficult sets of rapids called Boatbreaker can be inspected by driving east along the road on the south bank and looking upstream from the gauging station. This is a Class III rapid that should be scouted from the bank. Run left of center.

The first 1.5 miles from Pierce Bridge to Maplewood Dam contain easier Class II rapids that lead to the Maplewood Dam backwater. It is possible to take out on the right at this point to avoid the dam and the gorge. Otherwise, paddle 0.25 mile of deadwater to the abandoned 15-foot dam and portage on either side for 100 yards. The gorge below contains Class IV rapids, the most difficult usually run on this river. The hardest rapid begins 100 yards below the dam, and there is another difficult one adjacent to the old powerhouse. It is 0.75 mile from the dam to the NH 142 bridge in Maplewood.

Below Maplewood (8.25 miles) the rapids begin as Class III and gradually get easier. It is 1.75 miles to the Wing Road bridge, followed by 2.25 miles of Class II rapids to Hatch Brook (12.25 miles), where you can see a small, pink house on the right bank and hear some rapids ahead. **Caution!** A short distance below is the Class IV Alderbrook Rapid. At high water those who wish to avoid large waves can run down among the rocks on the right, while at lower levels the best channel starts near the left bank and moves in an S-shape to the center. Scouting either route is advisable.

It is 0.5 mile from the end of Alderbrook Rapid to the significant rapid, a series of rocky Class III drops adjacent to the railroad tracks which is best run near the right bank. Then there is 1.0 mile of easier rapids past a railroad bridge to a convenient take-out on the old road on the right bank (14.0 miles). Then there are 2.0 miles of quickwater to the 40-foot Littleton dam (16.0 miles), which spills water over the top.

Littleton ➤ Lisbon		13.0 mi
Description:	Class I–II	
Date checked:	2001	
Navigable:	High water (late April to end of May)	
Scenery:	Rural, towns	
Maps:	USGS Whitefield 15, Littleton, Sugar Hill, Lisbon	
Portages:	1.75 mi L unrunnable ledges (13.0 mi R dam in Lisbon 0.25 mi)	

Put in below the dam or at the Redington Road bridge 0.25 mile beyond. There are 1.5 miles of Class II rapids to the center of town, where there is a girder bridge on US 302. Below it there is a series of granite ledges that are normally unrunnable and can be most easily lined or carried on the left. Below the ledges there is a short Class III rapid, followed by 0.5 mile of Class II rapids to Bridge Street (2.5 miles). Put in at the sewage treatment plant just east of I-93 for an easier run.

The remainder of the run to Lisbon is unusual in that different routes in a rapid vary from Class I to Class III in difficulty, and skilled paddlers can choose between thrills and a dry boat. It is 4.5 miles to a bridge on a side road and then another 0.25 mile to the Gale River, which enters on the left under a railroad bridge.

The mouth of the Gale River (7.25 miles) marks the beginning of a particularly heavy rapid that is 0.5 mile long. In another 0.5 mile a yellow house on the right bank marks a ledge that extends across the river at an island, but this ledge can be run in several places. In another 2.0 miles you reach a US 302 bridge (10.25 miles). The last major rapid is just below it; then there are 2.75 miles of Class I rapids to Lisbon (13.0 miles). Take out well above the bridge on the right, because there is a dam just before it. There is an island above the bridge. If your car is spotted on the left, make sure you keep left.

Lisbon ➤ Woodsville		11.5 mi
Description:	Quickwater, Class I	
Date checked:	2001	
Navigable:	High or medium water (April and May)	

Scenery:	Rural, towns
Maps:	USGS Lisbon, Woodsville 15
Portages:	6.75 mi R dam at Bath 200 yd
	(11.5 mi dam at Woodsville)

Put in on the right at a ballfield 0.25 mile below the bridge. There is a fast current with occasional standing-wave rapids for 6.5 miles to Bath. Take out above the covered bridge on the right and carry 200 yards to a cove below the dam. There is a mile of fast current with one rapid to the mouth of the wild Ammonoosuc River (7.75 miles), which is followed in 0.25 mile by a railroad bridge.

Below the railroad bridge (8.0 miles), keep to the right bank to avoid a large wave adjacent to the gauging station. There are another 2.5 miles of fastwater to where a road on the right bank offers a potential take-out. The take out on the left is not good. Then a mile of smoothwater leads to the covered bridge (11.5 miles) in Woodsville. Just below it there is a dam, and at the foot of the dam is the Connecticut River.

Gale River NH

The Gale River drains the northern side of Franconia Notch and the surrounding mountains. Because the stream is confined in a narrow valley and the drainage area includes the steep slopes of Mount Garfield and Mount Lafayette, a summer rain sometimes raises the river to a runnable level. The stream's flow generally peaks twelve to twenty-four hours after a rain.

Off NH 18 ➤ Jesseman Road	4.0 mi
Description:	Class II
Date checked:	2001
Navigable:	High to medium water (late April
	through May and after heavy rains)
Scenery:	Forested, town
Maps:	USGS Franconia, Sugar Hill

Put in about 1.0 mile above NH 18 from a side road reached by taking Coal Hill Road up the south side of the river and following the leftmost road at a three-way fork.

The first mile to the NH 18 bridge is rocky, with occasional fallen trees, so much boat handling is required. Just below the bridge the river doubles in size as Lafayette Brook enters from the left at a heavy rapid. For the next 2.0 miles the river flows through Franconia Village, with NH 18 on the bank. The rapids are easy Class II.

The Ham Branch enters from the left just above the NH 117 bridge (2.5 miles). A concrete water gate on the right bank marks the point at which NH 18/116 leaves the river, although a side road continues on the right bank. Another mile of similar going brings you to the truss bridge on Jesseman Road (4.0 miles), the last take-out before the difficult rapids below.

Jesseman Road ➤ Ammonoosuc River   4.0 mi

Description:	Quickwater, Class III–IV
Date checked:	2001
Navigable:	High to medium water (late April through May and after heavy rains)
Scenery:	Wild, rural
Maps:	USGS Sugar Hill, Littleton 15

Below Franconia Village the Gale River drops through a winding valley to its confluence with the Ammonoosuc. The banks are uninhabited woods; the whole run is one of the more scenic and unspoiled in the White Mountains.

There is a hand-painted gauge on the left bridge abutment at the Jesseman Road put-in. A reading of 1.0 constitutes a low but runnable level. Always scout the run first.

To reach the put-in, travel north on NH 18 through Franconia. One mile past the center, go left onto Streeter Pond Road to Jesseman Road. Streeter Pond Road continues downstream to the take-out, but it does not follow the river.

The first 0.5 mile is quickwater through open fields. The rapids begin at a power-line crossing. They are Class III, with many large boulders in the streambed.

The rapids get a little harder. After 2.0 miles a sharp left turn brings you to the entrance of a gorge (2.5 miles), recognizable by rock walls on both sides below a pool. Take out on the right, well above the beginning of the gorge, to scout. The gorge contains four drops, each followed by a short pool.

Below the gorge there is a short drop. The chute is on the far left, with a total drop of about 6 feet. A final drop must then be negotiated to a railroad bridge where the Gale River joins the Ammonoosuc (4.0 miles).

Gale River (Ham Branch) NH

This scenic tributary of the Gale River drains the western slopes of Kinsman Ridge. The highway, NH 116, runs parallel to the river, but it is not close.

NH 116 ➤ Franconia		7.0 mi
Description:	Class I–II	
Date checked:	2000	
Navigable:	High water (May)	
Scenery:	Forested, rural	
Maps:	USGS Sugar Hill	

Put in at the northernmost NH 116 bridge. The trip is initially a twisting, rocky Class II run with some small, fallen trees, so take care on blind corners. After 2.25 miles the river splits around an island that has two barbed wire fences at the end. In another 0.5 mile you reach a truss bridge on a road to a farm.

Below the truss bridge (2.75 miles) the river has easier Class I–II rapids. There are good views of the Kinsman Ridge across the fields. Just above the third side bridge, Bickford Hill Road (5.75 miles), there is a washed-out dam that is easily runnable. A short distance below, where the river approaches NH 116 on the right, there is a ledge that is best run on the left. In another 1.25 miles the Ham Branch enters the Gale River (7.0 miles) just above the NH 117 bridge in Franconia.

Waits River VT

This is a sporty run in high water. The valley is narrow, and consequently the river rises quickly when there is moderate runoff.

The scenery consists of wooded hills and some pastureland; the water is clear. The stream is followed by VT 25 its entire length. Although the river is runnable from West Topsham, the usual trip is from Waits River Village to the fourth VT 25B bridge.

Waits River ➤ Bradford	11.5 mi
Description:	Quickwater, Class II
Date checked:	2001
Navigable:	High and medium water (late April to early May)
Scenery:	Rural, settled
Maps:	USGS East Barre 15, Woodsville 15, East Corinth, Mount Cube

Put in from a bridge on a side road opposite a very pretty church in the village of Waits River. The river is narrow, steep, and rocky, dropping 50 feet per mile. Below the first VT 25 bridge (2.0 miles) there are three ledges. The first one is around a sharp bend to the left, and it is usually run in the center. Below, the river widens, and the other two are recognizable from above. Look them over first, because the best channel changes with the water level. The second ledge is the most difficult, and the best route is usually near the right bank, which is difficult to scout because of barbed wire and a side stream. The pace slows below.

Just past the junction with the South Branch of the Waits River (just below the next VT 25 bridge) the current picks up. A large ledge creates a hole at some water levels that can best be avoided on the right. Strong rapids continue for a half-mile before easier rapids continue, with a gentle surprise or two to Bradford.

Take out under the VT 25B bridge. In Bradford, 0.5 mile below, is a high power-generating dam, below which the river meanders another 0.5 mile to the Connecticut.

Ompompanoosuc River VT

The main branch of the Ompompanoosuc rises in Vershire and flows generally south to meet the West Branch above Union

Village. Below the confluence is a large flood-control dam. The section of the main river above the dam contains many rapids; below, the going is easier. The mile or two just above the dam often is very overgrown and therefore difficult to navigate. Portaging the flood-control dam on foot is quite difficult. A dirt road, in good weather, runs along the east side of the river through much of the flood plain. Drive right up over the dam to get to it. Below the dam, the river riffles for a while before reaching the impounded Connecticut.

West Fairlee ➤ Union Village Dam	12.0 mi
Description:	Quickwater, Class I–II
Date checked:	2001
Navigable:	High to medium water (late April to early May)
Scenery:	Forested, rural
Maps:	USGS Strafford 15, Mount Cube 15
Portages:	2.0 mi R waterfall 50 yd
	8.0 mi L waterfall 100 yd

There are two bridges in West Fairlee providing access to the river. Neither is particularly satisfactory. From here to Post Mills is mostly smooth. Just above the VT 133 bridge in Post Mills is a 12-foot waterfall, which should be carried to the right. From here there are 4.0 miles of easy Class II rapids that lead to a high bridge on Sawnee Bean Road near Thetford Center (6.0 miles). There are three or four more difficult Class III drops in this section, the hardest being 0.5 mile above this bridge.

The 2.0 miles to the covered bridge in Thetford Center (8.0 miles) meander among fallen trees. **Caution!** The river goes over a 40-foot cascade just below this covered bridge. The portage is not easy. Below here, quickwater alternates with ledges that should be looked over carefully. Now away from any roads, at some water levels, these ledges should be carried around. The river gradually flattens out. Below where the West Branch enters, assuming there is no pool behind the flood-control dam, the river meanders below steep overgrown banks. Taking out below here, though it is another mile to the dam, becomes increasingly difficult.

Union Village ➤ Connecticut River   3.25 mi

This part can be run anytime. The rapids and riffles continue
for a distance, with the river gradually becoming wider and
slower as it reaches the Connecticut. You pass the VT 132
bridge (2.25 miles) and then I-91 before you reach the wide
mouth into the Connecticut.

Ompompanoosuc River (West Branch) VT

The West Branch rises in Strafford and flows southeast to join
the main river 1.0 mile above the flood-control dam. The river
rises to runnable levels only rarely, with the level frequently
becoming too low before the rain stops. Below Rices Mills, access
becomes increasingly difficult, and the quality of the river and
the view deteriorate as the flood-control-dam impoundment area
is reached.

Strafford ➤ Rices Mills   7.75 mi
Description: Class II, III
Date checked: 2001
Navigable: High water
Scenery: Forested
Maps: Strafford 15

Although it is possible to put in along the quickwater section
between Strafford and South Strafford, the usual put-in is in,
or just downstream from, South Strafford. From South
Strafford, for the next 3.0 miles, Class II rapids are reasonably
continuous. Look over very carefully the small gorge in Rices
Mills. The river here goes over a ledge and around a right
turn before narrowing to 10 feet or so. The currents bounc-
ing off the rock walls make balance precarious. There is a nice
pool below. The pool can serve as a take-out, or you can continue 100 yards or so to the VT 132 bridge.

Rices Mills ➤ Ompompanoosuc River   2.5 mi

Easy rapids continue under the VT 132 ridge, then dwindle to
quickwater. At the end of a left-turn loop is a drop over a
ledge, and farther on is a waterfall that must be portaged. The

river flows through pastureland, and the road visible along the bank is private and gated.

White River VT

There are more than 100 miles of good paddling on this river system, with nearly every kind of water, some of which can be run even in summer. The valleys are highly cultivated, and much of the river may not be attractive to those in search of wild surroundings. However, in the tributary valleys especially, one can see rural Vermont at its very best; the First Branch is perhaps the prettiest.

The main river rises north of Granville, flows south, then east, then southeast, finally emptying into the Connecticut River at White River Junction. At or near flood stage, some of the faster parts become Class III, but when the gauge at West Hartford reads 4.25 to 5.8 it is Class II.

There is another gauge under the bridge in Gaysville. When the gauge reads "0" the river is mostly large waves and Class III.

The river is the first in Vermont to witness the return of the Atlantic salmon. A vigorous program is in effect to restore the salmon to the Connecticut River Watershed. Remain alert for anglers in the river, and respect the multiple uses that coexist on this large river system.

Granville ➤ Stockbridge	14.5 mi
Description:	Quickwater, Class I–II
Date checked:	2001
Navigable:	High water (early April)
	Medium water (late April to mid-May)
Scenery:	Rural, towns
Maps:	USGS Hancock, Rochester

Begin on VT 100 at a bridge 1.0 mile north of the VT 100/125 junction in Hancock. The river above this point is small, but in high water it can be run for an additional 2.0 miles if you put in at another VT 100 bridge about 0.75 mile south of Granville.

For almost the entire distance from the bridge near the Granville-Hancock town line to Stockbridge, this shallow stream winds past farms at the bottom of a narrow valley. There are only a limited number of short Class II rapids, and the first is just below a bridge in Hancock (2.5 miles). After the VT 73 bridge (7.25 miles) it is 0.5 mile to the second and most difficult rapid, at a bridge beside VT 100. There is one more pitch in the remaining 6.75 miles to Stockbridge (14.5 miles).

Stockbridge ➤ Bethel   11.0 mi

Description:	Quickwater, Class II
Date checked:	2001
Navigable:	High water (early April)
	Medium water (late April through May)
Scenery:	Forested, settled
Maps:	USGS Rochester, Randolph 15

There are intermittent Class II rapids that extend over much of the distance to Bethel. Some of them can be scouted from VT 107, which occasionally is close on the right bank. In medium water this is not a difficult run, but in high water the current can be strong.

The most difficult section is 4.5 miles below Stockbridge at an S-turn just above Gaysville. The river swings to the left away from the highway and passes through a narrow cut. There are heavy waves, a submerged rock near the center that often cannot be detected as you approach, and a strong whirlpool at the bottom just before the river turns right. Under the high bridge at Gaysville (5.0 miles) there is another strong current where a rock ledge on the right deflects the river to the left.

Bethel ➤ Sharon   11.75 mi

Description:	Flatwater, quickwater, Class I–II
Date checked:	2001
Navigable:	Passable in all but dry summers
Scenery:	Rural, towns, forested
Maps:	USGS Randolph, Strafford 15

The river gets bigger in Bethel after the Third Branch enters and becomes a much larger stream suitable to summer running if the season is not too dry. Put in at the VT 107 bridge. The river is less rapid and is wider, and the valley is more open. However, for a long distance there are numerous traverse ledges that create sharp drops with fair current between. In 4.0 miles, North Royalton, where the Second Branch enters from the left, is reached. It is 2.0 miles more to Royalton and another 2.0 miles to South Royalton, where the First Branch enters. About halfway between these two towns there are ledges and a sharp drop. Just below the bridge at South Royalton there is a rapid, followed by 5.0 miles of easy river to Sharon.

Sharon ➤ Connecticut River	13.5 mi
Description:	Quickwater, Class I, II
Date checked:	2001
Navigable:	Passable in all but dry seasons
Scenery:	Rural, towns
Maps:	USGS Strafford 15, Quechee, Hanover

This section on the White River is similar to the section above, but the river is larger and the ledges closer together and more difficult. Below Sharon after 1.25 miles there is an old dam that can be recognized by its abutments. It can be run, but scout carefully. Line or carry on the left.

Below Sharon the 5.5 miles to West Hartford are characterized by numerous ledges with rather sharp pitches, but the river between is smooth. These ledges begin at a gravel pit below Sharon, and there are usually only one or two passable notches at each drop. The most difficult place is 1.5 miles below the gravel pit at a part known as Quartermile Rapids, which should be scouted. After approaching near the right bank, cross to the left of a large rock in the middle and to the left of haystacks below it. About 4.0 miles below Sharon there are several ledges; the first is open in the middle, the second on the far left. At the island below, the right channel is better, and the last rapid above West Hartford (6.0 miles) is best run near the right bank.

For the 6.0 miles to Hartford the river is wide, and there is a lot of picking around ledges at low water. An old dam/ledge is above the Hartford bridge. Then it is 1.5 miles to the bridges at White River Junction and the Connecticut River.

White River (Third Branch) VT

The Third Branch is the westernmost branch of the White River. It rises in Roxbury and flows south to the main river at Bethel. The Third has a more uniform gradient than the other branches, more like the main river, with only two small dams to break the continuity in the upper part. It provides a pleasant, easy run for its entire length.

Roxbury ➤ Riford Park	9.5 mi
Description:	Quickwater, Class I–II
Date checked:	2001
Navigable:	High water
Scenery:	Forested, rural
Maps:	USGS Barre 15, Warren, Randolph 15
Portage:	(9.5 mi ledge—may be run)

Put in at a bridge adjacent to a railroad underpass 0.5 mile north of the Roxbury/Granville town line. The Third Branch here is very small and fast, with overhanging alder and leaning and fallen trees. Class II rapids extend for 0.25 mile above and below a small bridge in East Granville. Quickwater, shallow rapids, and a few trees make the trip interesting. The river passes under a bridge (4.5 miles) above West Braintree and the VT 12A bridge (6.75 miles). Just above the small bridge near Riford Brook a rocky ledge should be scouted, but it can be run (Class III).

Riford Brook ➤ Randolph	3.75 mi
Description:	Quickwater
Date checked:	2001
Navigable:	High water
Scenery:	Rural, towns
Maps:	USGS Randolph 15
Portages:	3.25 mi dam at recreation area 15 yd
	(3.75 mi e dam at Randolph—liftover)
	3.75 mi R ledges below dam 100 yd)

Below the bridge at Riford Brook, which is the usual put-in for the upper segment, the river is still obstructed by trees, but not by rapids. A sharp turn under a railroad bridge 2.0 miles down may collect debris.

At the recreation area west of Randolph (3.25 miles) there is a dam that may open when the river can be paddled. Do not attempt to run or line the rip-rap below, because the rocks are extremely jagged.

The high VT 12 bridge at Randolph is just around a bend. The low dam below can be lined or run under favorable conditions. A series of Class II–III ledges is below, within sight of the bridge. Put in or take out at the dam from a side road on the right, or do so below the ledges behind the Vermont Castings Company on the right.

Randolph ➤ Bethel	10.75 mi
Description:	Quickwater, Class I
Date checked:	2001
Navigable:	Medium or low water
Scenery:	Rural, forested
Maps:	USGS Randolph 15
Portage:	(10.75 mi L dam at Bethel)

From the road on the right bank, put in below the VT 12 bridge in Randolph before or after the rapids, at your choice. The river is attractive, with clear water riffling over a sandy bottom, and it is generally out of sight of roads. Fallen trees are less of a problem, since the river is wider. Sandbars project here and there.

The railroad crosses the river 0.5 mile above a bridge on a side road (8.25 miles). Just below, a small rapid forms at the mouth of a side stream coming in from the right, and there are more easy rapids below.

The best take-out is on the right 0.25 mile above the bridge at the ballfield in Bethel (10.5 miles), which can be reached from VT 12. The dam in Bethel is immediately below the bridge. It is only another 0.5 mile to the confluence with the main river.

White River (Second Branch) VT

The Second Branch rises in Williamstown and flows through the scenic Williamstown Gulf, although it cannot be paddled until farther downstream. The valley is well cultivated, and VT 14 and many small roads follow the stream and cross it frequently. Covered bridges are the main attraction of this run.

East Brookfield ➤ East Randolph		8.75 mi
Description:	Quickwater, Class I–II	
Date checked:	2001	
Navigable:	Medium-high to medium water	
Scenery:	Rural	
Maps:	USGS Barre 15, Randolph 15	
Portages:	Near beginning many low farm bridges	
	5.25 mi old dam	
	6.75 mi old dam	
	(8.75 mi L dam at East Randolph)	

At the start, the Second Branch is still only a meadow brook wandering through farms. Besides the many alder and fallen trees, low farm bridges must be portaged. The remains of two old dams in North Randolph must also be scouted and probably carried. The first, just east of town (5.25 miles), is the steepest, and the other (6.75 miles) is west of the highway between the two VT 14 bridges. After the second dam, Class I–II rapids continue most of the way to the dam below the VT 14 bridge in East Randolph.

East Randolph ➤ White River		14.0 mi
Description:	Quickwater, Class I	
Date checked:	2001	
Navigable:	Medium-high to medium water	
Scenery:	Rural	
Maps:	USGS Randolph 15	
Portages:	8.75 mi L dam at East Bethel 100 yd	
	11.25 mi R waterfall 100 yd	
	12.0 mi ledge—can be lined	

Put in below the dam in East Randolph. The river is somewhat larger here, and although the trees still obstruct the channel, few block it completely. The stream often wanders well away from the highway past scenic high banks and through serpentine turns. Covered bridges cross the river at 1.0 mile, 2.25 miles, and 7.75 miles, while VT 14 crosses at 2.0 miles and at

6.25 miles. There are also more farm bridges, although all are high enough to paddle under.

At East Bethel check the dam below the second side-road bridge in advance to determine the best portage. The old mill downstream on the right is being restored. It may be best to take out on the left, cross the bridge, and carry down past the mill.

The Second Branch crosses under VT 14 again at 11.25 miles. Take out on the right well above the bridge to carry a steep ledge at an old dam site. After the next VT 14 bridge, a low ledge can probably be run. The high VT 107 bridge (13.75 miles) comes shortly above the confluence with the main river. A bridge 0.5 mile down the White River offers access.

White River (First Branch) vt

The First Branch of the White River, coming in from the north, is the easternmost of the three branches and has the steepest drop. Rising north of the town of Chelsea, it drops precipitously over ledges and empties into the main river at South Royalton. The valley is a lovely, highly cultivated part of rural Vermont. The covered bridges are an added attraction.

Chelsea ➤ Sawmill		3.0 mi
Description:	Ledges, Class III–IV	
Date checked:	2001	
Navigable:	High water only	
Scenery:	Rural	
Maps:	USGS Strafford 15	

Although the run is popular with expert ledge enthusiasts, water level is critical, so it is difficult to schedule trips—too much water is dangerous and too little is hopeless.

Put in below the lower VT 110 bridge in Chelsea from a side road by a creamery; ask for and obtain permission to access the river here. Rocky rapids alternate with steep ledges, all of which can be run by the right boat at the right water level. They should be scouted in advance from shore. The road follows the river closely for much of the way, so prior scouting is easy.

Take out where the river is near the road, well before the old sawmill dam.

Sawmill ➤ Tunbridge	3.75 mi

The river continues rapid, but the ledges diminish in frequency, if not in ferocity. Beside the dam at the sawmill, there is a dam at North Tunbridge (1.75 miles) and two dams at Tunbridge, one above and one below the VT 110 bridge. Two covered bridges add to the scenic run.

Tunbridge ➤ South Royalton		7.5 mi
Description:	Class I	
Date checked:	2001	
Navigable:	High water (early April)	
	Medium water (late April through May)	
Scenery:	Rural	
Maps:	USGS Strafford 15, Randolph 15	
Portages:	3.75 mi broken dam	
	6.25 mi dam	

A possible put-in is on the right side of the river just below Mill Bridge, the covered bridge just below the two dams in Tunbridge. The ledges and rocks that follow make this a walk-and-drag at low water levels, but more water can make this stretch a short but sporty, possibly Class II, rapid.

Just around the right corner is the Tunbridge Fairgrounds, and put-in is much easier here. Opposite the post office and next to the fire station an unmarked road leads down into the fairground. At the bottom take the first right, between some buildings, to the river. Park elsewhere, though, taking care not to block the fire station. Also, take time to notice the high-water markings on the fair buildings from the 1978 flood.

From here the river meanders with good current some 7.0 miles to the White River. Numerous ledges can provide some excitement, but this can be dampened by numerous downed trees that on occasion completely block the river. In 1.0 mile the river passes under the Cilley Bridge (another easy put-in if the fairground is closed) and in 1.75 miles under a concrete bridge, which is VT 110. Be especially careful of downed trees in this area. In 2.75 miles, the Howe bridge in South Tunbridge is reached. This bridge, the third and last of the covered bridges in this stretch, was built in 1879.

Following one another in short order, there are some ledges, another concrete VT 110 bridge, and a broken dam. It is an easy lift over the right side of the dam. At some water levels, a chute in the middle can be run solo, but check it carefully.

One mile after the second of two steel bridges and under another concrete bridge (6.25 miles), there is the first pair of dams. Without too much difficulty, boats can be lifted over the left side of the spillway. **Caution!** A breach in the middle of the dam may look runnable to some, but several steel rods extend downstream at various angles from the dam, and one of them dangles in this chute. Rather than lifting over the spillway, you can do a difficult but short carry on the right, around the dam and the bridge.

The second dam is 100 yards downstream. It also can be portaged on the right, but it is probably easier to lift over the spillway on the right and carry down the ledge. Stop on the right before the dam to scout this.

After entering the White River 0.75 mile farther on, paddle across and take out on the right just under the bridge at South Royalton.

Mascoma River NH

The Mascoma River basin drains a large area west of Mount Cardigan and flows into the Connecticut River in Lebanon. The river is more removed from highways than road maps indicate.

The upper section of the river is small until it is joined by the Indian River, which flows from Mount Cardigan along US 4 from Canaan. Scenery is a mixture of alder swamps, meadows, fields, and the town of Enfield.

For those who enjoy Class II and III rapids in attractive settings, the 4.0 miles between Mascoma Lake and the dam upstream from the Lebanon water treatment plant are highly recommended. A slalom and wildwater race occurs on this river each April.

The annual fall drawdown of Goose Pond frequently provides medium water for the upper section. Check with the Water Division (603-271-3406) for dates.

Canaan Center ➤ Mascoma Lake		12.0 mi
Description:	Quickwater, Class II	
Date checked:	2001	
Navigable:	High and medium water	
Scenery:	Forested, rural, town	
Maps:	USGS Mascoma 15	
Portage:	2.0 mi L dam 25 yd	

While it is possible, depending on water levels, to put in farther upstream, the bridge in Canaan Center is a convenient spot. Two washed-out dams here are evidence that a village once existed here. Meanders, downed trees, and deadfalls are common until the US 4 bridge (3.5 miles) is reached. The Indian River enters on the left shortly (4.0 miles), and the river increases in size to about 50 feet in width. Past the first railroad bridge, a 1.0-mile section of Class II water begins at a broken dam (the old sluiceway on the right now takes the overflow in high water); the best route depends on water level. The next drop runs best on the left but requires tight maneuvering. The next rapid, another broken dam, generally runs best on the right. After easier rapids, the second railroad bridge is passed. Here is an old gauging station that must have been reached by railroad, since there haven't been roads in here for many years. The river slackens as it passes under two more railroad bridges, then US 4 is reached in West Canaan (6.25 miles).

Quickwater runs by the entry of Goose Pond Brook (7.75 miles) and the next US 4 bridge (9.0 miles). This is a convenient spot to end or begin a trip. Twenty or 30 yards separate the US 4 bridge, a railroad bridge, and Blackwater Road bridge. Quickwater rapids lead under several bridges in

Enfield (where one can take out) and eventually bring one to Mascoma Lake (12.0 miles). If continuing downriver, keep to the right shore and pass under the bridge over the lake. Cross the lake where convenient on a Northwest course. The dam at the outlet of the lake can be carried most easily on the left.

Mascoma Lake ➤ Lebanon		5.5 mi
Description:	Class II–III	
Date checked:	2001	
Navigable:	High and medium water	
Scenery:	Forested, urban	
Maps:	USGS Mascoma 15, Hanover	
Portage:	(4.0 mi e dam)	

This is the classic whitewater section of the river. For more information, see AMC's *Classic Northeastern Whitewater Guide.* The scenery is quite good, but a requirement to maneuver will allow little viewing. If paddling across the lake, you will find the carry easier on the left shore. There is a nice parking lot there for those putting in. A large eddy under the dam on this side allows a comfortable put-in. The USGS gauge is at the put-in. A reading of 3.3 is low, 4.2 is medium, and 4.7 is high. Class II rapids begin immediately. Class II rapids pick up speed under the high US 4 bridge. An island is sighted; the right channel is frequently used for a slalom course. Please don't disturb the wires or gates if they are up. The river quickly passes under two more railroad bridges before slowing a bit. Along a straight section of river, one often sees the right bank breached and the river beginning to divert into a field. After the main course turns right, another section with many downed trees witnesses the wandering courses returning. Just past the high I-89 bridge (3.0 miles) the river turns right; watch for congestion and a hole at higher levels on the outside.

After the river leaves I-89, it narrows to pass under a small stone and metal bridge. The drop under this bridge is the beginning of the second race course. Many take out at this bridge on the right. The river bends left under a low railroad bridge. A sandy beach on the left is a good rest spot before an

S-turn that immediately follows. Because of ledgy pourers, these turns cannot be taken on the inside, so a middle course is the most conservative. Below this turn a 100-yard straight stretch leads to a right turn under a railroad bridge. There is an eddy under the bridge on the right which allows scouting of the next section. Excelsior Rapids follows, named for the defunct mill at the end of the drop. Excelsior is a Class III rapid at most levels, and it borders on Class IV as the water level rises. It is best scouted by climbing the right bank from the eddy, crossing the railroad bridge, and walking down the path on the left. The rapid contains no unusual features, but a variety of rocks, waves, and holes lead to some larger waves toward the bottom which are difficult to navigate in boats that have taken water above.

Below Excelsior is a river-wide low head dam. Exercise caution, and if you have any doubts, walk around Excelsior to avoid a swim over the dam. **Caution!** It is important, especially in high water, to observe the runout of Excelsior to the dam. The dam in medium water and higher is only 3 or 4 feet high, but it is very dangerous. In low water, it is easy to lift over on the right. In higher water, there is a path on the left that works best to portage.

Several hundred yards below the dam is the take out where the river turns right at a small parking area by the municipal pool.

Lebanon ➤ Connecticut River	4.0 mi
Description:	Quickwater, Class II
Date checked:	1988, NC
Navigable:	High and medium water
Scenery:	Rural, urban
Maps:	USGS Hanover
Portage:	(4.0 mi e dam)

Look over the rapid through the city of Lebanon. This has been run, but because of the dam partway down and the rough-cut rocks in the streambed, it is not recommended. Quickwater follows to a renovated power dam by an old mill building. One hundred feet downstream is another dam.

The best put-in is below this third dam is behind Dulac Hardware store (ask for and obtain permission to put in here) 0.25 mile below, where US 4 crosses the river. The river, with some easy Class II rapids, wanders through some rural, almost attractive sections of Lebanon. A difficult but runnable broken dam is reached around a left turn (2.0 miles), and just below, under a railroad bridge and the high US 4 bridge, is a low 1-foot weir that should be run with care or carried on the left—at high water it is very dangerous. Class II rapids continue alongside I-89. Below the next railroad bridge, around a left turn, is the next dam (3.0 miles). During 1988 this dam was being rebuilt to generate electricity. Scout carefully along Glen Road, which follows this section of the river. Much of the river is diverted to a generating plant 0.5 mile below at the NH 12A bridge. When there is sufficient flow, this half-mile is pleasant Class II paddling. Below this bridge, the river flattens out and meanders to the Connecticut. It is possible to take out behind the shopping center just beyond the NH 12A bridge or at the mouth at the Connecticut, reachable by some dirt roads behind the shopping center.

Ottauquechee River VT

The Ottauquechee River drains the east side of Sherburne Pass and flows east to the Connecticut River at North Hartland. The upper part offers a long run for novice paddlers. The middle section is broken by dams and the spectacular Quechee Gorge. The lower part is within the impoundment of a large flood-control dam.

Although the valley is one of the major east-west routes (US 4) across Vermont, the river itself is a lovely wooded aisle through its gorges large and small.

West Bridgewater ➤ Woodstock	13.5 mi
Description:	Class I–II
Date checked:	2001
Navigable:	High water (late April to early May)
Scenery:	Forested, rural, towns
Maps:	USGS Killington Peak, Plymouth, Woodstock South

Put in at the VT 100 bridge in West Bridgewater. The rapids are continuous and easy Class I and II. The river is crossed by bridges of both US 4 and side roads. However, as the river swings from one side of the valley to the other, the outside is a steep wooded bank or a shaley cliff. None of the rapids is especially notable, although you should, as always, watch for fallen trees.

The rapid immediately above Bridgewater is Class II. The dam is mostly gone, especially on the left side, and can be run. Below Bridgewater the valley and the river widen, although tributaries keep the water level up.

For an easy trip, take out where the river comes close to the road upstream of the US 4 bridge a mile west of Woodstock.

Woodstock ➤ Taftsville	4.5 mi
Description:	Flatwater, quickwater, Class I–II
Date checked:	2001
Navigable:	Medium-high water, medium water
Scenery:	Towns, forested
Maps:	USGS Woodstock South, Woodstock North, Quechee
Difficulty:	0.5 mi pipe at US 4 bridge—get out on R to scout
Portages:	1.0 mi e 2-foot waterfall under VT 12 bridge
	(4.5 mi L dam at Taftsville)

The rapid immediately above the first bridge in Woodstock is a difficult Class II, harder than those above. Just at the bridge, a pipe crosses but can be run. The river flows through town and under a covered bridge to the VT 12 bridge (1.0 mile) where there is a 2-foot drop with some rocks below.

The rapids gradually diminish to the backwater of the dam at Taftsville. A road on the left bank makes the take-out possible at various points. A covered bridge crosses the river at the dam.

Taftsville ➤ Connecticut River	12.0 mi
Maps:	USGS Quechee, Hartland, North Hartland

Below the Taftsville dam 4.0 miles of mixed rapids and smoothwater bring you to the dam and covered bridge at Quechee. It is 1.0 mile to the dam and cascade at Deweys Mills. The next mile is the spectacular Quechee Gorge, best viewed from the US 4 bridge midway down.

A dirt road on the left bank leads to the foot of the gorge. The formerly Class II–III lower gorge has been flooded out, and there are 4.5 miles of riffles and sandbanks to the North Hartland flood-control dam. At maximum pool Quechee Gorge will be filled nearly to the brim, and the dams at Deweys Mills and Quechee will be underwater. There is a boat ramp above, but access below is blocked by a chain-link fence. About 0.25 mile below the flood-control dam there are unrunnable falls above the US 5 bridge. It is 1.0 mile to a side road crossing a rock island with a dam on each side. One of the bridges is a covered bridge. It is then 0.25 mile to the Connecticut River.

Sugar River NH

This river drains Lake Sunapee. It begins with several dams and an unrunnable section, so the best part of the river starts at North Newport.

The river can often be run late in the season, because the drainage area is large and the flow is dam controlled. A good indication of the water level can be obtained from the NH 11 bridge at Kelleyville becaues the rapids there are typical of the rest of the river.

The Water Division (603-271-3406) draws down the level of Lake Sunapee every fall. The exact dates vary from year to year.

North Newport ➤ Kelleyville		2.5 mi
Description:	Class II–III	
Date checked:	2001	
Navigable:	High water (April)	
	Medium water—scratchy (May through June and wet falls)	
	Dam controlled (annual fall drawdown of Lake Sunapee)	

Scenery:	Rural, towns
Maps:	USGS Sunapee 15, Claremont 15

Put in at the covered bridge in North Newport. If the water is high, there will be standing waves and turbulence, with relatively few rocks visible. At lower levels you must dodge many moderate-sized rocks.

About 1 mile below the start, around the second right turn, there is a difficult Class III drop among boulders. It should be scouted from the right bank. The next corner is also more difficult than the first part, but the rapids ease off closer to Kelleyville. There is a USGS Gauge in Claremont. A reading of 2.76 (700 cubic feet per second) is medium. Always scout the run first.

Kelleyville ➤ Training tower 5.0 mi

Description:	Class I–II
Date checked:	2001
Navigable:	High water
Scenery:	Forested, settled
Maps:	USGS Claremont 15

Below the NH 11/103 bridge in Kelleyville the rocks are smaller and the run tends to involve a lot of picking around them at lower water levels. At higher water levels this section is likely to wash out into big waves. The outside corners tend to generate waves at all water levels.

The rapids gradually diminish, and access is possible at the fire department training tower, which is reached by a rough, dirt side road along the left bank.

Training tower ➤ Claremont 2.25 mi

Although there are no noteworthy rapids, the current is still swift and the run into Claremont is pleasant. Take out well above the NH 11 bridge on the right because the first dam is above it and the river is confined there between retaining walls. Park on the road.

Claremont ➤ Connecticut River	5.0 mi

Gorges and more dams highlight the river through Claremont. Resist the temptation to put in again, because there is still another dam in a gorge in West Claremont.

Croydon Brook (North Branch Sugar River) NH

This branch of the Sugar provides a taste of virtually everything. In 10.0 miles, one experiences lake paddling, quickwater, and whitewater up to Class III. The river rises north of Newport and Lake Sunapee and south of the Mascoma drainage basin. Longer stretches of relatively flat water, home to many beaver, are interrupted by bursts of whitewater, one section of which merits a trip by itself. It is important to emphasize that downed trees and low-hanging branches are a hazard the entire length of this river.

Grantham ➤ Sugar River		10.5 mi
Description:	Lake, quickwater, Class II	
Date checked:	2001	
Navigable:	High water	
Scenery:	Forested, rural, towns	
Maps:	USGS Sunapee 15	

The best put-in is on NH 10 just off Exit 13 on I-89 anywhere between the post office and the Grantham fire station. There is quickwater until Stocker Brook enters on the left, where Class II rapids start, continuing under NH 10 and past the foundation of an old mill on the left. Shortly, the river flattens out. Quickwater continues under Dunbar Hill Road (1.5 miles), which, if the water is quite high, you may not be able to pass under (carry on the right). The river then moves under a wooden footbridge (2.5 miles), which may also have to be lifted over. At the next NH 10 bridge (3.5 miles), just north of Croydon village, Class II rapids start. They parallel the road a short distance and then turn left. Obstructions in the middle may force the paddler to one side or the other. Below the next bridge (4.0 miles) the rapids diminish. Continue to and through Spectacle Pond (4.5 miles), which is aptly named for the view of the surrounding hills, especially craggy Grantham Mountain. The pond is really two ponds with a connecting stream on the far left. It is 0.5 mile long and may be covered with ice when the river is at its best.

Quickwater continues to where a bridge crosses the river (5.75 miles). This is 1.5 miles south of the Croydon fire station on NH 10. The bridge is on a side road off and visible from the paved highway. For those interested only in the whitewater stretch that follows, this spot is an excellent put-in. The rapids start almost immediately, are generally Class II, and continue uninterrupted to Croydon Flat, where NH 10 again crosses the river (7.5 miles). Keep in mind that if the river is high, much of this section may warrant a Class III rating. Suddenly there is a sharp right turn and a Class III drop that is actually two drops, with holes and obstructions on each side dictating a center route. It is helpful to approach from the right. This drop is easily scouted during the car shuttle; it is located where the road approaches the river 0.25 mile above the bridge in Croydon Flat.

Below this bridge the rapids diminish, and you can take out on the left where, after changing to quickwater, the river nears NH 10 on the left (8.25 miles). Quickwater continues to the main branch of the Sugar River. One can take out on the left under the covered bridge on the north Newport Road at the mouth of the Croydon Branch, or continue down the Sugar River toward Claremont.

Black River VT

The southern of the two Black rivers in Vermont starts from a series of lakes and runs southeast to the Connecticut River. Although sectioned by dams, it provides good runs on easy to moderate rapids. Below Cavendish the water level is controlled by release from the power dam.

Black River Lakes   6.0 mi

These lakes, situated near Tyson, begin about 6.0 miles south of the source of the river near Plymouth Union. Set deep among the hills, they offer attractive paddling in all seasons. VT 100 passes along the west side of all four lakes.

The paddler can put in directly from the main highway at the northern end of Lake Amherst. Lift over a low dam 1.0 mile below into the short river leading to Echo Lake, which is 1.0 mile long. At the southern end of the lake a mile-long river, which is rocky and presents problems except at high water, leads through Tyson to Rescue Lake. Rescue Lake provides another two-mile trip to Reservoir Pond, which is also 1.0 mile long. A low, 2-foot-high dam at the southern end is easily crossed into the river, or you can take out at VT 100.

Lakes ➤ Cavendish		9.75 mi
Description:	Quickwater, Class I–II	
Date checked:	2000	
Navigable:	High to medium water (April to early May)	
Scenery:	Forested, settled, rural, towns	
Maps:	USGS Ludlow 15	
Portage:	5.75 mi e 5-foot dam	

Put in at the dam at the south end of Reservoir Pond close to VT 100. The first 0.5 mile is Class II, but the rapids become easier and mix with quickwater until just above Ludlow (4.0 miles), where the dam is gone. A ledge under a small bridge east of town gives no trouble. Beyond the bridge near the sewage treatment plant watch for a small dam. The river riffles on past Proctorsville where the remains of a washed-out dam are still present. Approaching Cavendish, there is another small dam in the process of washing out which can be run; this one is visible from VT 131. Take out at the bridge on a side road in Cavendish.

Cavendish ➤ Whitesville		1.5 mi

The take-out above the dam is difficult, and a carry of 0.25 mile is necessary. Access below the gorge would be a problem.

Whitesville ➤ Perkinsville		7.75 mi
Description:	Class II–III	
Date checked:	2000	

Navigable:	High to medium water (late March to mid-May)
Scenery:	Forested, rural, striking rocky gorge
Maps:	USGS Ludlow 15
Portage:	(7.75 mi dam in Perkinsville)

The customary put-in for the run is at a side-road bridge in Whitesville. You can put in on the right below the ledge, but at favorable water levels, the river can be run through the extreme left channel.

The rapids are moderate Class II for 2.5 miles to an iron bridge. In another 0.5 mile, at the second pullover, with a big pine tree on the right, rapids start.

Approximately 2.5 mi below Whitesville, after arching southward, the river swings abruptly left (there is a highway pullout here). Rapids intensify for 0.25 mi passing a rocky feature which looks from the road and from downstream like knuckles on a fist. The flow turns right into a mile-long gorge which drops 40–60 feet below the road and narrows to a complex 4-foot drop "flush point" about 20 feet wide. Large shore and mid stream formations, with moss and ferns onshore make this section one of the most appealing of all riverscapes. After more-complex Class II–III features, the stream swings left and the banks become lower. Easy Class II water flows a mile to the covered bridge, a customary takeout for this section (0.2 mile on a dirt road west of the VT 131 and VT 106 intersection).

Perkinsville ➤ North Springfield flood-control dam 3.75 mi

The going is difficult below the dam in Perkinsville for a way, until the river comes into the ponding of an old power dam that is less than 1 mile downstream. The gorge is attractive, with high cliffs.

Pass the confluence with the North Branch (1.25 miles), with its earthen dam visible upstream, the river flows through grassy fields in the flood-control dam's recreation area. Since the permanent pond is less than 1 mile away, the paddle is pleasant but not exciting.

North Springfield ➤ Springfield   3.5 mi

Below the flood-control dam, starting at a put-in reached
from North Springfield, the river runs swiftly over a few rocks,
gradually becoming quickwater as it approaches Springfield.
This section can be run during much of the year. Take out at
the first bridge in Springfield.

Springfield ➤ Connecticut River   5.0 mi

The Black River through Springfield is a series of dams and
cascades. Below town a few rapids alternate with ledges before
flattening out into the Connecticut. Thrill seekers should
check the complex 10-foot drop approximately 1.0 mile below
Springfield. The lower part could be paddled as a side trip
from the Connecticut. All of the lower part of the river is followed by VT 11.

Williams River vt

The Williams River rises in Andover and flows to the
Connecticut. Most of the rapids are easy to moderate, and there
is also a terrific scenic gorge to admire. In high water, the river
can be paddled from above Proctor and the Middle Branch can
be paddled as well.

Gassetts ➤ Chester   3.5 mi

One can put in somewhere in the vicinity of the junction of VT
103 and 10 in very high water. The rapids are mostly Class II,
and the river follows the road fairly closely, so it can be inspected in advance. In North Chester a dam at an old gristmill is
adjacent to the VT 103 bridge and is a short and easy carry.

Chester ➤ Brockways Mills   7.5 mi

Description:	Quickwater, Class I, II, III
Date checked:	2001
Navigable:	High to medium water (early May)
Scenery:	Forested, rural
Maps:	USGS Ludlow 15, Saxtons River 15, Bellows Falls 15

Portages: 4.0 mi L ledge—liftover
                           (7.5 mi L waterfall 1.0 mi)

The Williams is suitable for beginners if they are protected and supported by a strong lead boat that can recognize ledges and fallen trees in sufficient time and can deal with them appropriately.

Put in from the VT 103 bridge in Chester. The river is small and shallow in medium water, with easy rapids. High water washes the rapids out to fast current. Watch for barbed wire and cows in the first mile to the VT 11 bridge. Only 0.25 mile below the bridge the middle branch enters on the right, greatly increasing the flow. Ferry across this junction in high water. After 1.0 mile more the railroad crosses. After lazing along for another 1.5 miles, the river wakes up as it passes under two bridges in quick succession, makes a sharp right turn, and roars over a rocky ledge that is perhaps Class II in high water.

The difficulty then decreases, with a few Class II spots, until the big ledge (4.0 miles). This ledge is difficult to recognize in advance and is hard to land above. Hug the left bank as you approach. It can be run, but most parties will wish to lift over at least the upper drop, even if they run or line the lower part.

Two more distinct Class II–III ledges interrupt the slightly more difficult rapids that run to the first covered bridge (5.0 miles).

The major rapids are past, but the river is still pretty, with high, wooded banks and gravel bars. There is another covered bridge at 6.25 miles, and the third railroad bridge is shortly below it. The best take-out is at the fourth railroad bridge on a road on the left bank that can be reached from Brockways Mills. A confident party can paddle another 0.25 mile and hope they can manage to take out above the next bridge. Immediately below, the river drops over a 30-foot falls into a gorge. A gauging station is on the left.

Brockways Mills ➤ Connecticut River   3.5 mi

Most of the next mile is in a deep gorge, with rapids that are only marginally navigable. It is possible to carry 0.75 mile on either side and relaunch down a steep bank into a swimming hole. In high water the Connecticut River ponds upstream for an indeterminate distance.

Another bridge is reached at 2.25 miles and I-91 at 3.5 miles. The Connecticut River is just below, with an access upstream on the left at the confluence.

Williams River (Middle Branch) VT

The Middle Branch of the Williams River rises in Londonderry and Andover and flows into the Williams just below the VT 11 bridge in Chester.

In high water it can be paddled for 3 or 4 miles, with rapids that are mostly Class II. Since VT 11 closely follows and crosses the river, you can scout easily to select a put-in. Unless you plan to continue down the Williams, take out at one of the three bridges in Chester.

Saxtons River VT

The Saxtons River rises in the hills of Windham, Vermont, and flows generally eastward to join the Connecticut River just below Bellows Falls. Both the South Branch and the main river above Grafton look as if they might offer interesting paddling at high water, but no description is available. The run from Grafton to the village of Saxtons River is a popular intermediate whitewater trip, but frequent dams discourage use of the rest of the river. Since there are no sizable swamps or lakes in the headwaters, spring runoff is shorter than on several nearby rivers.

Grafton ➤ Saxtons River Village	8.5 mi
Description:	Class II–III
Date checked:	2001
Navigable:	High water (April)
Scenery:	Rural, towns
Maps:	USGS Saxton River 15
Portage:	(8.5 mi ledge under bridge)

This run has about the same gradient as the nearby Cold River in South Acworth, New Hampshire, but is considered more difficult because of several steep drops spaced among easier rapids. VT 121 is usually nearby, although often out of sight.

Start at the VT 121 bridge about 0.75 mile northwest of the intersection with VT 35 in Grafton. In about 1.0 mile, the South Branch enters, doubling the size of the river; in low water it may be necessary to start below this point. The river reaches Cambridgeport 5.0 miles and four VT 121 bridges from the start. The next 3.5 miles to the village of Saxtons River have less gradient and generally are easier, although there are still some steep drops. Under the side road bridge in the center of the village there is a dangerous drop that allegedly has been run by a kayak, but it is easy to take out well upstream. There is a road to the river behind the fire station, but no parking is allowed, and a shallow rapid makes it difficult to reach by boat. Some parties choose to take out 0.5 mile west of town, where the VT 121 is near the river.

Saxtons River Village ➤ Connecticut River   5.25 mi
Scouted only

Maps: USGS Saxtons River 15, Bellows Falls 15

Put in below the ledge in the center of town. It is less than 0.5 mile to the next dam, which it is best to carry on the right. The rapids in the next section are easier than those above. It is 1.25 miles from the start to the covered bridge, then 1.75 miles to the VT 121 bridge. In another 0.5 mile comes the side-road bridge at North Westminster with a dam just below, which is best to carry on the right. In another 0.5 mile there is a 60-foot cascade with a difficult portage. Next is 1.0 mile of easy running to the US 5 bridge, where there is another dam (carry left), followed by a short rapid to the Connecticut River.

Cold River NH

There are many Cold Rivers in New Hampshire. This one originates in Acworth and flows west into the Connecticut below Bellows Falls. It offers a fine set of fairly continuous rapids that are broken into short segments by impassable obstructions.

At high water most of the rocks are buried and standing waves appear. At lower levels there will be considerable amount of rock dodging. Watch for blind corners and fallen trees.

East Acworth ➤ South Acworth	4.0 mi
Description:	Class II–III
Date checked:	2001
Navigable:	High water (early April)
	Medium water (late April)
Scenery:	Rural, towns
Maps:	USGS Lovewell Mountain 15
Portages:	(4.0 mi R dam and gorge at South Acworth 0.5 mi)

In the first mile below East Acworth, the river drops 100 feet; all of it is visible from the road. Put in at the first bridge 1.25 miles south of East Acworth where the rapids become very small and the gradient even, making a pleasant and exciting run. In medium water, this portion starts out scratchy, but the water level increases downstream as several side streams enter. This entire run is virtually continuous Class II rapids that require frequent rock dodging. Within the first 100 yards, there is a runnable rock dam. There are a few Class III rapids. A mile above South Acworth NH 123A crosses. Take out on the right above the dam in the town. Portage the dam and the gorge 0.5 mile along NH 123A.

South Acworth ➤ Vilas Pool	5.5 mi
Description:	Class II
Date checked:	2001
Navigable:	High water (early April)
	Medium water (late April)
Scenery:	Forested
Maps:	USGS Lovewell Mountain 15, Bellows Falls 15
Portages:	(5.5 mi L dam at Alstead 100 yd)

The put-in for the usual Cold River run is below the gorge, where the river comes close to NH 123A 0.5 mile west (downstream) of South Acworth. This portion of the Cold starts with quick current and easy Class II rapids that gradually increase in difficulty to hard, long Class II rapids toward the end.

The first 1.5 miles to the first bridge consists of quick current and up to easy Class II rapids, but watch for fallen trees. This bridge is on a side road and only 10 feet from NH 123A. An alternate put-in is in the field on the left bank upstream of this bridge. In another 0.75 mile NH 123A crosses. The next 1.75 miles to a covered bridge and a new adjacent bridge consist of frequent rapids with blind corners and fallen trees. NH 123A is often visible from the river, and sugar maple lines the banks.

Below this pair of bridges the rapids increase in difficulty. In 0.5 mile there is a particularly difficult spot with several channels and many fallen trees. Where a small slide appears on the left bank and the river turns right, get out to scout. In another 0.75 mile the river reaches the small pond and dam at Vilas Pool (9.75 miles), which is located on NH 123A just east of its junction near Alstead with NH 12A. Take out at the large pullover area overlooking the pond.

Vilas Pool ➤ Drewsville Gorge	3.25 mi
Description:	Class II–III
Date checked:	2001
Navigable:	Medium water (late April)
Scenery:	Rural
Maps:	USGS Bellows Falls 15
Portages:	0.75 mi frequent obstructions
	(3.25 mi R Drewsville Gorge 0.25 mi)

The first 0.5 mile consists of Class III rapids, a triple ledge, called Krystyna's Staircase, a very sharp right turn called Cave Sluice, and following a left turn, a Class IV at a broken dam called Glen Drop In. If you prefer not to begin in rapids, put in directly below them. The remainder of the run is followed by NH 123. This section and the following one can be run when the previous section is too low. The paddling is easier, but the take-out is tricky. Directly under a NH 123 bridge the river flows rapidly over 30-foot falls into Drewsville Gorge. Be sure to spot a landing in advance.

Drewsville Gorge ➤ Connecticut River   3.5 mi
Description: Class II–III
Date checked: 2001
Navigable: Medium water (late April)
Scenery: Settled
Maps: USGS Bellows Falls 15

Portage around the gorge is physically difficult, and it is also hard to get permission. It is relatively easy to put in from NH 123A on the right bank at a pull-off less than 0.5 mile downstream of the bridge.

The rapids below are Class II–III at the start, and the river here is a steep, rocky gorge. The rapids soon diminish to Class II, except for one Class III pitch 1.5 miles below near a gravel pit where the quarrying equipment is visible from the river. Three miles below the falls you reach the third NH 123 bridge at Cold River (3.0 miles). This is a good take-out for those who don't want to paddle the remaining 0.5 mile of quickwater past the NH 12 and railroad bridges to the Connecticut River (3.5 miles).

It is often possible to run the portion of the river below the waterfall when the water above it is too low.

Rock River VT

This small stream enters the West River just above the Maple Valley Ski Area. The upper part is a fine Class III run, while the lower section contains several Class IV drops which require scouting.

South Newfane ➤ West River   3.75 mi
Description: Class III–IV
Date checked: 2001
Navigable: High water only (late March to early
                           April)
Scenery: Town, forest
Maps: USGS Brattleboro 15
Portage: 1.5 mi L dam in Williamsville 50 yd—
                           approach carefully

Put in at the green iron bridge just below the village of South Newfane. The first mile, ending at a covered bridge, is continuous rapid, up to Class III in difficulty. Below the covered bridge, watch for a sharp left turn and a slide area on the right. **Caution!** This turn should be scouted, since the Class II rapid in turn leads immediately into a short pool above a 15-foot dam. Portage left. Below the dam, the rapids get tougher (Class IV). Take out on the right after the first corner to scout the first long rapid, which as a ledge which must be avoided.

A high concrete bridge is passed, followed shortly by a double ledge that should be scouted. Watch for houses on the left which herald the hardest rapid on the river (tough Class IV). Scout on the left. There are four ledges in this run. Eddy right below the first ledge and ferry to the left eddy below three large rocks. Run the second ledge right center, angling right. The third ledge which follows immediately must be punched through. The fourth ledge can be run either far right into an eddy, or just right of the undercut, and then left around a hole. A series of Class III rapids leads to a pool above the last big drop at an island. A sneak route exists left of the island, or run to the right through the drop.

The take-out is at VT 30 bridge (difficult) after another 0.25 mile of Class III rapids, or farther down the West River.

West River VT

The West River, known to the Indians and the early settlers as the Wantastigeset, rises in Weston and flows southeast to the Connecticut. It is almost continuous runnable rapids except where three dams block the flow. Although the river follows VT 100, the river's clear rocky bottom, fine banks, and wooded hillsides create the predominant scenery for the paddler.

For detailed information see AMC's *Classic Northeastern Whitewater Guide.*

Weston ➤ Londonderry		6.75 mi
Description:	Class II	
Date checked:	2001	

Navigable:	High water
Scenery:	Forested, rural
Maps:	USGS Wallingford 15, Londonderry 15
Portage:	(6.75 mi L dam at Londonderry)

Put in at the bridge in Weston. Although the river is channeled, it gives some indication of water level farther downstream. The rapids are nearly continuous for the first 2.0 miles. The S-turn rapids should be scouted because of the possibility of strainers in a blind corner. Take out on the right to scout just before a sharp right turn with a high bank on the left. The rapids soon moderate into quickwater. There is a good take-out just past a small bridge (6.0 miles) where VT 100 is close to the right bank.

Londonderry ➤ South Londonderry Ledges	5.25 mi
Description:	Class I, II, III
Date checked:	2001
Navigable:	High to medium water (April, May, after fall rains)
Scenery:	Settled
Maps:	USGS Londonderry

This is the famous Londonderry Ledges section. Most of the rapids are Class III at the usual level, with connecting sections of Class II and I. Put in at the dam or from a roadside turnoff on the VT 100 bridge south of Londonderry. The river gradually builds in difficulty to the first ledge section in the vicinity of the VT 100 bridge. Competent paddlers will find endless eddying and surfing opportunities in this section. A short pool under the bridge leads to a steep rapid with a strong eddy (Larry's Eddy) on the left halfway down. Easier going leads to the second VT 100 bridge. Dead Cow Rapids lies immediately under the bridge and provides good surfing opportunities. The ledge section starts shortly below, with a friendly hole on the right at the entrance and numerous ledges, waves, and holes throughout its length. Take out below the ledges from a dirt road on the right. This section often has water when the Winhall, the Rock, and the Wardsboro do not.

Below South Londonderry Ledges ➤
Ball Mountain Dam   6.5 mi
Description: Class II
Date checked: 2001
Navigable: High water, medium water (May or after
                          fall rains)
Scenery: Wild
Maps: USGS Londonderry 15
Portage: 6.25 mi Ball Mountain flood-control
                          dam—extremely difficult

This section is easier than the one above. The gradient is constant, with waves in high water and rocks in low. The mouth of the Winhall (1.75 miles) is a possible take-out, although it is not accessible in mud season.

The gradient steepens for the next 2.0 miles, ending suddenly at the backwater of Ball Mountain Dam. At low pond there are another 2.0 miles of gradually diminishing current and rapids to the portage trail on the right above the dam. Ice floes may block the river in the spring. The carry up is exceedingly strenuous: 250 vertical feet in 0.5 mile to the road. When continuing the run, you should scout the portage trail before putting in. There are better river sections in the area to paddle, considering the effort required in portaging.

Ball Mountain Dam ➤ Salmon Hole   2.75 mi
Description: Class III
Date checked: 2001
Navigable: Controlled release
Scenery: Wild
Maps: USGS Londonderry 15

This is the famous West River run, which has greatly increased in popularity with the water releases from Ball Mountain Dam. The normal white-water release is 1,500 cubic feet per second.

Access to the upper river is a problem. Kayakers sometimes carry across the dam and put in on the left below it, which is a long, steep carry. A dirt road on the old railroad bed along the left bank can be reached from Salmon Hole. Although narrow and muddy, it is the usual route. Access may be regulated.

A difficult drop lies just below the put-in, then the rapids moderate somewhat, with waves in high water and rock dodging at medium stage. The entire river can be seen from the access road.

The most difficult part is the Dumplings shortly above Salmon Hole. The river drops and swirls around huge boulders, to the delight of boaters and spectators alike. On water-release weekends even the bank is standing room only. The large pool below is Salmon Hole, the take-out.

This area is a state forest.

Salmon Hole ➤ Townshend Dam	5.5 mi
Description:	Class II
Date checked:	2001
Navigable:	Controlled release
Scenery:	Forested, rural
Maps:	USGS Londonderry 15, Saxtons River 15
Portage:	(5.5 mi R Townshend Dam 0.5 mi by car)

This section is somewhat easier to paddle than the one above and is more accessible.

Put in at Salmon Hole or at the bridge 0.25 mile below. At high water the waves are heavy; open boaters especially are advised to have proper flotation. Almost immediately the river divides around an island, with most of the water flowing left. In high water the right channel feels more like a small river, for those who prefer rocks to waves.

The most difficult spot is at the foot of the island, where the left channel drives toward the right shore around some large rocks. The spot is visible from VT 30.

The waves are heavy to the VT 30 bridge (2.5 miles) but moderate slightly to the VT 100 bridge (3.75 miles).

Below here is the nicest part of the run, where the river is not near the road and the waves are very large.

Townshend Dam ➤ West Dummerston	12.5 mi
Description:	Class I–II
Date checked:	2001
Navigable:	Spring, fall, wet summers; controlled release

| Scenery: | Forested, rural |
| Maps: | USGS Brattleboro 15 |

This section offers easy running for the less-experienced paddler. The water is regulated by the flood-control dam upstream, but natural water is usually allowed to flow through. The water releases above Jamaica raise this section to very high water.

Put in on the left from the dirt road across the dam and the covered bridge. The first part is narrow, curving and mostly away from the road. In low and medium water, easy rapids alternate with long smooth sections. Very high water washes out the smaller rapids and ledges, leaving only really big rocks as obstacles. The current is very fast.

Below the VT 30 bridge (3.75 miles) the river becomes wider, straighter, and less difficult. Below a bridge on a side road (6.25 miles) the river again approaches VT 30 and passes the site of the West Dummerston dam, of which little trace remains. Above the covered bridge and within sight of it is a series of ledges best run to the right at most water levels.

West Dummerston ➤ Connecticut River		6.5 mi
Description:	Class I–II	
Date checked:	2001	
Navigable:	Spring, summer, fall; controlled release	
Scenery:	Forested, settled	
Maps:	USGS Brattleboro 15	

The most difficult rapids in this section lie below the West Dummerston covered bridge. A ledge around the next corner can be dangerous in high water. Under any conditions but low water, hug the right bank. If the right channel can be run, the ledge will generate hydraulics. In low water the river funnels through a selection of channels with various obstructions, and some paddlers may want to try them all to practice technique. Farther on, many large rocks are scattered about the river.

If the water is low, take out at the next iron bridge (1.5 miles); below it the water is only spread thinly over the rocks. With sufficient water this section offers excellent practice in water reading and a pleasant run with riffles, fast corners, and islands. All of it is within sight of VT 30, which provides good access but destroys the aura of remoteness of the river above West Dummerston. A convenient take-out is directly below the high I-91 bridge (5.5 miles, no access).

The mouth of the West River is ponded from the Vernon Dam 7.0 miles down the Connecticut River, and it is filled with low islands that are interesting to explore. The US 5 bridge and a railroad bridge cross a rocky cut at the mouth.

Winhall River VT

The Winhall River is a small stream that rises on the north slope of Stratton Mountain and flows east to join the West River. With sufficient water it provides one of the longest advanced whitewater runs in Vermont. There is rarely enough water to paddle. All the rapids can be run by skilled open boaters, although most will portage Londonderry Rapids.

Off VT 30 ➤ West River		7.0 mi
Description:	Class III–IV	
Date checked:	2001	
Navigable:	High or medium water (April)	
Scenery:	Forested	
Maps:	USGS Londonderry 15	

A dirt road leads up the north bank from Grahamville School, which is a mile west of Bondville on VT 30. From one put-in at a large field on this road, there are continuous Class II–III rapids for a mile to the bridge at Grahamville School.

The next mile to the VT 30 bridge (2.0 miles) is about the same, with a more-difficult section around a big rock in the middle just above the bridge.

From Bondville to the VT 100 bridge in Rawsonville, 2.0 miles of Class III–IV rapids keep you very alert. Another mile of similar rapids brings you to a bridge on the unpaved Londonderry Road (5.0 miles). **Caution!** Pull out at this bridge and scout the difficult Londonderry Rapids in the next left turn. These rapids, at an old dam site, can be portaged on either side. For the more skillful paddler, routes exist on both the extreme left and the extreme right.

Below Londonderry Rapids (5.0 miles) there are 2.0 miles of easier Class II–III rapids to the confluence with the West River, but the waves can be heavy. Take out either just above or just below the confluence on the right, where there is a campground that is accessible from VT 100 to the north of Rawsonville.

Wardsboro Brook VT

This small stream enters the West River below Ball Mountain Dam, and it is paralleled by VT 100. It is a demanding Class IV run that requires high water. Since runoff here occurs rapidly, Wardsboro Brook is recommended for only a few weeks of the year.

Wardsboro ➤ West River	4.5 mi
Description:	Class III–IV
Date checked:	2001
Navigable:	High water only (early April)
Scenery:	Forested
Maps:	USGS Londonderry 15, Saxtons River 15

A put-in can be made below the bridge and the waterfall in the town of Wardsboro. Class III rapids make up the first mile of this run. Wardsboro Brook then passes under VT 100 and turns right with the first of many difficult Class IV rapids. This right turn should be scouted, as the channel changes with water levels may not exist at low water. The next 2.5 miles are continuous difficult rapids to the next VT 100 bridge, where they get even harder.

You can take out at a dirt road on the left just below the bridge. If you choose to run the last mile, take out at the bridge just above the confluence (4.5 miles). If you had difficulty up above, don't run the last mile.

Ashuelot River NH

The Ashuelot River is a beautiful tributary of the Connecticut, entering from the east only a short distance above the Massachusetts state line. The river offers such a variety of paddling that short trips can be arranged to suit just about anyone's taste.

The upper stretches are rapid and rough. The middle reaches are largely winding and placid, and the last few miles provide some of the wildest paddling in NH. The upper part must be done in the spring; the lower section can sometimes be run in the summer or fall. The middle section can be paddled during most of the year.

Power line ➤ Lower Stillwater	5.75 mi
Description:	Flatwater, quickwater, Class I–III
Date checked:	2001
Navigable:	High water (April)
Scenery:	Forested, towns
Maps:	USGS Lovewell Mountain 15
Portage:	2.5 mi R dam in Marlow 25 yd

Put in at a power dam 1.5 miles north of Marlow on the road to Ashuelot Lake. From here the river is mostly Class I, with a ledge 0.25 mile below the start, to the flowage from the dam in Marlow.

Below the dam a little fastwater runs to the next pond, which is about a mile below. After the pond there are some interesting rapids, but a reconstructed hydropower dam interrupts the section. After an old footbridge, warning signs herald the dam, which has a new footbridge over it. Portage on the left. The drop from the dam to the so-called Lower Stillwater is 36 feet in approximately 0.4 mile, ending at the power station for the dam. Some of that section may have to be lined.

Lower Stillwater ➤ Gilsum Gorge	4.5 mi
Description:	Class III–IV
Date checked:	2000
Navigable:	High to medium water (April)
Scenery:	Forested, town

Maps:	USGS Lovewell Mountain 15,
	Bellows Falls 15
Portage:	(4.5 mi L Gilsum Gorge [cross river in
	200 yd] 0.75 mi)

This section, known as the Upper Ashuelot, makes a good whitewater run for intermediate or expert paddlers. The scenery is somewhat marred by NH 10, which is almost always present on the bank, but this makes put-ins and take-outs easier.

Just below Lower Stillwater, there is a small bridge over the river which offers a possible put-in. This spot is recommended only for those who like to start with a bang: the most difficult regularly run pitch in the river is about 200 yards below the put-in. Called Surprise Rapids, this stretch can be examined from NH 10, and it should definitely be scouted.

Surprise Rapids is followed by much easier Class II–III rapids. The river bends to the right and is followed by an old elbow of NH 10 (0.5 mile), while the newer road continues straight ahead. This old loop is the usual put-in, since most groups do not want to start off with Surprise Rapids. The rapids here are easy Class II. The river passes another small bridge, and the easy rapids flatten out to smoothwater (1.0 mile).

Below a short pool the current speeds up considerably, marking the beginning of 2.0 miles of continuous rapids. The river is narrowed by the road embankment to the left. The 2.0 miles contain many difficult Class III and IV rapids and require a great deal of maneuvering, even at high water levels. Fortunately, NH 10 and its older loops are also nearby for an emergency take-out.

At the end of this 2.0-mile stretch, the river becomes relatively calm and splits around an island. The right side should be taken to get into position for a small broken dam below. The broken dam is about 1.5 feet in height, and it is best to run it from the far right. One hundred yards below, near the NH 10 bridge in Gilsum (3.5 miles), the sawmill on the left provides a possible take-out.

Rapids continue through Gilsum, with the road or houses fairly close on the right. The rapids in this section are less difficult than those above, but they can have heavy waves, particularly near the end. Take out just below the NH 10 bridge (4.5 miles) at a picnic area on the left. Plan and execute this landing with caution because the current is strong and the gorge begins about 200 yards below.

An old stone bridge just off NH 10 marks the actual entrance to the gorge. From the bridge, the gorge and its first drop are very impressive. The main current undercuts and deflects off an enormous rock in the center. Gilsum Gorge has been run in relatively low water, but the run is a difficult stunt. At higher levels it is very dangerous.

Gilsum Gorge ➤ Shaw's Corner	4.0 mi
Description:	Class II–III
Date checked:	2000
Navigable:	High to medium water (April)
Scenery:	Forested
Maps:	USGS Bellows Falls 15

This is a popular intermediate trip, with continuous rapids, but it is closely followed by a road.

Water levels required for this section are about the same as for the stretch above Gilsum Gorge. If the gauge above the stone bridge at the head of the gorge reads 3.5, the river is low but runnable; at 5.5 or higher you can expect a number of Class III rapids.

A put-in can be made where the river first approaches the road below Gilsum Gorge. The small May Brook enters the river at this point, and there is a short island in the stream.

Class II rapids continue to a small bridge (0.25 mile). Just below this bridge is a shallow rapid: if this spot is passable, then so is the rest of the run. The Ashuelot bends away from the road. The next stretch contains many Class II rapids and some tight turns. **Caution!** Watch for trees and logs in the river in this stretch. The river then returns to the road (1.75 miles). The rapids become slightly more difficult, approaching Class III at water levels of 5.0 and higher.

About 2.5 miles from May Brook there is one spot where the river rounds a right bend with large boulders blocking the left side. The channel then empties back into the left. This is the most difficult spot except for Shaw's Corner Rapids, farther downstream.

For a long distance above Shaw's Corner, the road remains close beside the river. The river turns left (3.5 miles) and passes a long straight stretch with a field on the right. Then the stone remains of a bridge abutment come into view on the right bank, marking the beginning of Shaw's Corner Rapids. The river turns sharply left with a ledge on the left. A short, rocky section is followed by three ledges, with waves or hydraulics, depending on the water level. Novice and intermediate paddlers should scout this area.

A suspension bridge (4.0 miles) just below Shaw's Corner Rapids is the usual take-out.

Shaw's Corner ➤ Surry Mountain flood-control dam   5.25 mi

The Class II rapids continue for about a mile to an old abutment, after which they gradually change to fastwater, undercutting the banks. In the spring, when the water is high, there is a good-sized impoundment above the dam, but what little water there is may be frozen. Also, there is a gate on the road. Off-season take-out is possible (with an uphill carry of perhaps 100 yards) via Surry Village Road. It might be best to run this section after a fall rain.

Surry flood-control dam ➤ West Street, Keene   6.75 mi

Description:	Flatwater, quickwater
Date checked:	2000
Navigable:	Medium-high for upper part
Scenery:	Rural, towns, forested
Maps:	USGS Bellow Falls 15, Keene 15
Portage:	(6.75 mi R dam in Keene 10 yd)

Put in at a bridge below the dam. The Ashuelot River here is a winding brook with a sandy bottom. It runs swiftly through a golf course (watch out for flying golf balls) and then gradually slows down approaching the dam in Keene, which is above the first bridge to the north of town. There is a large island just above the dam and just after a new footbridge in Ashuelot River Park. It is easy to take out on the left, but the shorter carry is to the right.

West Street, Keene ➤ West Swanzey	8.75 mi
Description:	Flatwater, quickwater
Date checked:	2000
Navigable:	Passable in all but driest weather
Scenery:	Forested, rural, towns
Maps:	USGS Keene 15
Portage:	(8.75 mi L dam in West Swanzey)

The river flows through Keene. It is less clear and less enjoyable for a short while, but that soon passes. It is scratchy for the first few yards, but is always passable. There are several bridges in town, and at least two of them have gauges.

Otter Brook comes in on the left shortly below the last bridge, near where sewage once flowed into the river from a huge conduit. One covered bridge is passed at Swanzey Center. A dam is near the next one, the Thompson covered bridge, in West Swanzey. There is an automated gauge on the bridge. Call 603-358-5349 for a recording which yields the flow in cubic feet per second.

West Swanzey ➤ Ashuelot	13.25 mi
Map:	USGS Keene 15

Below the dam at West Swanzey the river continues placidly for 3.0 miles to a point 0.5 mile below the Westport bridge, where there is a broken dam. This is easy to run at ordinary water levels. The next 8.0 miles to Winchester are all flatwater. The dam there can be carried on the left. The dam was scheduled for at least a partial breach in 2001. Stillwater continues for another 3.0 miles to Ashuelot Village covered bridge. This section has been very polluted in the past but has been cleaned up considerably.

Ashuelot ➤ Connecticut River   5.0 mi

Description: Quickwater, Class III–IV
Date checked: 2000
Navigable: Medium water (spring and after heavy
                        rains)

This section of the Ashuelot has distinct advantages and disadvantages. On the positive side, the rapids are heavy and challenging, and the water level is often high enough for summertime paddling. As drawbacks, frequent dams necessitate short and difficult portages, the water is polluted, and many factories abut the river.

At any runnable level the lower Ashuelot is one of the larger and more forceful whitewater runs in New England. Often the waves are too large and the dams too close together for safe sport in open boats.

Put in at the covered bridge in Ashuelot. Here the river is wide, with a good current but no real rapids. The first dam (0.25 mile) has washed out and can be run in the center. Mostly smooth river continues to the second dam (0.5 mile). There are several long, wavy Class III rapids to the next dam (1.5 miles), which requires a short but tough portage on the right. The rapids here are typical of the Lower Ashuelot—turbulent and powerful in high water.

Below the third dam (1.5 miles) the Ashuelot passes under a bridge to the Ashuelot Paper Company. In the next right turn lies the heaviest rapid of the trip, Class III–IV even at lower water levels. This rapid should be looked over from the side road on the right bank. More rapids continue to the fourth dam (2.25 miles), which lies on a diagonal across the river, from upstream left to downriver right. It can be run safely after scouting, but for those who prefer to try, use the right side for portage. Approach with caution because of the strong current above the dam and because there is a diversion canal on the right.

More large rapids in several stretches bring you to the backwater from the fifth dam. This last dam (3.0 miles) is just below a steel bridge in Hinsdale. Below it there is a sharp drop, then some easier rapids to the NH 63 bridge (3.5 miles) in the town. Rapids diminish to smoothwater, and the river flows through a gap into the broad Connecticut River (5.0 miles).

Otter Brook NH

Otter Brook is a small tributary of the Ashuelot and is sometimes called the East Branch, or just the Branch. The water is often clear, particularly above the Otter Brook flood-control dam, making the stream very appealing. The upper part of Otter Brook is an excellent advanced whitewater run when it has water. The lower portion also holds intermediate rapids before giving way to quickwater in Keene.

East Sullivan ➤ Otter Brook State Park	3.25 mi
Description:	Class III–IV
Date checked:	2001
Navigable:	High water only (early April)
Scenery:	Forested
Maps:	USGS Monadnock 15

For one or two weeks in the year this section of Otter Brook is runnable. It is definitely a small stream, averaging 10–15 yards in width. Expert boaters who catch it will find Otter Brook an enjoyable but not intimidating Class III to easy Class IV run.

There is a hand-painted gauge on the upstream side of the NH 9 bridge abutment, but unfortunately the water piles up against it, so accurate readings are had to get. From East Sullivan to Otter Brook State Park, NH 9 is next to the brook.

Put in just below the NH 9 bridge in East Sullivan. The rapids are Class II for the first 100 yards, and then the difficulty increases to Class III. The rapids are continuous. A long stretch of rapids follows, with no pools in which to rest.

The most difficult drop in the river comes when it bears slightly left away from the road and plunges 1 foot and then 3 feet over an angled ledge (1.0 mile). There is another Class IV drop shortly below, where the river turns right and returns to the road. Rapids continue past an old iron bridge (1.75 miles) to the bridge at the old Pinnacle Ski Area.

Below the ski area (2.5 miles) the rapids diminish in intensity, but they remain continuous. Here, as above in Otter Brook, a capsized boat can be swept a long way downstream.

The suggested take-out is at the next bridge (3.25 miles), which is the access road to Otter Brook State Park. Picnic tables here provide a pleasant lunch spot. Boats will have to be carried 200 yards or so from the river to NH 9 if the gate is locked.

The rapids flatten out quickly below Otter Brook State Park, with mostly quickwater to the pool behind the flood-control dam. A 0.5-mile flatwater paddle brings you to the dam itself (5.0 miles), which is a long, steep carry.

Flood-control dam ➤ Ashuelot River	5.0 mi
Description:	Quickwater, Class II–III
Date checked:	2001
Navigable:	High to medium water (April)
	Dam controlled
Scenery:	Forested
Maps:	USGS Monadnock 15, Keene 15

Below the dam Otter Brook contains continuous intermediate rapids. The amount of water for the run is controlled completely by the dam, which is managed by the Army Corps of Engineers.

Put in right below the spillway from the dam. The put-in can be found by following signs to the Otter Brook dam from NH 101 just east of Keene. Rapids begin immediately, with a wavy Class III drop in a right turn. Otter Brook passes the stone abutments that remain of an old bridge and continues southward with Class II rapids. After 2.0 miles NH 101 is visible ahead. The most difficult drop of the trip begins just before Otter Brook reaches NH 101. The river turns right and is joined by Minnewawa Brook on the left. A green house appears straight in front. Just at this point there is a ledge that should (and at times must) be run on the right.

After the NH 101 bridge (3.0 miles) the rapids diminish quickly as the river flows to a high railroad bridge, followed by a dam (3.5 miles). This dam has cement flanges that extend upstream on either side, and the stream has cut a new channel above the right flange. Before entering, scout this passage for overhanging brush or fallen trees. To avoid this potentially blocked section of the brook, take out on the left just past the bridge.

After the dam the brook is mostly quickwater, with a good current and a sandy bottom. Take out on the right just before the NH 12 bridge in Keene (4.75 miles) or continue to join the Ashuelot River (5.0 miles).

Ashuelot River (South Branch) NH

The South Branch of the Ashuelot River is a small stream that rises in Troy, rushes steeply northward to Webb, and then flows more smoothly westward to a junction with the Ashuelot River in Keene. The rapid, upper part is only runnable for a few days of the year.

Troy Gap ➤ Webb		3.0 mi
Description:	Class IV	
Date checked:	2000	
Navigable:	High water (April)	
Scenery:	Forested	
Maps:	USGS Monadnock 15	

This portion of the stream is hemmed in by very steep banks, and it contains many difficult rapids. The river drops 300 feet in these 3.0 miles. The railroad and NH 12 follow the river closely, although they are not always visible. When runnable, the South Branch is so narrow that paddlers find it a challenge to avoid running on top of one another. This problem is accentuated by the possibility of fallen trees, which can be a real hazard.

The South Branch is a difficult run. It should not be attempted by inexperienced paddlers or open boats.

Put in from NH 12 about 1.5 miles north of the center of Troy. Here there are two bridges close together where the South Branch loops under a road. The stream immediately passes under a railroad bridge, with flatwater for the first 100 yards.

The rapids begin, become continuous, and increase to Class IV in the next 0.5 mile. The river then turns left under a railroad bridge and crosses twice under NH 12 (0.75 mile). These bridges mark the most difficult rapids in the river. Paddlers must first contend with a large crosswave off the railroad-bridge abutment, then a very steep drop, followed by extremely rocky going between the two road bridges. Because this stretch has steep, rocky walls, it should be scouted from the road bridges before you put in. Highway construction may alter this area.

The next 1.25 miles to a small pool and dam (2.0 miles) contain many more Class IV rapids. The dam, easily visible from NH 12, has a notch in the center that makes it runnable. Rapids moderate in the next mile to a culvert that is on a construction company road in Webb. This spot is reached by leaving NH 12 and following the road toward East Swanzey for a few hundred yards to a side road on the left, which leads in 100 yards to the river.

Webb ➤ Ashuelot River	9.0 mi
Maps:	USGS Monadnock 15, Keene 15

Put in where the stream turns south away from NH 12 and follows the road to East Swanzey. It is about 2.0 miles to the millpond above the dam just below East Swanzey, with rapids for much of the way. Below here the South Branch has good current and few rapids, winding through pastureland until it joins the main Ashuelot near Swanzey, some 7.0 miles down.

Green River VT, MA

The Green River is a crystal mountain stream that descends a narrow valley through the hills north of Greenfield, Massachusetts, and empties into the Deerfield River near Greenfield. Rising to the west of Governors Mountain in

Guilford, Vermont, it is large enough to paddle during the spring by the time it reaches the Green River Post Office. There are excellent swimming holes and plenty of opportunities for trout fishing. It is an unusually beautiful stream and a delight to the nature lover.

Green River ➤ West Leyden	8.0 mi
Description:	Class III
Date checked:	2001
Navigable:	High water (early April)
Scenery:	Forested
Maps:	USGS Brattleboro, Colrain
Portage:	8.0 mi L dam

The access and car shuttle are as difficult as the paddling on the Green River because the best water level for paddling coincides with the last part of mud season in the dirt access roads. A dirt road follows along the right bank; it is often passable only by four-wheel-drive vehicles. Even the long way around is not particularly easy.

A boat can be launched a short distance below the mill dam at Green River from the dirt road on the right bank. All the pitches can be run at ordinary high water levels. The river is small, steep, and full of ledges, particularly in the uppermost part where it rounds Pulpit Mountain. It is best to proceed cautiously, inspecting each bad chute before you run it.

The Massachusetts State line is at 3.25 miles. At Stewartsville the dam at the sawmill is carried on the left.

Chapter 5
Merrimack Watershed

CANADA

MAINE

Memphremagog

Upper
Connecticut

Androscoggin

Champlain

Saco

Merrimack

Piscataqua

Hudson

NEW
YORK

MASSACHUSETTS

MERRIMACK WATERSHED

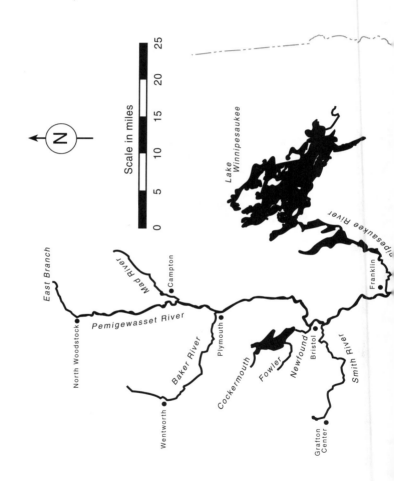

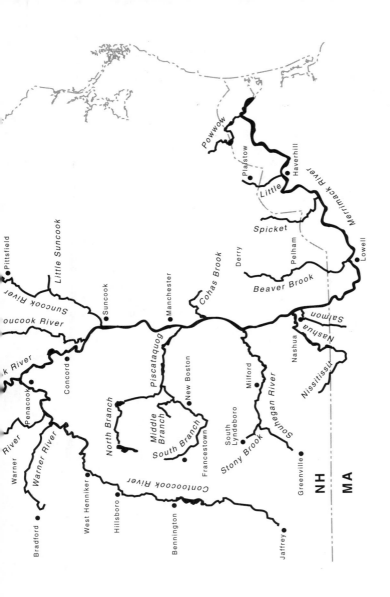

The Merrimack Watershed dominates central New Hampshire. It encompasses and borders large population centers, so the Merrimack and its tributaries are local rivers to many people and are frequently paddled. In the past the larger rivers suitable for summer paddling were badly polluted, but they now are cleaned up significantly and are quite pleasant for recreational use.

The divides are low to the east and west, so the tributaries have many miles of quickwater and easy rapids, as well as difficult drops to challenge experts. Many of the rivers provide easy paddling throughout the summer.

Merrimack River NH

The Merrimack River begins in Franklin, New Hampshire, at the confluence of the Pemigewasset and Winnipesaukee rivers. It flows south into Massachusetts and then turns east and runs into the sea at Newburyport.

Except in the large cities, the banks are still rather nice from a distance. Suburban sprawl usually does not reach the river's edge. From Franklin to Concord, the river has a sandy bottom. The closer you get to the sea, the muddier and more polluted the river becomes.

Almost all of the river is runnable throughout the paddling season. However, it should be avoided at high water when the current is fast, since the landings are difficult, and the approaches to the dams are dangerous.

Most of the big drops have been harvested for power. When the river's natural flow is low, the water level is affected by the demand for electricity. Low water has the biggest impact on the paddler below Franklin and below Amoskeag Dam in Manchester. Information on daily flows can be obtained by calling the water flow information line at the Public Service Company of New Hampshire (603-634-3569).

The Merrimack is close to many large population centers, and launching ramps provide access to all sections of the river.

In Penacook, at the mouth of the Contoocook River, sits Hannah Duston Island. It was there that Hannah Duston, who was captured by Native Americans in a raid on Haverhill, Massachusetts, on March 15, 1697, a week after the delivery of her eighth child, escaped her captors. On the morning of March

31, with the help of Mary Neff, who had been taken prisoner at the same time, and a youth who had been captured in a raid in Worcester, Massachusetts, she killed and scalped ten of the twelve Native Americans guarding her. The other two Native Americans fled, and the three prisoners went downriver by canoe to reach Nashua that night. Hannah later received a bounty of twenty-five pounds per scalp from the Massachusetts General Court.

Franklin ➤ Concord	24.0 mi
Description:	Flatwater, quickwater, Class I
Date checked:	2001
Navigable:	Passable at all water levels
	Dam controlled, peak power generation on Pemigewasset River
Scenery:	Forested, settled
Maps:	USGS Penacook 15, Concord

Put in on the Pemigewasset River below Eastman Falls Dam, if you want to begin with 1.0 mile of Class II rapids, or on the Winnepesaukee River behind the high school in Franklin, if you prefer 0.5 mile of quickwater.

From the confluence of the Pemigewasset and Winnipeasukee rivers, there are Class I rapids for the first 0.5 mile. Then there is a moderate current to Boscawen (10.5 miles), where the first bridge (closed) is located. Another 4.5 miles of meandering river brings you to Penacook, the US 4 bridge off Exit 17 of I-93 (poor access), and the mouth of the Contoocook River on the right.

In the mouth of the Contoocook River (15.0 miles) there is an island, joined to the mainland by two railroad bridges, a monument to Hannah Duston. In 2.0 miles there is another bridge with a launching ramp downstream on the right. From that point it is 1.0 mile to Sewall Falls Dam, which has been breached and no longer needs to be portaged. Beware of assorted debris and a new set of standing waves now rated as Class III. Consider scouting this run. A nice sand beach on the right shore just above the dam offers a fine landing place. The dam itself is old, and care should be used when using it as a vantage point.

Below Sewall Falls Dam (18.0 miles) there is a Class III rapid that is 0.25 mile long and rocky in low water. In another 3.5 miles there is a railroad bridge and an I-93 bridge, just upstream from which there is a launching ramp that can be reached from Exit 16. The remaining distance to the Bridge Street bridge (24.0 miles) was shortened in 1976 when a new channel was cut across a meander. A new launching ramp is on the right bank near the cloverleaf of I-393, 1.0 mile above Bridge Street.

Concord ➤ Manchester	18.25 mi
Description:	Flatwater, quickwater
Date checked:	2001
Navigable:	Passable at all water levels
	Dam controlled, good flow all year
Scenery:	Forested, settled
Maps:	USGS Concord 15, Suncook,
	Manchester North
Portages:	5.0 mi L Garvin's Falls Dam 100 yd
	10.5 mi L dam at 0.25 mi
	(18.25 mi R Amoskeag Dam 200 yd)

There are boat-launching ramps just above the Bridge Street bridge and the US 3 bridge (1.5 miles) on the left. After 2.25 miles of meandering, you pass under a railroad bridge, below which there is some turbulence, then Garvin's Falls Dam (5.0 miles) comes in sight. Portage on the left. There is a short Class II rapid below it.

In the next 5.5 miles to the dam at Hooksett, you pass the mouth of the Soucook River (5.75 miles) and the Suncook River (8.75 miles). About 0.25 mile above Hooksett Dam there are two nice boat-launching ramps on the left, but experienced paddlers who are carrying by hand can continue in low water as far as the abutment on the left (10.5 miles). Carry past the parking area to another launching ramp below the dam.

There is some turbulence around the bridge abutments below the Hookset dam, then 7.25 miles of smoothwater to Manchester. Amoskeag Bridge and the Manchester skyline can be seen from a long distance upstream. Take out at the bridge on the right to portage Amoskeag Dam. Look for concrete "steps" by the river and the Holiday Inn.

Manchester ➤ Nashua	17.75 mi
Description:	Flatwater, quickwater, Class II–III
Date checked:	2001
Navigable:	Passable at most water levels
	Dam controlled, peak power generation
Scenery:	Forested, settled, urban
Maps:	USGS Manchester North, Manchester South, Nashua North

Water flow information at Amoskeag Dam in Manchester can be obtained by calling the Public Service Company recorded line (603-634-3569). Flood stage is anything over 20,000 cubic feet per second (cfs). Spring runoff typically produces 12,000–15,000 cfs. Early summer levels run around 5,000 cfs, and dry summers bottom out at 1,200–1,300 cfs. At 5,000–12,000 cfs, the two most difficult rapids, Goffs Falls and Griffins Falls, are easy to moderate Class III; at high water, they wash out. The Merrimack moves a lot of water, but it does so with a constant current of strong quickwater, rather than through rocky drops.

There is a mile of Class II rapids through Manchester. On the left bank the walls of old factories rise straight up from the river, and on the right there is a limited-access highway. In high water, keep to the right.

Past two highway bridges and shortly below the rapids, the Piscataquog River (2.0 miles) enters on the right in South Manchester. A cascade of sewage, attested by a crowd of herring gulls, comes in on the left just above the Queen City Bridge, which is the third highway bridge below Amoskeag Dam. In 1.5 miles there is a riffle, and soon the I-293 bridges come into sight.

Land under the I-293 bridges (4.25 miles) to scout the Class III drops, Griffins Falls and Goffs Falls, which can be run on either side but not in the middle. This spot can be reached on the right via a dirt road. In another 0.75 mile there is a railroad bridge with a ledge starting just above it. It too can be run on either side but not in the middle, where there is an island. This ledge can be inspected in advance from dirt roads on either side.

Below the railroad bridge (5.0 miles) there is smoothwater for 1.25 miles to a short Class II drop, and then more smoothwater for another 2.0 miles to a longer Class II rapid just below a big power line. After 2.25 miles of smoothwater the Souhegan River (10.5 miles) enters on the right. Almost 3 miles downstream of the confluence with the Souhegan, on the right, are the best preserved remains of the old lock and canal system. In another mile there is a Class II rapid, followed by 3.25 miles of easy paddling to the NH 111 bridge (17.75 miles) in Nashua just below the mouth of the Nashua River on the right.

Nashua ➤ Lowell		14.0 mi
Description:	Flatwater, quickwater	
Date checked:	2001	
Navigable:	Passable at all water levels	
Scenery:	Forested, settled, towns	
Maps:	USGS Nashua South, Lowell	

From the NH 111 bridge in Nashua, it is only 1.0 mile to the south end of town, where Salmon Brook enters on the right. The river now is all smoothwater. It passes between tilled fields and meadows for some distance, finally entering a section with wooded banks before it reaches the next bridge, MA 113, at Tyngsboro, Massachusetts, 5.0 miles below. There are more signs of human habitation in the next 4.0 miles to North Chelmsford, where Stony Brook enters on the right. In another 3.0 miles one arrives at Lowell. Take out at the public launching ramp above the dam.

The river is followed by the railroad. Watch for interesting old stone bridges and culverts spanning small tributaries.

Pemigewasset River NH

The Pemi is a born-again river. In the mid-twentieth century, much of it was fetid and frowzy. Today it is clean and clear.

Analysis of the river water in the mid-1960s yielded results typical of severe pollution. Some tests in 1966-67 showed less than 10 percent saturation of oxygen. But completion of several wastewater treatment facilities resulted in a significant improvement in water quality. The Pemigewasset is now a Class B river, which means it is suitable for swimming and fishing.

The Weeks Act of 1911 authorized the federal government to purchase land in the White Mountains to protect watersheds. By that time many of the steep slopes in the Pemigewasset watershed had been denuded by logging, which in some cases was followed by forest fires. Thus, there existed the possibility of severe flooding caused by rapid runoff into the Pemigewasset River. This potential threat to the many communities downstream along the Pemigewasset and Merrimack rivers helped lead to the establishment of the White Mountain National Forest.

During and after a heavy rain the water level can change very quickly, sometimes by several feet in a couple of hours. Be conscious of this if you are camping along the river, for there is plenty of evidence that the islands are flooded each year.

Most of this river consists of swift current over a gravel bottom, but there are two stretches with challenging rapids. The popular one begins at North Woodstock. It is usually a good Class II run, but in very high water there are large waves and usually a few fallen trees hazardously sticking out into the main current. Above Livermore Falls in Campton there are more fine rapids, but high water produces high waves that must be handled carefully in open boats. The danger is that the pools of calm water, which are present at medium water, cease to exist when the water is high, so that the heavy rapids and fast-moving water continue right up to the lip of the falls.

The river is attractive and seemingly remote, which is surprising considering that there are three highways, a railroad, and transmission lines following the narrow valley. All of these are obvious on occasion, but on the whole the trip is a scenic one. In many respects this section is similar to the Saco River from Bartlett to North Conway.

North Woodstock ➤ Third NH 175 bridge   4.5 mi

Description:	Class I–II
Date checked:	2001
Navigable:	Medium to high water (May)
Scenery:	Forested
Maps:	USGS Lincoln

This section of the Pemigewasset is most responsive to rainfall and melting snow. The gradient is not so steep that it requires a heavy runoff, as is the case with the East Branch, yet it is just enough to require a good flow for easy passage. A soaking summer rain usually raises the river to medium levels and provides a day or two of pleasant boating. Most of the river below Woodstock remains passable at moderately low water, although travel may be slow because some walking down will be necessary. Between Plymouth and Woodstock, I-93 crosses the river four times, so you have a good opportunity to check the water level as you drive along.

Put in just below the stone bridge on NH 112 just east of NH 3, and park your car out of the way. At the start of the run the river is shallow and rocky, but it is immediately joined by the East Branch, which forces the water against a cliff on the right, creating large waves that may sink the unwary. The ensuing 0.25 mile of Class II rapids (III in high water) ends just before a NH 175 bridge, which serves as a alternate put-in for less-experienced boaters.

For the next 4.0 miles the river flows through intermittent Class II rapids and around islands where the channel changes frequently. Frequent sharp corners with many fallen trees pose the only special danger for competent whitewater paddlers.

Below the second NH 175 bridge (4.0 miles), where I-93 comes in sight on the left, the river makes a sweeping S-curve. Pull in at the old abutment to scout the ledges above the third NH 175 bridge. These ledges constitute the most difficult rapids in this section. They may be carried on either side or run in various places, depending on water level. The easiest route is an obscure channel on the left. The banking on the right also provides take-outs above and below the ledges. There is a small parking lot on the right below the bridge.

Third NH 175 bridge ➤ Blair Road   14.5 mi
Description: Quickwater, Class I–II
Date checked: 2001
Navigable: Medium water
Scenery: Forested, rural
Maps: USGS Lincoln

The rapids in this section are not as difficult as the ones above. Class I rapids and riffles are interspersed with more and more quickwater the farther you go downstream. The banks are still largely wild, although bridges cross more frequently. As in the previous section, countless bends with inconveniently located downed trees are a hazard.

Access to the West Thornton NH 175 bridge (5.0 miles) is via Robbin's Nest Road off NH 3 just north of the bridge. This leads to a launching ramp under the bridge, which is an excellent site for rainy day picnicking or for loading boats in foul weather.

There is more of the same past the second railroad bridge (10.25 miles) and the second crossing of I-93, a bridge in West Campton near a gravel mill (12.75 miles). The mouth of the Mad River (13.75 miles) has some turbulence, with a rock garden on the right shortly below. I-93 crosses a third time, and finally you reach the Blair Road covered bridge (off Exit 27, I-93).

Blair ➤ Plymouth   4.0 mi
Description: Quickwater, Class I–III
Date checked: 2001
Navigable: Medium water, dangerous in high water
Scenery: Forested, towns
Maps: USGS Lincoln, Plymouth 15
Portage: 2.0 mi R Livermore Falls—dangerous
                          landing above

Class II–III rapids begin a mile below the covered bridge at Blair and continue to the top of the falls. Be sure to scout this stretch in advance from a side road to the old power station off US 3. This must be done by foot, however, as vehicle access and parking in the area of the falls are restricted. These restrictions also eliminate this spot as a convenient take-out.

The falls are dangerous. Take out well above them on the right and line to the beach opposite the lip of the falls. Portaging is difficult but not impossible. It involves carrying along the railroad tracks next to the right bank, with steep ascents and descents to the river, or, in low water periods, carrying along the ledges next to the falls.

The water runs smoothly through a sheer gorge below the falls, then separates around an island where the Class II rapids to the left are easier than those to the right. Shortly below the I-93 bridge, the Baker River enters on the right. Below the bridge in Plymouth, behind the Plymouth business district, a municipal parking lot lies next to the river. A short dirt road from it to the river provides a good take-out 0.25 mile below the bridge on the right.

Plymouth ➤ Bristol	15.75 mi
Description:	Flatwater, quickwater
Date checked:	2001
Navigable:	Passable at most water levels
Scenery:	Forested, rural
Maps:	USGS Plymouth 15, Holderness 15
Portage:	(15.75 mi R Ayres Island Dam 0.5 mi)

This section is attractive and easy. The section above Squam River is mostly shallow, with sandy banks and bottom, offering very pleasant swimming throughout the summer. There are only a few houses along the banks, and roads are only occasionally visible. For much of the distance, however, I-93 lies close enough to the left bank so that traffic is frequently heard, though it is seldom seen.

The best put-in for this section is reached from a municipal parking lot on the right behind Main Street buildings in Plymouth, an area mentioned earlier as a take-out for the Blair-Plymouth section.

From the bridge in Plymouth the river has a fast current for many miles. Good current continues past the US 3 bridge in Ashland (4.25 miles) to the mouth of the Squam River (6.25 miles), where there is a small ledgy island. Low water at this point exposes some more ledges that normally are not noticeable. There is access on the west bank at the Sawhegenet Falls Park Recreation Area, on River Road in Bridgewater, New Hampshire. The current weakens in the next 3.0 miles as you approach the deadwater behind Ayres Island Dam.

There is public access to the river on the west bank beside the NH 104 bridge in New Hampton (12.75 miles). Portage the dam (15.75 miles) on the right.

One mile east of the center of Bristol, on NH 104, a road to the right leads past some highway department buildings and down the hill. Turn left near a water treatment facility and follow the dirt road to the river just below the dam.

In the first 1.5 miles there are several nice Class II rapids that have heavy Class II waves at high water levels. The last important drop is 0.5 mile below the Bristol bridge at a right turn. This rapid may be run on the inside of the bend to avoid the waves. If you wish to run only the rapids, there is a road along the left bank, or you can put in at this road for an easier run.

Bristol ➤ Franklin	15.0 mi
Description:	Flatwater, quickwater, Class II–III
Date checked:	2001
Navigable:	High water, heavy waves (spring runoff)
	Medium water (1,500 cfs)
	Low water, scratchy (550 cfs)
	Dam controlled, peak load hydroelectric stations
Scenery:	Forested, rural
Maps:	USGS Holderness 15, Penacook 15
Portages:	12.5 mi L Franklin Falls flood-control dam 0.5 mi
	14 mi R Eastman Falls Dam 200 yd
Restriction:	No camping

Start at the end of the rapids below the bridge where the road is close to the river.

The best run on this portion of the river is the 7.5-mile section from the Bristol dam to Hill. There are rapids and quickwater most of the way. It is a scenic trip, with secluded shorelines altered somewhat by the effects of periodic flooding.

Hill has a ghostly atmosphere. Back from the river a short distance, the main street, somewhat dilapidated but complete with a sidewalk, is lined with maple and elm trees that are aged and in poor health. The driveways are lined with old trees also, and lone apple trees dot the farmyards. But there are no houses and no people, only cows and corn; the town is gone. It was moved when the Franklin Falls flood-control dam was built downstream. Today, standing in the still-fertile fields, you can almost feel a part of the past.

Quickwater continues for the next 3.5 miles past the mouth of the Smith River (3.5 miles) and around a large island. One mile after the flatwater begins, the valley widens and there are fields on the right. This is Hill. At the other end of the town there are some old bridge abutments (7.5 miles). The river at this point cannot be reached from NH 3A.

Flatwater continues to the Franklin Falls flood-control dam (12.25 miles). Road access to this dam is off NH 127 at a sign north of Franklin where a gated road comes down to the water. Ask for and obtain permission at the office to put in here.

Franklin Falls flood-control dam ➤ Merrimack River   2.5 mi

After this dam there is more deadwater above the power dam at Franklin (14.0 miles). Portage on the right. There is a 1-mile Class II rapid in the remaining distance to the confluence with the Winnipesaukee River (15.0 miles).

Eastman Falls Dam at Franklin is also operated by the Public Service Company. The generating schedule is about the same as that at Ayres Island Dam in Bristol.

A call to the dispatcher at the Public Service Company of New Hampshire at 603-634-3569 can give you current information.

Pemigewasset River (East Branch) NH

This large, clear river drains the Pemigewasset Wilderness. There are several miles of difficult whitewater above the Kancamagus Highway bridge, but you must carry your boat. The rapids are continuous below the bridge. For detailed information, see the AMC's *Classic Northeastern Whitewater Guide.*

Kancamagus Highway ➤ North Woodstock		6.0 mi
Description:	Class IV	
Date checked:	2000	
Navigable:	High water, difficult (April)	
	Medium water (May)	
Scenery:	Forested, settled	
Maps:	USGS Mount Osceola, Lincoln	
Portage:	4.5 mi L dam at Lincoln	

There is a fairly even gradient of over 70 feet per mile in this section, but the large drainage basin gives the East Branch a long season. There is a painted gauge on the center abutment of the Kancamagus Highway bridge. Because of the clarity of the water and the size of the riverbed, the river always looks lower than it really is.

For the first 2.0 miles from the put-in, the river is fairly continuous Class III–IV, with a good rapid in every corner. Upper Condo marks the end of this section, with the heaviest waves of this section. The next rapid, First Island, finds you blasting down a chute at the end of the island heading toward a large boulder. Go right. Second Island should be scouted. The right channel has three large boulders, with various routes around them, and the remains of a metal culvert.

Upper Loon Mountain Rapid is extremely technical. Take out just above the Loon Mountain bridge on the left to scout Lower Loon Mountain Rapid. Recent floods have channeled the river down a deep chute to the right of the abutment, which is slightly easier than it looks. The runout of Lower Loon is on the right into an extremely small pool above a boulder sieve. The boulder sieve can be run right or portaged on either side. The next 1.5 miles are harder than those above.

There's no decision to Decision Rapids anymore, since the channel goes right with a series of steep, tight turns on the right bank marking two very technical rapids: Ethel's Back Yard and Lower Ethel, which are separated by a nice pool. The current continues to the dam, which is an easy portage on the left. It is sometimes possible to scrape down on the left. Watch out for the next island. Closed boaters should go left, and open boaters right. There is a bridge halfway down the island. Take out just past the bridge to scout Lower Condo, a staircase with a sharp left turn if you go left, a technical run with bow pinning possibilities if you go right. Class III rapids continue to North Woodstock.

Mad River NH

The Mad River, a tributary of the Pemigewasset River north of Plymouth, provides many miles of continuous rapids. The steepness of the terrain around it means that runoff occurs very quickly.

Waterville Valley ➤ Campton	12.0 mi
Description:	Lake, Class III–IV
Date checked:	2001
Navigable:	High to medium water (mid-April to early May)
Scenery:	Forested
Maps:	(12.0 mi L dam at Campton 30 yd)

This portion of the river flows through Waterville Valley, one of the most beautiful in the White Mountains. It does not often have enough water for boating, but on a few days of the year it provides a long and continuously interesting whitewater run. The season for flexible boats is somewhat extended. The river contains a multitude of small- and medium-sized rocks that force paddlers to dodge rocks constantly.

Begin near the town of Waterville Valley. Follow NH 49 through the town, and shortly after passing the tennis courts, make a sharp left turn by the library. This road soon crosses the river and continues on to join the Tripoli Road to North

Woodstock. The Tripoli Road is not plowed in winter, so NH 49 from the south is usually the only route into the Mad River basin in the spring.

The West Branch of the Mad River, which enters shortly below, is visible from the put-in. Rapids begin almost immediately, with the difficulty reaching Class III. A mile and a half of rapids brings you to the Mount Tecumseh (Waterville Valley) ski area bridge, which can also be used as a put-in, but access there is more difficult.

Below the ski area bridge (1.5 miles) there are 3.0 miles of continuous Class III rapids with a couple of drops that are slightly harder than the rest. The hardest rapid is in a right turn about 1.5 miles below the bridge. It is actually a little easier than it looks: a fairly straight course in the center is the best route in medium to high water. A turn-off makes it easy to scout this drop from the road.

There is a nice view of Welch Mountain on the right bank (4.5 miles), after which the rapids become continuous Class III–IV. The river narrows, and even resting or rescue places are hard to find. The rapids are continuous for 2.0 miles to Six-Mile Bridge, where take-out access can be found. A paddlers' gauge is painted on a rock on river left slightly above the bridge. Boatable levels range from 1.5 (low) to 3.5 (high). Always scout the run first.

From Six-Mile Bridge (6.5 miles) there are 2 miles of Class III–IV rapids with larger waves but fewer rocks. At Goose Hollow (8.5 miles) there is a single bridge. The best take-out is at an unmarked rest area just below Goose Hollow at a White Mountain National Forest campground.

In the next 3.0 miles to Campton Pond, the rapids ease steadily from Class III to Class I. Take out at NH 49, which follows along the western shoreline.

If you are continuing downstream, portage the dam (12.0 miles) on the left.

Campton ➤ Pemigewasset River   2.5 mi

Description:	Quickwater, Class III–IV
Date checked:	2001
Navigable:	High to medium water (mid-April to mid-May)
Scenery:	Forested
Maps:	USGS Plymouth 15

In Campton there is a steep gorge. The rapids there are created by steep drops over and around ledges as well as by boulders. Campton Pond tends to make the flow in this section steadier and more dependable.

Just below the bridge there is a partially washed-out dam that should be scouted and probably lifted over. Past an old factory on the left, the river swings right and enters Campton Gorge, where there is 0.5 mile of Class III–IV rapids. They can be run by skilled paddlers but should be scouted first.

Below Campton Gorge there are 2.0 miles of quickwater to the Pemigewasset River (2.5 miles). The first take-out is 1.5 miles downstream on US 3 (4 miles), a short distance above the I-93 bridges.

Baker River NH

This river was named for Thomas Baker, a lieutenant from Northampton, Massachusetts, who traveled along it in 1712 on a raid against the Native Americans. It rises on the south slopes of Mount Moosilauke in Benton and runs south, then east to the Pemiegewasset in Plymouth.

The scenery is rural and very attractive. A main highway follows up the valley, but it usually cannot be seen from the river. An abandoned railroad grade is scarcely noticeable.

NH 118 ➤ Wentworth   6.0 mi

Description:	Quickwater, Class II–III
Date checked:	2001
Navigable:	High water (April)
	Medium water, scratchy above Warren (early May)

Scenery:	Forested, rural, towns
Maps:	USGS Rumney 15
Portage:	(6.0 mi L ledge at Wentworth 100-200 yd)

The river has been channeled from NH 118 through the town of Warren, an indication that runoffs are often fast and furious. The watershed is mountainous, and the gradient initially is steep, making boating for the first 2.0 miles very dependent on the weather. If the spring is early or dry, the water needed for good Class III rapids above Warren will already be in the Merrimack by mid-April.

Put in at the NH 118 bridge north of Warren. The gradient is steepest in the first 0.75 mile, where there are Class III rapids as the river drops steadily over small boulders. The river widens, and the rapids become easier as the town of Warren comes into view.

The first bridge in Warren, Studio Road (1.25 miles), can be used as a starting point if the rapids above are too shallow. The current through Warren to the NH 25 bridge is swift. Much of the remaining distance is quickwater, with wide turns where overhanging trees are an occasional hazard. Below the second NH 25 bridge (3.5 miles) there is a short Class II rapid. In Wentworth (6.0 miles) take out above the old truss bridge, because underneath it is a very turbulent Class IV drop. It can be carried on the left under the bridge, unless the water is very high.

Wentworth ➤ Plymouth   21.0 mi

Description:	Flatwater, quickwater, Class I–II
Date checked:	2001
Navigable:	High or medium water (April through May and after moderate rains)
	Low water, passable below West Rumney
Scenery:	Forested, rural, town
Maps:	USGS Rumney 15, Plymouth 15

The farther downstream you start on the Baker River, the more it becomes a leisurely float trip, with less and less water required to keep you off the bottom. The river is clean, and the riverbed is sandy in many locations. With a little helpful rain, the part below West Rumney makes a nice summer trip.

The river winds through a rural valley hemmed in by wooded hillsides. It frequently undercuts banks, dumping trees into the current. These obstacles are hazardous, but you can almost always paddle around them. Noise from the highway is most noticeable as you near the end.

Put in below the NH 25 bridge on the north bank. There are short Class I–II rapids and quickwater 6.0 miles past two bridges to the girder bridge on a side road in West Rumney. Below here the river generally is wider with less current. In 1.25 miles there is a highway rest area on the right, followed in 0.5 mile by an overhead cable at a gauging station, which precedes a short Class II rapid at the site of an old dam. More quickwater continues for 6.75 miles past the Stinson Lake Road bridge (10.0 miles) to an old bridge site in an S-turn by Polar Caves (14.0 miles). Stinson Mountain occasionally is visible. The river is more sluggish for the next 2.25 miles to the Smith Road covered bridge (16.75 miles).

There are 4.0 more miles of flatwater to the truss bridge on US 3 (20.75 miles) in Plymouth. Access is not good here, however. It is easier to continue to the Pemigewasset. The half-mile of river between the US 3 bridge and the confluence of the Baker and Pemigewasset rivers tends to be shallow in summer and may require some wading. It is less than a half-mile from the confluence to the Holderness Road bridge in Plymouth and less than a quarter-mile to a good take-out on the right bank, which is reached via a dirt road from a municipal parking lot next to the river in downtown Plymouth.

Newfound River NH

This river drains Newfound Lake and flows into the Pemigewasset River at Bristol. It is a short, narrow river, with continuous and difficult rapids. In one section the drop is 50 feet in 0.5 mile, a challenging run in high water for covered boats. In medium water, this is an ideal section for a small inflatable canoe, which, being flexible, can easily slither past the rounded boulders.

The annual fall drawdown of Newfound Lake does not provide sufficient water for this run.

Newfound Lake ➤ Bristol	1.75 mi
Description:	Class II–IV
Date checked:	2001
Navigable:	High water (early April)
	Medium water (late April)
Scenery:	Forested, settled
Maps:	USGS Cardigan 15
Portage:	1.25 mi L hydroelectric dam 20 yd

Begin on the left bank below the dam at the south end of Newfound Lake. The rapids that follow are Class II–III for 1 mile to the first millpond. The most difficult drop in this section is just above the first bridge. Portage the dam on the left.

Below the first dam (1.25 miles), the rapids soon become Class IV. **Caution!** Just 50 yards below the first US 3A bridge, there are two large, nasty spikes sticking straight up from a shoal in the middle of the river. Fortunately for the inflatables, the spikes are exposed at medium water. The Class IV rapids extend for 0.5 mile on the east side of the highway, from which the whole section can be scouted. The most difficult pitch is behind a restaurant near the end. Take out at the second millpond beside the lower bridge (1.75 miles).

The remainder of the river is tame by comparison. If curiosity impels you to run it, carry the second dam on the left and begin again in the millrace, which is deeper and more accessible than the main channel. The Class I rapids soon end, and they are followed by quickwater. Take out at the NH 104 bridge (2.75 miles), the second in this section. Do not continue, because the river is not easily accessible from the Main Street bridge, and below that there is a steep, unrunnable cascade that continues the rest of the way to the Pemigewasset River.

Cockermouth River NH

This small river empties into the northwest end of Newfound Lake. Its water is clear, and the valley through which it flows typifies rural New England at its best. It takes about two hours to run.

Groton ➤ Newfound Lake	3.5 mi
Description:	Flatwater, quickwater
Date checked:	2001
Navigable:	High to medium water (early spring, after heavy rains)
Scenery:	Rural
Maps:	USGS Cardigan 15

Start in Groton where the road to North Groton crosses the river, which at this point is about a canoe-length wide. The current is fast as the stream winds along the edges of fields. Just above the second bridge (2.0 miles) there is a short and easy Class II rapid. In the last 0.75 mile the river is flat and wide. It flows under a road along the northern end of Newfound Lake 0.5 mile before it empties into Hebron Bay (3.5 miles).

Fowler River NH

The Fowler River rises on Mount Cardigan and flows to Newfound Lake. Welton Falls is on the upper reaches. For most of its length it is too steep for paddling, but the lower part is navigable at high water, or make a short side trip from the lake. Refer to the USGS Cardigan quadrangle.

Crawford School ➤ Newfound Lake	2.25 mi

The first few rapids might be Class II, but the gradient decreases rapidly, and the river meanders along most of the way, becoming flatwater by the time it reaches the bridge 0.5 mile above the lake.

Smith River NH

The Smith River rises near Grafton as a small stream and flows east to the Pemigewasset River near Bristol. The upper part is a pleasant quickwater trip, and the lower part contains difficult rapids. There is a scenic waterfall below the part that normally is run. The banks are wooded, and there are frequent road and railroad crossings, so trips of varying lengths can be planned.

Grafton Center ➤ NH 104   13.0 mi

Description:	Flatwater, quickwater, Class I
Date checked:	2001
Navigable:	High water (April)
Scenery:	Forested, rural
Maps:	USGS Cardigan 15

Put in from the road to the Ruggles Mine just west of Grafton Center. In the next 6.5 miles to Fords crossing, where there are adjacent railroad and road bridges (the first of two such pairs), the river is a winding meadow brook, with overhanging bushes and occasional fallen trees. There is often quickwater under bridges. The next 6.5 miles are more open and less obstructed, and the lead you past the US 4 bridge (9.25 miles) to the girder bridge on NH 104.

Just above the NH 104 bridge (13.0 miles) there is a short Class II rapid, which can be avoided by taking out just above it at the Eastern District Road bridge.

NH 104 ➤ Profile Gorge   8.0 mi

Description:	Flatwater, Class III–IV
Date checked:	2001
Navigable:	High to medium water (April to mid-May)
Scenery:	Forested, town
Maps:	USGS Cardigan 15, Holderness 15

The river in this section offers some very fine whitewater boating. The rapids above South Alexandria are the most challenging, but the nearby Smith River Road provides an easy retreat. Below South Alexandria the pitch is more moderate, and civilization is less evident from the river. The gorge and waterfall at the end of the trip deserve exploration, on foot. See AMC's *Classic Northeastern Whitewater Guide* for details on this stretch.

There is a hand-painted gauge on the left abutment of the Cass Mill Road bridge in South Alexandria. Boatable levels range from 0 (low) to 1.5 (high). Always scout the run first.

To reach the river, proceed west from Bristol on NH 104 to Cass Mill Road, then turn left. Continue until you see the river. At the crossroads there, a turnoff on old NH 104 leads to the start, while a left turn goes to the takeout. Old NH 104 parallels the river and intersects the new NH 104, where a trip may also begin.

Below the NH 104 bridge there is 0.25 mile of Class III ledges, including an old dam. Then there is 0.75 mile of smoothwater to the bridge on Murray Hill Road.

Below the Murray Hill Road bridge (1.0 mile) there is a short stretch of flatwater; then comes the first rapid in a left-hand bend. This is the first of two brief Class III rapids, each followed by quiet stretches. Next comes a Class IV section, full of small rocks and crosscurrents, which rushes past a picnic area on the right shore and down to the next bridge (1.75 miles) on Smith River Road. For a shorter and slightly easier run, this bridge is a possible put-in.

Below the second bridge there is 1.0 mile of continuous Class III–IV rapids with a very fast pace in high water. At the end of this mile there is a short drop in a right turn, with a large rock and hole sitting in the center, forcing boaters to one side or the other. The left side is preferable, although another rock upstream of the main hole must be avoided. Below this drop the river divides around an island just before the Class Mill Road bridge. The right side contains the hardest rapids on the river, a tough Class IV over large rocks and ledges; scout it before running. The left side descends much more gradually and is much easier to navigate.

The first 0.5 mile below the Cass Mill Road bridge in South Alexandria (3 miles) contains Class III–IV rapids, and it is often run with the stretch above. A set of power lines (3.5 miles) marks the point where the rapids moderate. This power-line crossing can be reached from Smith River Road, which follows the left bank from South Alexandria.

Below the power lines (3.5 miles) there are 2.0 miles of Class III rapids, then 0.5 mile in which the rapids diminish to mere current. At this point the river passes the bridge to Smith River Campground (6.0 miles). Then there are 2.0 miles of smoothwater to a broken dam (8.0 miles), which can be run on either side at certain water levels. **Caution!** It is best to take out above the dam: the river below is more suitable for sightseeing than boating.

Shortly below the broken dam (8.0 miles), the Smith River foams through Profile Gorge, a 150-yard rock-walled stretch that can be viewed from a high cement bridge at the gorge entrance. Moderate rapids follow to a bad drop just above the NH 3A bridge. Beneath the bridge is the beginning of Profile Falls (8.5 miles), where the Smith River slides over ledges for 100 yards before plunging down a 30-foot vertical drop. A road on the left bank leads to a parking area at the foot of the falls. The river from there to the Pemigewasset River (9.0 miles) is Class II.

Winnipesaukee River NH

The Winnipesaukee is a river of intermittent rapids, and some are long and difficult. The water is clear, although rebar is a threat below Tilton, requiring caution. A hydro dam in Tilton further complicates the run. The upper part, from Silver Lake to Tilton, is excellent for training beginners, as the lakes in the headwaters provide a dependable flow. The river below Tilton is isolated and flows through a narrow, wooded valley with continuous Class III–IV rapids below the Cross Road bridge. River flow is controlled by Lochmere Dam, located between Winnisquam and Silver lakes. Each fall the Water Resources Board draws down the levels of Winnipesaukee and Winnisquam lakes about 3 feet, which provides medium to high water levels for several weeks, generally after Columbus Day.

NH 140 ➤ Franklin   6.0 mi
Description: Flatwater, Class I–II, III–IV
Date checked: 2001
Navigable: High water (late March to early April)
                           Medium water (late April, May, and
                               annual fall drawdown)
Scenery: Forested, settled, town
Maps: USGS Penacook 15
Portage: 2.25 mi L dam in Tilton

This segment begins very close to Exit 20 off I-93. There is a launching ramp on Shaker Road just east of the NH 140 bridge that provides access to Silver Lake, located upstream.

The first 0.5 mile is flat, followed by 0.5 mile of Class I–II below the I-93 bridge, followed by more flatwater, then followed by easy Class II to Tilton. Take out on the left in Tilton (2.25 miles). If you wish to continue, carry across the bridge, down NH 3, and put in below the hydro dam. Ask for and obtain permission to put in here. A 100-yard Class II rapid leads to smoothwater, punctuated by another Class II.

The difficult rapids begin at the Cross Road bridge (4.5 miles), where the river enters a steep, narrow valley. At first there is a series of rapids and pools as the river flows over runnable, washed-out dams and past ruined factories. There are many turns in the river, and the rapids get longer and harder, up to Class III, as you approach and pass under a covered railroad bridge (5.5 miles). Class II–III rapids continue and end abruptly, with the most difficult rapid just above the NH 3 bridge in Franklin. Take out at the millpond just below the bridge.

Contoocook River NH

The Contoocook River is one of the principal tributaries of the Merrimack River. It rises in Rindge east of Mount Monadnock and flows generally northeast to join the Merrimack in Penacook.

The greatly differing sections of the Contoocook hold appeal for both flatwater and whitewater paddlers. In the upper section there are easy rapids, but only in high water, in the early spring. Flatwater follows as the river's volume increases. Heavy rapids above Henniker give way to pleasant flatwater, with a few rapids near the confluence. The calm stretches and even some of the rapids provide opportunities for summer boating.

Jaffrey ➤ Peterborough	6.75 mi
Description:	Class II
Date checked:	2001
Navigable:	High water (late March to early April)
Scenery:	Forested
Maps:	USGS Monadnock 15, Peterborough 15
Portages:	2.0 mi L Class IV gorge 400 yd
	5.0 mi R Noone Dam 10 yd
	(6.75 mi L Peterborough Dam 30 yd)

From Jaffrey the Contoocook flows through easy rapids interrupted only by a small gorge. These rapids are a good training ground for beginning whitewater paddlers. This section, very small and winding, contrasts noticeably with the lower river in breadth and volume.

There is a dam at the outlet of Cheshire Pond, and put-in is possible from the US 202 bridge just below. Easy Class II rapids start immediately. The river crosses several times beneath the railroad and the old US 202 bridges. The old road can be followed beside the river. After 2.0 miles the river makes a sharp right turn into a hemlock grove, and there is a wooden bridge 30 yards beyond.

Caution! Make a steep, short take-out on the left above the bridge (2.0 miles) because there is a gorge below. The gorge contains difficult rapids that can be run only at certain water levels. At higher levels the rapids are Class IV and can be navigated by closed boats. At somewhat lower levels open boats can proceed from drop to drop in the gorge, lining or lifting around any drops judged impassable. The gorge should be scouted, particularly since a fallen tree or jammed log would create a hazard. To portage, carry down the road on the left for 0.25 mile, and upon passing the first house on the right return to the river. A car certainly eases this portage.

Below the gorge are another 1.5 miles of Class II rapids. For the next mile rapids alternate with smooth stretches to a side road bridge (4.5 miles) above the millpond in Noone. The dam at Noone (5.0 miles) requires a short portage on the right. Another mile of mixed rapids and flatwater continues to Peterborough, where there is a little drop next to the Peterborough Plaza. A take-out can be made at the new NH 101 bridge (6.25 miles) or, after a little more smooth paddling, at the dam above a stone bridge in Peterborough (6.75 miles).

Peterborough ➤ Bennington	12.0 mi
Description:	Flatwater, quickwater, Class I
Date checked:	2001
Navigable:	Passable at most water levels, especially toward Bennington
Scenery:	Forested
Maps:	USGS Peterborough 15
Portages:	2.0 mi R North Village Dam 10 yd (12.0 mi R first of several dams in Bennington)

The paddle from Peterborough to Bennington is one of the prettiest on the river. Most of this stretch, particularly the second half, is navigable whenever the river is free from ice.

From the stone bridge and dam, it is a 2.0-mile paddle to the dam in North Village. Portage on the right. The Contoocook then flows under US 202 and snakes swiftly around some low islands. This portion might be impassable in low water. Smooth paddling for 5.5 miles past woods and meadows leads to a small side-road bridge (7.5 miles). In another mile the Contoocook empties into Powder Mill Pond, the backup from a dam in Bennington. A half-mile down the pond there is a covered bridge at a narrows (9.0 miles). Continuing down the pond, a railroad bridge crosses at another narrows (10.75 miles) and then comes to the first dam in Bennington (12.0 miles). Take out on the right bank.

Bennington Portage   1.5 mi

On the river through Bennington there are at least four dams and impassable rapids. In addition, the Monadnock Paper Mill sometimes diverts water and leaves the riverbed almost dry.

Bennington ➤ Hillsboro   12.0 mi

Description:	Flatwater, Class I–II
Date checked:	2001
Navigable:	Passable at all levels
Scenery:	Forested
Maps:	USGS Hillsboro 15
Portage:	12.0 mi two dams in Hillsboro 0.5 mi

This stretch is not quite as appealing as that above Bennington. The current is slow and the river winds considerably.

Put in below the last dam in Bennington, at the bridge near the Monadnock Paper Company. It is 2.5 miles to Antrim and another 8.25 miles to the entrance of the North Branch of the Contoocook (10.75 miles). About a half-mile past the North Branch, Class II rapids begin and continue right up to the dam (12.0 miles) in Hillsboro, making a difficult and dangerous approach.

Take out on the right where the river comes close to the road 0.5 mile above the dam and just before the mill buildings. It is also possible to take out upstream before the rapids at private docks; ask for and obtain permission to take out here.

Hillsboro ➤ West Henniker   6.5 mi

Description:	Flatwater, quickwater, Class III–IV
Date checked:	2001
Navigable:	High and medium water (spring and after heavy rains)
Scenery:	Forested, settled
Maps:	USGS Hillsboro 15
Portage:	6.5 mi R West Henniker Dam 10 yd

The heaviest rapids on the Contoocook are found in this section—the river at this point is one of the largest whitewater rivers in New England. The water level here is more reliable than it is on other rivers, making the rapids runnable all spring and after heavy rains.

There is a USGS gauge on the right bank 1.0 mile above the dam in West Henniker. When it reads up to 8.0, all rapids except Freight Train Rapids near the end are difficult Class III. Freight Train Rapids are always Class IV. At water levels above 8.0, all the rapids become more turbulent. This section can be run with open boats at water levels up to 9.5 with great care. At virtually any water level, capsizing in the Contoocook can lead to a long swim and a difficult rescue.

A mill dam directly under the NH 149 bridge in Hillsboro makes it advisable to put in just below the village. Reach the river from the left bank near the railroad trestle. The first 0.5 mile consists of Class III rapids, then the river becomes smooth, with one rapid shortly above the NH 202 bridge. From there quickwater continues to the bridge (3.0 miles). Access to the river is good from either old NH 202 on the right bank or from a dirt road on the left bank, which you can drive on in dry season with four-wheel-drive vehicles.

Another smooth 0.5 mile leads to the start of the rapids. Those just starting a trip can go through the woods and put in from old NH 202 at the beginning of the rapids. This is the usual starting point.

The first rapid of the lower section (3.5 miles) begins in a slight left turn, where the current goes from being imperceptible to irresistible. There are no rocks here, but the waves can be very turbulent at high water. The river bends right with rapids and returns to the road (4.0 miles). The next left turn holds another difficult rapid, the shallowest in this portion; if this rapid is passable, then the whole stretch can be run.

When the river leaves the road, there is a very challenging rapid ahead. The right turn is the beginning of a heavy and continuous 0.5-mile rapid known as the "S-turn." In this rapid, swimming and rescue are extremely difficult. S-turn is the most technical rapid and is often scouted from the right. Easier rapids follow, with a USGS gauge on the right bank (5.0

miles). Those who wish to avoid the last and toughest of the Contoocook rapids should take out here where the road is near.

From this calm spot (5.0 miles) the river turns left with easy Class II rapids. Where it turns right the ferocious Freight Train Rapids begin, a Class IV pitch in medium water. Take out on the left bank at the turn to scout. The route is basically through the biggest waves and holes in the center. The last 0.5 mile is quickwater running to the dam in West Henniker (6.5 miles). A take-out can be made on the right bank on old NH 202. This dam is very dangerous; take-out well upstream.

West Henniker ➤ Henniker		2.0 mi
Description:	Quickwater, Class II–III	
Date checked:	2001	
Navigable:	Medium water	
Scenery:	Settled, towns	
Maps:	USGS Hillsboro 15	
Portage:	2.0 mi R broken dam 20 yd	

From the old NH 202 crossing in West Henniker (just below the dam) only one rapid interrupts the smooth course to the new covered bridge at New England College. Starting under the stone NH 114 bridge just below, the river runs through a series of Class II–III rapids for 0.5 mile to a broken dam. This dam is in the process of washing out and should be inspected in advance from the steel truss bridge 100 yards below.

Henniker ➤ Hopkinton flood-control dam		6.5 mi
Description:	Flatwater, quickwater	
Date checked:	2001	
Navigable:	Passable at all water levels	
Scenery:	Forested	
Maps:	USGS Hopkinton	
Portage:	(6.5 mi L two dams 0.5 mi)	

Below the steel truss bridge the river flows sluggishly, with only one rapid, just around the first corner, which is flooded-out in high water. At low water levels the pollution is notice-able, and the attractiveness of the river depends on recent fluctuations in the water level at the dam. This dam is one of the larger flood-control projects in New England and can back up water all the way to Henniker. The best access is at a boat ramp on the right at the bottom of the southern loop, 3.0 miles above the dam. Portage on the dirt road on the left, starting above the second boom.

Hopkinton flood-control dam ➤ Rowley Bridge   0.5 mi

The 0.5-mile section of Class II rapids running to the Rowley covered bridge offers a place to practice technique in an enjoyable setting.

Rowley Bridge ➤ "the Island"   15.25 mi

Description:	Flatwater, quickwater
Date checked:	2001
Navigable:	Passable at all water levels
Scenery:	Forested, settled
Maps:	USGS Hopkinton, Penacook 15, Concord
Portage:	5.0 mi R dam in Contoocook 10 yd

The Contoocook flows swiftly for only a short distance below the Rowley Bridge, gradually slowing to the dam at a small park with picnic tables in Contoocook Village. The dam is an easy carry when the water is not too high.

Immediately below the dam, and past a covered bridge, there is a short Class I rapid. The difficulty of the rest of the river depends on the water level: at low water it is essentially flat, with some boat traffic; at high water the current is swift, with considerable turbulence and strong eddies.

The Warner River joins on the left (6.0 miles), and the Tyler Bridge (7.5 miles) offers very poor access. On the south bank near the bridge are Gould and Rattlesnake hills, where timber for the Civil War warship USS Kearsarge was cut.

The riverbanks were uninhabited above the Blackwater River (9.0 miles), but now a few cabins are visible on the way to a side-road bridge in the locality known as Riverhill (13.75 miles). The river is lined with houses for the next 1.5 miles, to a park in Penacook known appropriately as "the Island" (5.25

miles). Reach the Island by taking Washington Street out of Penacook and following a marked turn-off. There is a public landing on the upstream tip of the island for easy take-out. Although it is possible to continue to the Merrimack, it is not recommended because of the dams and the rapids. Most paddlers terminate their trip here.

"The Island" ➤ Merrimack River   2.5 mi

There are dams on both sides of the Island, and each requires a short portage. The next mile to the US 3 and 4 bridge in Penacook (1.25 miles) has some Class II–III rapids. Just below this bridge is a broken dam that sometimes can be run as a stunt, but as a rule it should be portaged. In low water you can land on the right just above the dam to portage, but avoid this in high water when the current is strong.

Easy rapids follow for 0.5 mile to another bridge (1.75 miles) where a take-out should be made on either side above the bridge. Directly below this bridge is an island with an old bridge abutment. To the left of the island, there is a very sharp drop, followed by an unrunnable dam. On the right side of the island, the descent is more gradual and possibly runnable, but a difficult Class IV. Look this over carefully. The right bank offers a long but gradual portage of 400 yards that avoids all the difficult rapids. When the two channels rejoin, there are more Class IV rapids, with a line of old mill buildings on the left bank. Rapids diminish quickly to the confluence with the Merrimack River, where the Contoocook splits to form Hannah Duston Island.

Warner River NH

The Warner River flows eastward from Bradford toward Concord. It empties into the Contoocook River a little below the town of Contoocook. The upper part contains thrilling rapids for covered boats or open boats with maximum flotation, the middle portion has easy rapids, and lower down, the river meanders through wild swamps. It passes under two covered bridges and runs down the median of I-89.

Bradford ➤ Roby   6.5 mi

Description:	Quickwater, Class II–IV
Date checked:	2001
Navigable:	High water (March)
Scenery:	Forested, towns
Maps:	USGS Mount Kearsarge 15
Portage:	5.0 mi R dam

Put in at the NH 114 bridge southeast of Bradford. The broken mill dam at Melvin Mills (3.0 miles) can be run. After leaving the pond below the mill, the river flows through continuous Class III rapids that require many quick decisions. The river is small, and there are many sharp turns. In about 1.0 mile and around a left turn the river splits and part of it goes into an old millrace on the extreme left. Immediately below is the first tough rapid, with approximately 0.5 mile of uninterrupted Class IV drops. These drops terminate in a chute between cement abutments directly above a small bridge, which is easily visible from NH 103. Approximately 150 feet above the chute between the cement abutments is a low dam. Run it in the chute to the far left in medium water, but scout it first. Just above the dam is a small pool (another 100 feet) and before that the worst of the drops in this section.

After this first difficult pitch, the river eases to Class II for about 0.5 mile before entering the second and most difficult rapid, which is a series of five closely spaced Class IV drops in a gorge beyond an old mill site that adjoins a small picnic area. There is an old tar road on the left, which can be used for scouting or portage. Below the second difficult rapid the river eases up. Soon, behind some houses, there is a stretch of water that turns out to be a millpond. Portage the small dam by the abandoned mill on the right.

Below the dam (5.0 miles) there is quickwater for about 1 mile as the river meanders in a big loop, passing under NH 103 twice. At the second bridge another long section of Class III–IV rapids starts. These are beautiful and continuous rapids, with one-boat eddies. There are no pools for rescue, but there are no sharp drops either, except near the end where the river makes a sharp right turn and goes over a 3-foot ledge. This ledge is hard to diagnose from the boat and difficult to run without scraping. Directly below the ledge there is a bridge on a small dirt road (6.5 miles).

Roby ➤ Warner		2.5 mi
Description:	Quickwater, Class I–II	
Date checked:	2001	
Navigable:	Medium water (April)	
Scenery:	Forested, settled	
Maps:	USGS Mount Kearsarge 15	
Portage:	1.5 mi L dam in Waterloo	

Below the bridge the rapids quickly lighten from Class II to quickwater. In 1.5 miles, just below the covered bridge at Waterloo, there is a dam that is followed immediately by a short Class IV drop. Take out on the left and portage along the old railroad as far down the rapids as you wish. It is another 1.0 mile to the I-89 bridge (2.5 miles).

Warner ➤ Contoocook River		10.0 mi
Description:	Quickwater	
Date checked:	2001	
Navigable:	High or medium water (April through May)	
Scenery:	Forested, towns	
Maps:	USGS Mount Kearsarge 15, Penacook 15, Hopkinton	
Portage:	7.5 mi L dam in Davisville 0.25 yd	

The river below here makes a very pleasant run, with only a few fallen trees to present problems. The old put-in at the junction with Stevens Brook is difficult since NH 103 was improved.

There are a few riffles through Warner and several bridges through the next 3 miles. The interstate highway crosses twice, and the river flows for a while through its median. After a couple of miles through a swamp, where the insects can be vicious, it reaches the bridge at Davisville (7.5 miles). Take out here and portage 0.25 mile down a road on the left bank. This route bypasses an old, partly washed-out dam site and the Class IV rapid below it.

From the dam (7.5 miles) it is a pleasant 2.5 miles to the Contoocook River (10.0 miles). Watch for frequent strainers. Paddle down the Contoocook for 1.5 miles to the bridge at Tyler (11.5 miles). The take out here is difficult.

Blackwater River NH

The sandy bottom of the Blackwater Valley is not as rich for farming as other parts of New Hampshire, which perhaps explains why this valley is so sparsely settled. The river rises in Wilmot north of Mount Kearsarge (Merrimack County) and flows southeast to meet the Contoocook River not far from Concord. Most of the river is a delightful, easy paddle in a scenic area.

Medium water levels, spring or fall season, are required. The river should be avoided in high water because the many fallen trees are definitely hazardous—inexperienced paddlers have had to be rescued from them.

Wilmot Flat ➤ Cilleyville   3.25 mi

This upper part of the river makes a pleasant run when the water in the lower Blackwater River is too high. See USGS Mount Kearsarge 15.

Put in below the Tannery Pond dam at Wilmot Flat. To reach the put-in, take US 4 west for 4.0 miles from Andover Center. Take Village Road on the right approximately 0.5 mile to Tannery Pond on the right. Please note that this area is mostly private property, with no easy put-in. Remember to ask for and obtain permission before crossing property lines. The brook is small, with a slow current and many downed trees. Some small bridges are low and require ducking or possibly portage in extremely high water. Before the covered bridge you pass the confluence with the North Branch on the left.

Take out near the covered bridge in Cilleyville, above the broken dam.

Cilleyville ➤ West Salisbury   9.0 mi
Description: Flatwater, quickwater, Class I
Date checked: 2001

Navigable:	High water needed above Andover (early spring)
	Medium water (late spring and wet fall)
Scenery:	Forested, town
Maps:	USGS Mount Kearsarge 15
Portage:	(9.5 mi broken dam at West Salisbury)

Below the old dam site Class III rapids run for 100 yards to a pool below the old NH 11 bridge. Quickwater continues to the covered bridge in Andover. Fallen trees are the major hazard. There is an easy rapid under a railroad bridge, and a small laid-rock dam. For an easier trip, put in at the covered bridge in Andover (3.0 miles).

After the covered bridge you come to Beech Hill Road bridge, which has a hand-painted gauge on the left.

The current becomes slower, with occasional riffles, as the river wends its way, passing twice beneath US 4. After 4.5 miles it enters the slackwater of the Bay, where the river broadens into a 1.5-mile series of marshy ponds. You can take out at the end of the Bay on a dirt road to the left, which can be reached by traveling west out of Salisbury Center on US 4. Take the first left (West Salisbury Road). This comes out at the end of the Bay.

The Bay ➤ Peters Bridge   1.5 miles

There is a steep, rocky drop at the end of the Bay, then less than 0.5 mile to the next bridge, where there is a broken dam with jagged masonry in the river. The Class II rapids below the dam diminish to quickwater within the next mile to Peters Bridge, the best place to put in for this section.

Peters Bridge ➤ Flood-control dam   12.0 mi
Description:	Quickwater, flatwater
Date checked:	2001
Navigable:	Medium water (late spring and wet fall)
Scenery:	Wild
Maps:	USGS Mount Kearsarge 15, Penacook 15
Portage:	12.0 mi L flood-control dam

From Peters Bridge there are 4.0 miles of quickwater to Sawyers Bridge. It is a beautiful stream that meanders through a swamp above and below Sawyers Bridge, but there are fallen trees. Some of them are dangerous in high water because you may be swept under them; others are a nuisance at low water because they must be lifted over.

When the dam is drawn down, there are a few rocks and a faster current below the old abutment, just before the ponding before the dam.

Take out at an access road on the left.

Flood-control dam ➤ Snyder's Mill	4.0 mi
Description:	Flatwater, quickwater, Class III–IV
Date checked:	2001
Navigable:	High water (April)
Scenery:	Forested
Maps:	USGS Penacook 15, Hopkinton

This section is recommended only for covered boats, open boats with maximum flotation, and a strong party of at least four boats which has Class IV experience. People who never tip over in the Contoocook in Freight Train Rapids above Henniker often swim in one of the two Class IV rapids above Snyder's Mill.

Put in on the right at the foot of the cascade under Swettis Mills Bridge on NH 127. The put-in is just past the salt shed of the highway department on a dirt road next to the town hall and library. Below the cascade the river splits around an island where there is a shallow, rocky rapid. This is more water on the right. If you do not hit any rocks here, the rapids farther down the river past Dingit corner will be extremely exciting. Below the island there is an easier put-in behind the Webster Elementary School (0.25 mile).

The river then riffles through an attractive, forested area. One and a half miles below the school the river turns left and tumbles through a Class III rapid that has a couple of large rocks and a nice set of three-foot standing waves with a pool at the bottom.

At that point the river squeezes through a 15-foot-wide notch in a ledge and drops 4–5 feet into a messy hole, which, again, is recommended only for advanced closed boaters or those open boaters with maximum flotation. It should be scouted and/or portaged on the left. It is quite exciting and often results in nosestands and Eskimo rolls. The water below the hole is fast and deep. This can be seen upstream from Clothespin Bridge (2.0 miles).

Below Clothespin Bridge there is a Class III ledge. The river rounds a sharp left corner, passes the USGS gauge (2.5 miles), and drops over a rocky Class III rapid best run near the left bank. The gauge can be checked from the road by taking Clothespin Bridge Road off NH 127. After crossing the bridge, follow the river 0.2 mile downstream. Pull over at a roadside pull-off.

The first set of Class IV rapids (2.75 miles) is rocky and continuous, with only small eddies, big enough for one boat. This area can be scouted or portaged on the left side. There is a trail going upstream from Snyder's Mill on the left (downstream) approximately 0.75 mile upstream for those who wish to view this very difficult set of rapids. The river swishes from side to side around the rocks like a downhill ski run. After rounding a sharp right turn, the river drops into a 0.25-mile stretch of flatwater, the lull between storms. If the first rapids are not to your liking, do not run the next set.

The second set of Class IV rapids is very turbulent, tricky to run upright, and hardly enjoyable swimming. It could be described as a hard Class IV washing machine, followed by a 4-foot ledge onto a 0.25-mile washboard which is made up of shallow, bony rapids that run down under Snyder's Mill Bridge (4.0 miles). There is a dirt access road on the right, which was the take-out until it was marked as private property. Instead, take out on a small trail directly downstream from this road or take out at the bridge. Neither option is a great take-out, however.

Snyder's Mill ➤ Contoocook River		6.0 mi
Description:	Flatwater, quickwater	
Date checked:	2001	
Navigable:	Medium water	
Scenery:	Forested	
Maps:	USGS Penacook 15, Hopkinton	

The lower section of the Blackwater is a pleasant run, with the only hazard being occasional fallen trees. Bridges cross at 4.5 miles and 5.5 miles. There is no access at the confluence (6.0 miles), but in any case many paddlers will want to continue 3.25 miles down the Contoocook to Broad Cove, on the right.

Blackwater River (North Branch) NH

This is an easy trip, possible in wet summers, and ideal for beginners or bird watchers.

Start at the launching ramp above the dam at Cilleyville near the junction of NH 11 and NH 4A on the right bank. Paddle upstream for about a mile through Bog Pond and then on upstream another 1.5 miles to the bridge at West Andover near Winslow Eaves Sculpture Studio. Then return. You may encounter beaver dams at the north end of Bog Pond, but they are a minor problem.

Soucook River NH

North of Loudon near Pearls Corner, Bumfagon Brook and Gues Meadow Brook join to form the Soucook River, which flows south to the Merrimack River below Concord. It is a pleasant, winding stream, with a good current and largely undeveloped banks.

It is possible to begin 0.75 mile upstream from Pearls Corner at the second bridge on Pearls Corners Road, but that section has Class II rapids that remain blocked by deadfalls.

The last 11.0 miles beginning at the NH 9 bridge east of Concord are especially recommended because there are no carries. This lower portion of the Soucook is more difficult at medium water levels, when there are several Class II rapids and innumerable riffles. At high flows many of them are washed out, so there are only occasional rapids. If there is not enough water to run the rock dam just above the bridge, the river below is too low for an enjoyable trip.

Pearls Corner ➤ NH 9 Bridge	11.0 mi
Description:	Quickwater, flatwater, Class II
Date checked:	2001
Navigable:	High water (April)
Scenery:	Forested, towns
Maps:	USGS Gilmanton 15, Suncook
Portages:	5.0 mi L dam at Loudon 50 yd
	8.5 mi R Cascade Camping Area 200 yd

Put in below the confluence at a bridge on a side road east of Pearls Corner. There are 2.5 miles of good current in a winding meadow stream to the first bridge, then another 2.5 miles, half of which is deadwater, to the dam in Loudon. The first NH 106 bridge is just before the dam. Take out on the left and carry across the road. Put in on the right. The short, rocky Class II rapids below can be lined if necessary. The portage trail goes to the end of the rapids. Immediately following the end of the rapids, the river is blocked by downed trees. There are 2.5 miles of good current and occasional rapids between wooded banks to the new (second) NH 106 bridge, which is just before the dam.

Below the NH 106 bridge (7.5 miles) there is about 1 mile of flatwater to a rocky Class IV rapid that can be run only under favorable conditions. Portage 200 yards on the right through the Cascade Camping Area to a pool below. It is 0.5 mile to the next side-road bridge (9.0 miles), below which the river forms the eastern boundary of the city of Concord. In 2.0 miles there is a 1-foot dam at a gauging station just above the US 4 bridge. The gauge house no longer has a readable gauge.

NH 9 Bridge ➤ Merrimack River	11.0 mi
Description:	Quickwater, Class I–II
Date checked:	2001
Navigable:	High water (April)
Scenery:	Forested, rural
Maps:	USGS Suncook, Concord

Below the NH 9 bridge the river passes almost immediately under an old truss bridge, and just under the NH 393 bridges is a Class II rapid. More quickwater flows as the river winds behind steep, wooded banks that are often 100 feet high. Watch out for fallen trees, particularly at high flows when the current is strong.

After the NH 106 bridge (4.75 miles) Class II rapids occur more frequently, ending with a fast Class II drop at a ledge 0.5 mile above the high US 3 bridge (7.5 miles).

Occasional Class I–II rapids start 2.5 miles below the US 3 bridge. Just beyond the old railroad grade you reach the Merrimack River (11.0 miles).

Take-out is on the left bank 0.5 mile below the confluence and is reached from a side road in Pembroke.

Suncook River NH

The Suncook River flows from Crystal Lake in Gilmanton through the two Suncook lakes and then southwest to the Merrimack River at Suncook. Although there are four dams, there is some fine quickwater in the 29.25 miles described below. There is also a substantial amount of flatwater that can be run throughout the paddling season.

Lower Suncook Lake ➤ Pittsfield	7.75 mi
Description:	Lakes, quickwater, Class I–II
Date checked:	2001
Navigable:	High water needed for rapids (April)
Scenery:	Forested, towns
Maps:	USGS Gilmanton 15
Portages:	4.25 mi e dam in Barnstead 50 yd
	(7.75 mi R dam in Pittsfield 300 yd)

The river becomes runnable below Lower Suncook Lake. Put in from a side road upstream of NH 28. There is 0.5 mile of Class II water to the NH 28 bridge. From the bridge there are 1.25 miles of Class I rapids that lead to an old dam site just above the first bridge in Center Barnstead (1.75 miles). There is a Class II rapid for a short distance in the vicinity of that bridge. The current gradually eases off in the next 0.5 mile, and then there are 2.0 miles of flowage to the dam in Barnstead.

Below the dam (4.25 miles) there are some rapids for 1.5 miles to a 2.0-mile backwater behind the Pittsfield dam (7.75 miles).

There is access to the river at several points above both dams from side roads.

Pittsfield ➤ Epsom Circle   8.75 mi

Description:	Quickwater, Class I–II
Date checked:	2001
Navigable:	High water (April)
Scenery:	Forested, towns, settled
Maps:	USGS Gilmanton 15, Gossville

In medium water it is possible to relaunch above the bridge. In high water carry across the bridge and relaunch below or put in on the left 200 yards downstream from the Pittsfield dam. The river is small and fast, and there is evidence of beaver activity. It is an easy Class II run for the first 2.0 miles to a sharp left turn at a ledge. Just above the bridge at Webster's Mills is the most difficult drop, which is best to run on the right in high water.

Below the bridge (3.0 miles) the river broadens. There are big waves in high water, but in medium water the river is scratchy. Class II rapids continue for 1.0 mile before ending abruptly, followed by 1.5 miles of quickwater to the bridge at North Chicester (5.5 miles). Just below the bridge a low dam can be run under favorable conditions.

In the last 3.25 miles to Epsom Circle (8.75 miles), meandering through meadowland, the river is easy and enjoyable.

Epsom Circle ➤ Short Falls   4.0 mi

Description:	Flatwater, quickwater, Class II–IV
Date checked:	2001
Navigable:	High water needed for rapids (April)
Scenery:	Forested, settled
Maps:	USGS Gossville, Suncook
Portage:	1.25 mi R dam at Bear Island

After 0.25 mile the Little Suncook River comes in on the left. The river becomes ponded by a dam, which is 1.25 miles below the bridge near Epsom Circle. This dam is located at the head of Bear Island on the topographic map.

The island is about a mile long. The channel on the left starts by going over a low dam and has a number of tricky Class III and IV drops that local covered boaters find exciting. The righthand channel requires a portage around a dam on the right. The rapids on this side of the island are Class II.

The rapids end shortly below the island. Fast water continues for about 1.75 miles to the bridge at Short Falls, where there is a riffle just above the bridge (4.0 miles), with some small surfing waves.

Short Falls ➤ Suncook	8.75 mi
Description:	Flatwater, quickwater
Date checked:	2001
Navigable:	Spring, summer, fall
Scenery:	Forested, settled
Maps:	USGS Suncook
Portage:	4.0 mi e dams at NH 28 bridge
	(8.75 mi dam at Suncook)

Below the bridge the water is ponded, and there are big estuaries at the mouth of all the tributaries. The left bank is mostly wild, but in many places on the right there are cottages and trailer parks.

In 4.0 miles a bridge on NH 28 is followed by an island with a dam on each side. Take out on either side of either dam. The best portage is on the island. There is current only for a short distance before you reach a backwater that extends for the remainder of the 4.5 miles to the US 3 bridge (8.5 miles) in Suncook. Below the bridge are a small pond and a high dam (8.75 miles).

From the dam the river drops nearly 100 feet in the first half of the remaining mile to the Merrimack River.

Little Suncook River NH

This small, exciting stream is the outlet of Northwood Lake in Northwood. It flows almost due west to the Suncook River just below the traffic circle in Epsom. US 4 follows nearly on the right bank, but the highway is usually out of sight. See the USGS Gossville map.

The first convenient put-in is the NH 107 bridge 0.5 mile below the outlet from Northwood lake. Since you immediately encounter numerous blind turns and narrow Class III–IV rapids that are frequently blocked by downed trees and barbed wire fences, this put-in is not recommended. A better choice is a roadside picnic area on US 4, where the river approaches the road. From here there is 0.5 mile of quickwater to a small concrete dam (0.5 mile), which is visible down a side road from US 4. Below this dam are rocky Class III–IV rapids that require just the right water level, which is found only a few days of the year after heavy rains and during the annual drawdown of Northwood Lake. There are many sharp corners, which sometimes hide a snowmobile bridge or a fallen tree. Take out at the bridge in Gossville (1.75 miles), since the next 0.5 mile to the Suncook River is congested with fallen trees, alder thickets, and grapevines in the middle of a swamp.

There is an annual fall drawdown of Northwood Lake by the NH Water Division (603-271-3406).

Piscataquog River NH

The Piscataquog River is formed west of Goffstown by the union of the North Branch, which rises in Weare, and the South Branch, which rises in Francestown. The main river then flows eastward to the Merrimack in Manchester. The rapids can be run later in the year than those on the branches, and the smooth sections can run whenever they are free from ice.

Confluence ➤ Lower dam   3.0 mi

The first 1.5 miles to Goffstown are described under both the North and South branches because it would be run as a continuation of one of those trips. The first dam lies just below the bridge in Goffstown. Water is backed up by the second dam, a high power dam, forming the recreational Glen Lake.

Power dam ➤ Grasmere   1.0 mi

Description:	Flatwater, quickwater, Class II–III
Date checked:	2001
Navigable:	High to medium water
Scenery:	Settled
Maps:	USGS Goffstown

Below the power dam, which can be reached from the south, there are continuous rapids that are Class II in medium water and generate very large waves in high water. It is best to run this stretch when the upper river is low.

Grasmere ➤ Merrimack River   6.0 mi

Description:	Flatwater, quickwater, Class I–III
Date checked:	2001
Navigable:	Spring, summer, fall
Scenery:	Settled, forested
Maps:	USGS Goffstown, Manchester South
Portages:	4.0 mi L Kelleys Falls dam

The rapids ease at Grasmere Bridge. The next 2.5 miles are mostly quickwater, with occasional Class I rapids between attractive wooded banks to the backwater from the Kelleys Falls dam, where cottages line the shore.

The dam is located almost beneath the Pinard Street bridge. Take out at the boat ramp on the left, or continue below the railroad bridge to portage.

Below Kelleys Falls the river runs briskly through a ravine so deep that the houses in Manchester can scarcely be seen on the banks above. The river drops over a series of ledges separated by quickwater. The third ledge, a mile down, contains the remnants of an old dam, which can be scouted or carried on the right.

Several islands can be run on either side, including the large one at the confluence. The banks of this lower section are littered with shopping carts and other debris. None of the lower bridges offers access, but a convenient take-out is on the left bank of the Merrimack under the Queen City Avenue bridge. A road heading into the old factory area south of Queen City Avenue leads under the bridge. A more pleasant take-out is on the Merrimack from side roads near the I-293 bridge 2.25 miles downstream.

Piscataquog River (South Branch) NH

The South Branch rises southwest of Concord in Francestown and flows east and northeast to join the North Branch just above Goffstown. The upper river has too many obstructions to be popular, but the lower river is frequently used as a whitewater practice run. Someone who is going to "run the Piscataquog" is usually referring to the section below New Boston.

Francestown ➤ Old bridge   7.5 mi

This section is not popular because it contains a mixed selection of water, including two gorges. See the USGS Peterborough 15 and New Boston quadrangles.

Put in at the NH 136 bridge east of Francestown. Following a steep rapid below the bridge, the river winds through a marshy area with beaver dams. Shallow, pleasant Class II rapids, with steep drops between two bridges, are interspersed with fallen trees. Easy rapids, and occasional more-difficult spots, continue to the second NH 47 bridge (3.75 miles), becoming smooth as they approach a bridge on a side road (4.25 miles). Below this bridge there is a broken dam with 100 yards of Class III rapids, which come into a pool. Take out here, since the unrunnable gorge starts above the next bridge (5.0 miles). Haul the boats up a steep bank on the left. Carry by car to the next bridge.

A quarter-mile below the end of the gorge is an old mill site. A large boulder in the center and a large drop may have to be lifted over or portaged. Shallow rapids lead into quickwater through a swampy area. Rapids start again above the next bridge, and continue intermittently to a small bridge (6.5

miles) at an old paper mill site. The bridge spans an awkward chute that reputedly contains old machinery. Portage to the right. It is another mile to the usual put-in for the run to New Boston.

Old bridge ➤ New Boston	3.5 mi
Description:	Class I–II
Date checked:	2001
Navigable:	High water (March to early April)
Scenery:	Rural, towns
Map:	USGS New Boston
Portages:	0.75 mi R small dam
	2.5 mi R first dam in New Boston 50 yd
	(3.25 mi R second dam in New Boston 300 yd)

This area can be reached by a side road to the west of NH 13 a mile south of New Boston. Proceed for approximately 2 miles, crossing the river midway. Put in whenever it is convenient—where the river is near the road.

Class I rapids continue nearly to the side-road bridge crossed en route to the put-in. Below this bridge Class II rapids lead in 1.25 miles to a dam, which should be portaged on the right. Rapids continue for 0.25 mile to the NH 13 bridge, just below which there is a millpond. Carry the dam in the center of New Boston (3.25 miles) on the right, go down the street for 300 yards, and put in near the next NH 13 bridge. In 0.25 mile, the river passes a bridge by the old railroad station (3.5 miles).

New Boston ➤ Goffstown	7.5 mi
Description:	Quickwater, Class I–II
Date checked:	1983
Navigable:	High water (March to early April)
Scenery:	Rural, towns
Maps:	USGS New Boston, Weare, Goffstown

The dam in New Boston has washed out. The most convenient starting point in New Boston is the old railroad station across the second bridge below the town. In about 0.25 mile there is another side-road bridge.

For the next 5.0 miles NH 13 is often in sight on the right bank. Many of the rapids in this section are artificial because rocks have been placed in the river to improve the fish habitat. The rocks present no problem at high water, but they require careful route selection at lower levels. It is 2.5 miles to the next bridge. The Middle Branch enters below on the left (3.0 miles). The next 1.5 miles to a bridge (4.5 miles) and a gauging station are somewhat easier. This is a popular take-out spot.

One mile below the gauging station the road leaves the river, and the rapids end. This is the last take-out before Goffstown. The river meanders, with a fast current, fallen trees, and many channels. The North Branch (6.0 miles), indistinguishable from other channels, enters on the left. From there it is 1.5 miles to the bridge at Goffstown (7.5 miles), with little current into the ponding from the Goffstown dam. Take out at the ballfield on the right, accessed from the one-way road along the river.

Piscataquog River (Middle Branch) NH

The Middle Branch rises in Francestown and flows northeast to a marshy area, where it makes an abrupt turn and flows south to meet the South Branch about 2.0 miles below New Boston.

Five Corners ➤ South Branch	5.75 mi
Description:	Flatwater, quickwater, Class I–III
Date checked:	2001
Navigable:	High water (April)
Scenery:	Forested, marsh
Map:	USGS Concord 15
Portage:	5.0 mi e dam 50 yd

Put in below the gorge at the five corners over a mile west of NH 77. The trip starts slowly, then a gorge follows, with some Class II–III rapids and a sharp right turn. Below the NH 77 bridge a steep drop may have to be lined or carried. After a few more rapids, the river enters a swamp where two other brooks join and makes its turn to the south. A small bridge on a closed road crosses at the end of the marsh, and the going is easy to the backwater of a dam. Easy rapids continue below the dam for the 0.75 mile to the South Branch.

Piscataquog River (North Branch) NH

The North Branch rises southwest of Concord in Deering and flows east and south to join with the South Branch just above Goffstown. The upper part is steep and rocky, with many ledges and old dam sites, and the lower portion is a pleasant quickwater run. The two are separated by a large flood-control dam in Everett.

Lake Horace ➤ Everett Dam		9.0 mi
Description:	Class II, III, IV	
Date checked:	2001	
Navigable:	High water (April)	
Scenery:	Forested, towns	
Map:	USGS Hillsboro 15, Weare	
Portages:	2.25 mi R dam at North Weare 50 yd	
	(9.0 mi flood-control dam)	

All but one of the twenty-two milldams that formerly obstructed the river are gone, but the steep drops that engendered them remain. Since the old sites are still in the process of change, and the problems are different at different water levels, this section should only be run by competent paddlers who are willing to assess problems as they come up. Almost everything can be run at the right water level, but many people would prefer to line or carry some of the drops.

Put in just below Lake Horace. The river is very small, with some overhanging bushes. Two old dams are located above the bridge a short distance down. Then a series of more than six ledges follows to the millpond of the dam in North Weare, which sits atop a complicated ledge.

Another ledge lies under the New Boston road, and then easy Class II rapids run to the gorge below the old NH 77 bridge. There are a few more steep drops. Then some easier drops (Class II+) and some quickwater past the bridge on the road to the reservoir (6.0 miles) bring you to the old abutment (7.25 miles). The river splits around an island, where the route is not obvious. Take out from the old road on the left near Choate Brook (7.75 miles). You can reach this point from Pages Corner, turning south on Sugar Hill Road and continuing past the Road Closed sign.

Everett ➤ Goffstown		8.5 mi
Description:	Quickwater	
Date checked:	2001	
Navigable:	High or medium water (spring and after moderate rains)	
Scenery:	Rural	
Maps:	USGS Weare, Goffstown	
Portage:	5.25 mi R dam in Riverdale	

Put in just below the flood-control dam. The bridge 0.5 mile below is an alternate put-in. The river winds with gentle current through meadowland to Riverdale, where the dam above the bridge should be carried on the right. Be considerate of the landowner, and ask for and obtain permission before crossing property lines.

Below the dam (5.25 miles) there are 1.25 miles of easy river to the NH 114 bridge (6.5 miles), where there is a boat ramp, and to another bridge at Goffstown (8.5 miles), 1.5 miles below.

Cohas Brook NH

Cohas Brook flows along the south end of Manchester and enters the Merrimack at Goffs Falls. The banks are so thickly wooded that nearby settled areas are usually out of sight, but I-93 is audible for a portion of the trip. See the USGS Manchester North map.

The upper portion is full of dense thickets, fallen trees, wire mesh, and electric fence. Also in store is a mile of paddling in the median strip of I-93. The median strip can be paddled upstream and back from the Bodwell Road bridge, just after the river leaves the median. Small beaver dams, fallen trees, and some low brush should be expected.

An acceptable, 4.0-mile portion begins at the second Bodwell Road bridge. Expect a few fallen trees and/or log jams. The stream, soon enlarged by the outlet of Massabesic Lake, passes under I-93 in 0.75 mile. Shortly after passing the NH 28A bridge (1.25 miles), the stream meanders through a large wet marsh west of NH 28A. Around the corner below is a Class II–III rapid that runs continuously for about 100 yards and is runnable only in high water. Take out on the right just after these rapids where Goffs Falls Road approaches on top of a high, steep bank (4.25 miles).

The lower portion is not recommended. It contains smooth-water and rapids. In the middle of a Class III–IV rapid (5.25 miles) there is a difficult access on the left. This access is from Perimeter Road, just opposite and downstream of the north end of Manchester Municipal Airport's main runway. This rapid can be portaged on the right. Smoothwater and rapids continue to Pine Island Pond (5.75 miles), which can be accessed publicly only via Perimeter Road up a very high bank. Below the dam (6.5 miles) there is 0.25 mile of unrunnable cascades to the Merrimack River.

Souhegan River NH

The Souhegan rises in the Pack Monadnock and more souther-ly ranges and flows north and east to the Merrimack River between Manchester and Nashua. The upper portion offers a good intermediate whitewater trip; farther down, the river has a mixture of smoothwater and rapids. Riverbanks usually are unset-tled except near towns.

Although it may be possible to canoe above Greenville, it is not recommended because there is an impassable gorge below town. Although old rebar has been removed from the gorge, it is reported that there is a partly submerged pipe that presents a dangerous hazard.

Greenville ➤ NH 101 bridge	5.75 mi
Description:	Class II–III
Date checked:	2001
Navigable:	High water (late March to early April)
Scenery:	Forested
Map:	USGS Peterborough 15

This is a very popular section of rapids, because the parts are of consistent difficulty, and the road is close by, offering opportunities for scouting and rescue.

Put in at the site of the old hydroelectric plant on a short side road off NH 31, 1.0 mile north of Greenville and 0.25 mile north of a railroad overpass. The first mile to the NH 31 bridge is the most difficult (Class III). The rapids are rocky, with several small ledges, and they generate considerable waves in high water. Eddies are small, and rapids are continuous.

Below the bridge, the river follows the road closely for a while. The first drop is rocky, then the river becomes slightly easier, offering choices among the rocks.

Where the river turns away from the road, a huge boulder sits in the river to the right. A sharp left turn shortly below concerns boaters, but the large rock on the right has a pillow that makes it easy to miss.

At the large island, the left-hand channel tends to be blocked by fallen trees. The right-hand channel has a ledge where a zig-zag course may be easier to plan after scouting.

Below the island, the river becomes easier, splitting again in several places. Many parties take out at a bridge on a side road (4.5 miles), since access is good and the rapids diminish to the NH 101 bridge.

NH 101 Bridge ➤ Wilton	1.25 mi
Description:	Class III–IV
Date checked:	2001
Navigable:	High water
Scenery:	Forested
Maps:	USGS Peterborough 15, Milford
Portages:	0.75 mi ledge—lift over
	1.0 mi L first dam in Wilton
	(1.25 mi second dam in Wilton)

The Class III rapids beginning at the NH 101 bridge are more difficult than those below the old power station. Paddlers must dodge rocks in a very swift current. In 0.75 mile there is a sharp Class IV drop over a ledge, which is best to run on the left. A dirt road that leads away from the river on the left can be used for scouting, carrying, or taking out.

After the second section of difficult rapids there is 0.25 mile of fastwater to the first dam in Wilton (1 mile). Portage on the left and continue through 0.25 mile of rocky Class III rapids to a bridge and the mouth of Stony Brook on the left. The second dam is just below.

Wilton ➤ Milford	5.75 mi
Description:	Quickwater, Class II
Date checked:	2001
Navigable:	High water
Scenery:	Forested, towns
Map:	USGS Milford
Portage:	(5.75 mi R first dam in Milford)

At the second dam there are two options. You can carry 0.5 mile along the road through Wilton, to the bridge at the east end of town. Doing this avoids a series of dams and a stretch of river that is often dry because of the diversion of the water into a power canal that parallels the river. However, if there is water in the river, you can put in below the final dam by following a steep dirt road over the railroad tracks and run 0.5 mile of Class II rapids to the bridge mentioned above, near which the power canal rejoins the river.

From the bridge at the east end of Wilton, Class II rapids continue for 0.75 mile, ending just past the truss bridge at Jones Crossing. This marks the end of the rapids on the upper river, and it is the usual take-out for paddlers interested primarily in whitewater.

From Jones Crossing (1.25 miles), there are 4.5 miles of winding stream, with a fast current and a few fallen trees, to Milford (5.75 miles). Take out at the ballfield off NH 101.

Through Milford   1.0 mi

To avoid the carry around two dams, it is recommended that you portage by car, since buildings and retaining walls make hand-carrying each dam difficult.

Milford ➤ Turkey Hill Bridge   10.0 mi

Description: Flatwater, quickwater, Class I–II
Date checked: 2001
Navigable: High water (spring)
Scenery: Rural, towns
Maps: USGS Milford, South Merrimack,
                      Nashua North

Put in by carrying down between the houses opposite a supermarket on NH 101A. Remember to ask for and obtain permission before crossing property lines. Except for a rocky Class III rapid beneath the high NH 101 bridge, this section begins with 2.0 miles of quickwater.

Below the NH 122 bridge (2.0 miles), there are 5.5 miles of meandering quickwater past two more bridges to a sharp right turn, where there is a Class II ledge. The river then splits around two low islands, below which is Indian Ledge, a Class III rapid that should be scouted. The best carry starts on the right above the islands, but you also can run the Class II rapids on the left and then line the main drop down a side channel. Then there are 2.25 miles of smoothwater to the Turkey Hill bridge.

The Turkey Hill bridge (10.0 miles) is a recommended takeout point if you wish to avoid the portage at Wildcat Falls farther downstream.

Turkey Hill Bridge ➤ Merrimack   3.25 mi

Description: Quickwater, Class II–III
Date checked: 2001
Navigable: Medium water
Scenery: Forested
Map: USGS Nashua South
Portages: 2.0 mi L Wildcat Falls 0.25 mi
                      (3.0 mi dam at Merrimack)

Three-quarters of a mile below the Turkey Hill bridge there is an easy Class II rapid, followed by 1.25 miles of deadwater to Wildcat Falls (2.0 miles). Take out on the left and carry 0.25 mile around the falls, which are doubly hazardous because they are likely to be jammed with debris. Then it is 0.25 mile with two short Class II rapids to the high Everett Turnpike bridge, under which there is a short Class III rapid. A half-mile farther is the dam and the US 3 bridge at Merrimack (3.0 miles). Only 0.25 mile of fast water brings you to the Merrimack River (3.25 miles).

Stony Brook NH

Stony Brook, a small stream west of Manchester and Nashua, is a tributary of the Souhegan River. Because of its size, it is less reliable and less frequently runnable than the Souhegan. When there is enough water, Stony Brook provides a short run comparable, in the last part, to the tougher stretches of the Souhegan.

South Lyndeboro ➤ Wilton	3.0 mi
Description:	Class II–III
Date checked:	2001
Navigable:	High water (late March to early April)
Scenery:	Forested
Maps:	USGS Peterborough 15, Milford
Portage:	2.75 mi L sawmill 20 yd

From the put-in at the NH 31 bridge just below South Lyndeboro, there are 1.5 miles of Class II rapids to the next NH 31 bridge. The river then turns left under a railroad bridge and drops through Class III ledges, which should be looked over from the highway nearby. The next mile has many more such ledges, all runnable (cautiously) at the right water levels.

The dam at the sawmill (2.75 miles) above Wilton can be portaged on the left. More rapids continue to Wilton (3.0 miles). Take out on the right where there is an artificial embankment made of stone.

In the next 100 yards to the Souhegan River there is a dam and a short, steep portage on either side. Most boaters will not want to make this portage.

Nashua River

The Nashua River has two principal branches, the South Branch, rising near Worcester, and the North Branch, formed by the junction of the Whitman and Nookagee rivers in West Fitchburg. The two branches meet at Lancaster Common and flow north to the Merrimack River at Nashua, New Hampshire. The South Branch is dammed at Clinton to form the Wachusett reservoir, which supplies water to Boston, Massachusetts. There is, therefore, usually little or no flow through the old riverbed between Clinton and the junction with the North Branch at Lancaster Common, so this branch has now become the principal headwater of the river.

The Nashua River has enjoyed a major restoration in the last twenty-five years. The industrial pollution is gone now. Birds, wildlife, and fish are returning, and paddling the Nashua River is now an enjoyable experience. For further information on the river contact the Nashua River Watershed Association (NRWA), 592 Main St., Groton, MA 01450. They print a river guidebook that locates access points and points of interest.

Leominster, MA ➤ Lancaster, MA	10.5 mi
Description:	Quickwater, Class I, II
Date checked:	1998
Navigable:	High water (spring into mid-June)
Scenery:	Forested, settled, towns
Maps:	USGS Fitchburg, Shirley, Clinton
Portages:	2.0 mi L dam

This section is clear but extra caution must be taken because of numerous sweepers and strainers.

Put in at the Searstown Mall. The paddling is easy through an open valley not far from the birthplace of Johnny Appleseed. The first dam is hard to see around a right-hand turn. Land on the left to carry. One Class II rapid is under a power line around a double island. There is one last riffle before the MA 117 bridge, although the current continues, and curves and snags still trouble unskilled paddlers. Take out at Lancaster Canoe Launch at the Main Street Bridge, or continue a little farther to the railroad trestle on river right.

Lancaster, MA ➤ Ayer, MA   10.5 miles

Description:	Quickwater
Date checked:	1998
Navigable:	Passable at most water levels. Generally runnable anytime
Scenery:	Forested, settled, towns
Maps:	USGS Clinton, Shirley, Ayer
Portage:	(10.5 mi L dam)

Here the river sharply reverses itself and starts its northward swing. Below the confluence with the South Branch (0.5 mi) the river is much larger, with a strong current and fewer meanders. It passes under MA 117 (2.0 miles) by the mouth of the Still River on the right, and under MA 2 (8.5 miles) and finally approaches the dam at the Ayer Ice Company. Do not approach the dam on the right. Portage over a low cement wall on river left just above the dam.

Ayer, MA ➤ East Pepperell, MA   11.0 mi

Description:	Flatwater, quickwater
Date checked:	1998
Navigable:	Passable at most water levels
Scenery:	Forested, towns
Maps:	USGS Ayer, Pepperell
Portages:	(11.0 mi R dam 0.5 mi)

Nonacoicus Brook enters on the left in one mile, and the Squannacook River enters on the left at three miles, just below the MA 2A bridge. It flows easily past MA 225 (5.5 miles) and MA 119 (8.25 miles), where it enters the extensive ponding behind the dam at East Pepperell. The Stony Wading Place was here before the bridge was built. The old dam remains are barely visible at low water. Ruins of the 1841 Oliver Howe paper mill are adjacent to the Groton Canoe Launch here on the right.

Pepperell Pond is one of the more beautiful and interesting segments of the entire river. Although less than three miles in length as the crow flies, the maze of oxbows, islands, backwaters, and meanders make it possible to spend an entire day here. A survey by a wildlife biologist hired by the NRWA confirmed that this area is unique in the diversity of its plant and animal life. Waterfowl and other birds are particularly abundant. Conservation restrictions and public land purchases will ensure that Pepperell Pond will remain protected. The Nashua River repeatedly has been cited by the EPA and many other state, regional, and federal agencies for its remarkable progress. The growing NRWA greenway program has thus far protected approximately sixty percent of the river bank.

The long portage is best made by car for 0.5 mile to the covered bridge on the Nashua River. Alternately, people continuing during medium water may put in at the Mill Street bridge on the Nissitissit River just to the North, and run down the last mile of it to the Nashua. Or, you may put in on the Nissitissit behind Lower Industrial Park off MA 111, 0.25 mile from the Nashua.

East Pepperell, MA ➤ Mine Falls, NH		9.75 mi
Description:	Flatwater, quickwater	
Date checked:	1998	
Navigable:	Passable at all water levels	
Scenery:	Forested, settled, towns	
Maps:	USGS Pepperell, Nashua South	
Portages:	5.25 mi e old dam at Ronnells Falls	
	(9.75 mi R Mine Lot Falls (difficult)	
	0.25 mi)	

On April 19, 1775, when the men of Pepperell had gone to Concord to answer the alarm, the women dressed in their husbands' clothing and armed themselves with whatever they could find. They patrolled the Mill Street bridge in East Pepperell and arrested a Tory, Captain Leonard Whiting of Hollis, who was bearing dispatches to the British in Boston.

From the put-in below the dam in East Pepperell it is only 0.75 mile to the junction of the Nissitissit. The current is moderate as far as the broken dam at Ronnells Mills, just below the NH 111 bridge. Besides the obvious problems, some spikes still protrude. This can be run on river right, but only with scouting and good safety precaution.

The main flow of the river is on the right, which is free of debris from the old dam. At high water this is a short Class III run. There is convenient access on the right above or the left below the dam.

From here to the first dam 1.0 mile west of Nashua the current slows. The take-out at Mine Lot Falls is a 700-foot carry, so one might be better advised to take out at the Horrigan Conservation Area off NH 111, about three-quarters of the way down.

Mine Lot Fall ➤ Merrimack River	5.5 mi
Description:	Flatwater, quickwater, possible rapids
Date checked:	1998
Navigable:	Passable at most water levels
Scenery:	Forested, settled, urban
Maps:	USGS Nashua South
Portages:	3.75 mi L dam (difficult footing) 200 yd along railroad track

Portage Mine Lot Falls on the right. This is the dam that forms the Nashua Canal.

The first rapids below the dam should not be run. A good path leads high above the river, with a trail down over boulders to the river at almost the end of the rapids, about 0.25 mile.

Below the rapids the river wanders peacefully in a big loop to the left under the Everett Turnpike and a prize-winning pedestrian bridge.

Just before the last loop, a factory comes into sight on the right, with a solid line of factories around the next bend. Water from the canal exits under these factories. Below the stone-arch Main Street bridge is another dam that can be portaged on either side, although the right is shorter, and the bank is steep in either case.

The river is quickwater for the remaining 1.75 miles to the Merrimack. The chief obstruction is shopping carts.

Alternate Canal Trip   3.0 mi

Portage into the canal on the right (east) side of the Nashua River. The canal is sluggish and pleasant, passing under the same turnpike and pedestrian bridges as the river.

At the far end, the canal goes down the drain and emerges from underneath the factory. You can carry to the right down the railroad track and then straight ahead, bearing right to the Standard Hardware parking area by the river.

A more-desirable carry is under a power line 0.5 mile upstream, where the river is only a short distance down the bank through the bushes.

River Canal Circle Trip   about 6.0 mi

Put in the canal from the parking area behind the high school. There is also a convenient take-out for people coming downstream, better than at Mine Falls. Paddle left upstream toward the dam where a carry can be made, with some effort, over to the river. Continue downstream to where the factory comes into view. There is a culvert on the right (the upstream end of the oxbow shown on the maps). Carry up to the canal and paddle back to the start.

Nissitissit River NH, MA

The Nissitissit River rises in Lake Potanaipo in Brookline, New Hampshire, and flows southeast into the Nashua River in Pepperell, Massachusetts. Although the entire river may be run in high water, the section from Lake Potanaipo to the NH 13 crossing is not recommended.

This is a trout stream with clean water within 50 miles of Boston. Sharp turns, beaver dams may present difficulties.

Brookline, NH ➤ West Hollis, NH   4.75 mi

Description:	Quickwater, Class I
Date checked:	2001
Navigable:	High water
Scenery:	Forested, rural
Map:	USGS Townsend

The first good put-in is behind the fire station in Brookline, New Hampshire. If the water looks too low at this point you may wish to put in at Bohannon's Bridge about 2.0 miles farther downstream. A short distance before that bridge there is a single Class II drop that should be scouted and can be lined or portaged. From Bohannon's Bridge you will be out of sight of civilization for about 2.5 miles, winding through Campbells Meadows and over a dozen or so beaver dams.

After 2.5 miles the river turns right at a house on the bank. Below there is an old mill site with a drop that may be up to a Class II. The mill site is on private property; ask for and obtain permission before crossing property lines. If you cannot run this drop, you should take out on the conservation property upstream and portage by car to the West Hollis bridge 0.5 mile downstream.

West Hollis, NH ➤ Pepperell, MA	3.5 mi
Description:	Quickwater, Class I
Date checked:	2001
Navigable:	High water
Scenery:	Forested
Map:	USGS Pepperell
Portage:	1.25 mi e small dam
	3.5 mi R dam at Pepperell

Some paddlers consider this the most scenic part of the river, with its good current and wooded banks. Much of this land is in the Nissitisset Wildlife Management Area. A small dam at a human-made pond can usually be run. Below the Prescott Street bridge (2.0 miles) there are some shallow rapids and then a long deadwater section above the dam, bordered by several houses. There is a carry of a few hundred feet to MA 111. Take out on the right on private land, but remember to ask for and obtain permission before crossing property lines.

Pepperell, MA ➤ Nashua River, NH   1.0 mi

The rapids below the dam can be run. Most of them are Class II, and they end shortly below the MA 111 bridge. The next bridge, at Mill Street (0.25 mile), is the last access before the

Nashua River, which is an additional 0.75 mile of pleasant quickwater paddling.

From the confluence it is another 4.5 miles to the next bridge on the Nashua River, the NH 111 bridge.

Salmon Brook MA, NH

Salmon Brook is a very small stream that rises in Groton, Massachusetts, and flows northward to enter the Merrimack River in Nashua, New Hampshire. The section above Massapoag Pond is very difficult because of the obstructions and alder swamps. There are no real rapids. The river is of chief interest to swamp- and culvert-lovers.

Massapoag Pond, MA ➤		
Simoneau Plaza (Main Street), NH		6.5 mi
Description:	Flatwater, quickwater	
Date checked:	2001	
Navigable:	Anytime except extreme low water; high water is more difficult	
Scenery:	Forested, rural, settled	
Maps:	USGS Pepperell, Nashua South	
Portages:	Frequent at bridges and culverts—depends on water level	

Below the Massapoag Pond dam lies a lovely swampy pond—Lower Massapoag Pond—which has no development and no dam. The low culvert at MA 113 can be run. The next section is a nice marsh that gradually becomes very narrow; the brook meanders back and forth between high pine banks on both sides.

All the bridges are low, and some are so low that portages are mandatory. Most of the culverts can be run, though. The only bridge that presents a real problem is a stone bridge with a rapid above and parallel to it: take out above the rapid.

The mile above Harris Street is the least desirable and is also more obstructed by alder and meanderings. The last mile is nicer.

The river runs underneath a shopping plaza, so it is necessary to take out above the gate on the west side of Main Street or at the playground farther upstream.

The river is not particularly accessible for paddling for the remainder of its distance to the Merrimack. A stone at a little park near the Alds Street bridge marks where Hannah Duston spent the night on her return (see page 146). The river then flows through a factory to the Merrimack.

The first settlement in Nashua was at the mouth of Salmon Brook, but it was later moved a mile north to the mouth of the Nashua River.

Beaver Brook MA, NH

Beaver Brook is a pleasant, winding stream that flows from Beaver Lake in Derry to the Merrimack River at Lowell. There is a good current for most of the distance, with lots of small beaver dams, some minor rapids, and occasional fairly frequent short carries. The brook flows through several suburban communities, but few of the settled areas are visible from the river.

Derry ➤ West Windham	7.0 mi
Description:	Flatwater, quick water
Date checked:	2000
Navigable:	High water (April); fine in October also
Scenery:	Forested, towns
Maps:	USGS Derry, Windham
Portages:	4.0 mi R dam at Kendall pond 100 yd
	7.0 mi R dam at West Windham 40 yd

The original put-in on NH 28 is not recommended because of numerous dead falls along the river. An alternative put-in is off Gilcrest Road in Londonderry. In less than 1 mile, Beaver Brook enters Kendall Pond (3.5 miles). Gilcrest Road can be reached by taking Exit 4 off I-93 onto NH 102 toward Londonderry, and then taking the first third left. Gilcrest crosses Beaver Brook just before intersecting with Kendall Pond Road.

Put in on the right side of the road, avoiding the No Trespassing signs and a large deadfall about 25 feet in.

A half-mile across the pond is the outlet (4.0 miles), where there are a dam and a bridge. Take out on the right and carry across the road. Beware of snowmobile bridges just past the dam. For the next 3.0 miles the stream winds through meadows where there are logjams and beaver dams. Portage the dam at West Windham (7.0 miles) on the right. The NH 128 Bridge is just below it.

West Windham ➤ Second 128 bridge   3.0 mi

Description:	Quickwater, Class I
Date checked:	2000
Navigable:	High water (March, April, or wet fall)
Scenery:	Forested
Map:	USGS Windham

The river bottom is gravelly, and numerous rocks give practice reading water, but the current is so slow that they present little hazard. Fallen trees in the river present another navigational problem for paddlers in this section. It is 1.75 miles to the NH 111 Bridge, 0.25 more to the next bridge, and then 1.0 mile to the second NH 128 bridge. The usual easy run on Beaver Brook is from Kendall Pond to this point. To continue, take out on the right avoiding the No Trespassing signs, cross NH 128, and return to the brook on the right.

Second NH 128 Bridge ➤ Collinsville   10.0 mi

Description:	Flatwater, quickwater, Class II
Date checked:	2000
Scenery:	Forested towns
Maps:	USGS Windham, Lowell
Portages:	0.75 mi L broken dam
	3.75 mi small dam
	(10.5 mi R dam in Collinsville)

This section of Beaver Brook is more demanding than the sections above; it has a few rapids and two interesting stone-arch bridges.

A house marks a left turn at a broken dam. Although the locks are jagged, it can be run, or it can be lined and portaged on the left. Deal with it as you choose and continue promptly. The second of two closely spaced bridges (Tallant Road) offers good access upstream on the left (1.25 miles). Quickwater follows 1.25 miles to a bridge, now closed, and then for another mile to a small concrete dam (3.75 miles), which can be lifted over on either side or run in the middle.

One half-mile past the second dam a steel-beam bridge (4.25 miles) on NH 111A may have to be carried at high water because of low clearance. It is 0.75 mile to a stone-arch bridge and another 0.5 mile to the bridge on Bridge Street (5.5 miles) opposite the shopping center in Pelham.

From the shopping center it is 0.75 mile to the Willow Street Bridge, and from there the river winds 4.5 miles, mostly through meadowlands.

One mile after the last Pelham bridge there is a working gravel quarry. Shortly after a very small pond, you will encounter a steel-span bridge that is impassible at high water. Unfortunately there is 10-foot chain-link fence on either side. If this bridge is impassable you can turn back and get out at Willow Street.

There are some Class II rapids above the demand bridge at Collinsville. From the steel-span bridge to the demand bridge (10.5 miles) in Dracut, the ride is interesting and gentle. Takeout 200 yards above the dam, on the right, at a launching ramp.

On the other side of the demand bridge, there are year-round Class II and Class III rapids for the first 0.25 mile. After that it meanders quietly through backyards for a couple of miles. Taking out is rarely an option (because of 10-foot fences) until a bridge just before the old farmers dam. Take out here and drive to the put-in in Lowell to finish the trip to the Merrimack.

Spicket River NH, MA

The Spicket River rises in Island Pond in Hampstead and flows south to reach the Merrimack at Lawrence. The upper and lower parts are not practical to paddle, but the middle section offers a more-pleasant quickwater run than might be expected in such a settled area.

Island Pond ➤ Methuen, MA	10.0 mi
Description:	Quickwater
Date checked:	2000
Navigable:	High water (March and April or after rain)
Scenery:	Wooded, settled
Maps:	USGS Ayers Village, Lawrence

The Spicket River, named after the Spiggott Indians of Methuen, rises from Island Pond in Derry and flows through Salem and Methuen before joining the Merrimack in Lawrence. The river actually joins the waters from the North Canal before flowing into the Merrimack. It flows over a total of six dams including the first dam at Island Pond. These dams (plus the Millville Lake dam on the Hitty Titty Brook tributary) originally were built to store and control water flow for the Arlington Mills in Lawrence. The water is not required as it once was and may be reduced at the dams to a trickle during the dry summer months (July and August) and paddling may not be as pleasant (or even possible).

The uppermost section is a very narrow brook and the former site of many water-powered mills. It is not navigable except in very early spring and during the fall drawdown of Island Pond (after Columbus Day weekend). After the river passes under NH 111 and approaches Cow Bell Corners in North Salem (intersection of North Main Street and Haverhill Road), it becomes a fast, narrow brook with several rapids up to Class II. The more-significant problem is the strainers from the trees that easily can cross the river. The river quickly calms down to a meander before backing up behind the Taylor Pond Dam. A short 100 yards after the dam, the river enters Arlington Lake just under North Main Street. A Class II rapid will also show up here when an old, normally submerged dam pops up when Arlington Lake is lowered.

After the Arlington Lake Dam the river pools in a human-made lake dug in the 1970s (just off North Main Street), and then into several miles of pleasant, flatwater-paddleable waters. A significant river cleanup has been going on in recent years through this section. The best put-in is on Town Farm Road (2.0 miles) just after a floodplain area and the confluence of the Hitty Titty Brook (a.k.a. Widow Harris Brook), the most significant tributary. There is parking available, which can be reached from MA 97, to North Main Street (near the Methuen line) for 0.5 miles; turn right onto Town Farm Road.

The river through Salem does not drop enough to have been exploited, and the river is mostly untouched as it meanders past residential and business areas. Very little signs of civilization exist past the bridges. An old bridge abutment (3.0 miles) is still standing just pass the current Main Street bridge.

Continuing downstream, the river occasionally comes up to residential backyards. You pass under Lawrence Road (6.0 miles, reasonable access) and then behind the businesses on NH 28. An official river access has been created behind Home Depot, but parking is limited. A better access is behind the Fun House Pizza and Chili's restaurants (7.0 miles). The best day's paddling will end here.

The river continues under NH 28 and down to Hampshire Road (9.0 miles). There is an access just about on the NH/MA border; you can paddle downstream to an interesting wildlife area and up to the first dam in Methuen (11.0 miles). Access is possible from a factory parking lot on river right, upstream of the dam and the Pelham Street bridge. It is also possible to paddle back upstream. It should be noted that the first 0.5 mile (11.0 to 11.5 miles) is a boring straight canal dug to alter the riverbed when they built I-93. The old riverbed is accessible under the highway, but it is now a dead end. The drainage of this area was permanently affected.

Paddling past this point is not practical as it is a thickly settled urban area and there are three dams. The first dam in Methuen Center is very difficult to get around; the second is a low head dam by the Methuen Music Hall that can create a dangerous hydraulic; and a 15-foot dam in the middle of the Malden Mills complex makes a difficult, dangerous portage.

Little River NH, MA

This stream is runnable from Plaistow, New Hampshire, to within a mile of the Merrimack River in Haverhill, Massachusetts, at which point it runs into a culvert. It is a small, quickwater stream that is runnable only at high water.

Begin the run from Main Street in Plaistow (NH 121A) just east of NH 125. In 0.5 mile the stream passes beneath Westville Road, and within another 0.5 mile beneath two bridges, the second of which is NH 125. It passes under NH 121 (1.5 miles) just above the state line. The stream remains small until it passes underneath I-495 (3.0 miles) and enters the backwater of a dam in Haverhill. Much of this flowage is paralleled by railroad tracks. The best take-out points in Haverhill are: at a playground (5.0 miles) on the right, 150 yards past a railroad bridge; and 0.5 mile above the dam; or at Benjamin and Apple streets, just above the dam. See the USGS Haverhill map.

Powwow River NH, MA

The Powwow River runs from southeastern New Hampshire through Amesbury, Massachusetts, to the Merrimack River. The more-rural parts of the river are home to deer, at least one fisher, and varied bird life, including several great blue herons. The upper river passes through rural fields and woodlands, with a minimum of settlement until it reaches Lake Gardner. Several public open spaces line the banks of the upper Powow above the Lake Gardner dam, including Sargent Farm, Woodsom Farm, Camp Kent, Battis Farm, and Powwow Hill.

The lower section of the Powwow River, below Lake Gardner, historically was a source of power for many industries. It runs through downtown Amesbury, with a spectacular waterfall in the millyard and another waterfall running under Main Street. Below the mills, the river was once navigable by small steamboats. Although much more shallow now, the river is passable by small boats when the tides are right. Amesbury intends to develop a river walk along the Powwow River below Main Street, which will include improved public access for small boats. Public access from Camp Kent is another future possibility.

Tuxbury Pond ➤ Lake Gardner		3.75 mi
Description:	Flatwater	
Date checked:	1998	
Navigable:	Water level between the Tuxbury and Lake Gardner dams has been dropped until repairs are made to the dam. This entire stretch should be passable in high-water times, and the river within 1.5 to 2.0 miles of Tuxbury Dam should be passable all of the time.	
Scenery:	Woodlands, fields, marsh, sparsely settled	
Map:	USGS Newburyport West	
Portages:	Two bridges and a very small dam	

Put in below the Tuxbury Pond outlet dam and the Newton Road bridge. A parking lot is located at Tuxbury Pond on Newton Road. This section is mostly wooded and may have some branch/tree obstructions. In approximately 0.75 mile, you will pass the water-treatment plant on your right. You will then need to portage, on your right, over the next Newton Road bridge. This is an alternate put-in with on-street parking for a few cars. Very shortly (about 0.1 mile) you will come to a very small dam, with an easy portage on the left.

The river now continues without obstruction for approximately 1.5 miles with a very slow rate of flow (it's not unreasonable to paddle both down- and upstream). While wandering past wooded sections of Sargent Farm on a recent trip, we were privileged to see a fawn sunning itself just a few feet from the riverbank. The river next winds past Woodsom Farm, then past wooded banks again with sparse settlement.

The next two bridges are passable, with lovely old colonial homes along the banks. Put-in/take-out is possible on the right side of the first bridge, at West Whitehall and Whitehall

Roads, but parking is very limited. After the second bridge, the water becomes quite shallow in dry periods and may not be passable for a few hundred yards.

Around the next corner, it deepens and widens, as you enter the mouth of Lake Gardner, which extends for the next 1.5 miles. The river turns a sharp right into Lake Gardner, where there is a small, sandy beach on the left. The beach is part of Camp Kent, which, although it does not have restroom facilities, is worth a stop.

After stretching your legs, continue down the length of Lake Gardner, which is settled on your right but bordered by Battis Farm and wooded Powwow Hill on your left. Powwow Hill is the highest point in Essex County, with an elevation of 332 feet. Take out either at Battis Farm, which has rather steep banks and a bit of a walk to the parking lot, or, if the gates are unlocked, at the town beach next to the Lake Gardner dam. At low tide, if the town beach on Lake Gardner is unlocked, you may be able to park here. There is limited public access and multiple obstructions, including a dam (which is listed on the National Register of Historical Places). Some parking is available, although the banks are steep. At low tide it may not be passable for several hundred yards. The river continues from this point on without obstruction. Historic mill buildings soon give way to woods and marsh. Great blue herons frequent this section of the river. Just before the bridges there is a sharp right turn. On the left of this turn there is a small inlet into a tidal sanctuary where wild rice grows. When the tides are high enough, it's a worthwhile detour.

Chapter Six
Piscataqua Watershed

PISCATAQUA
WATERSHED

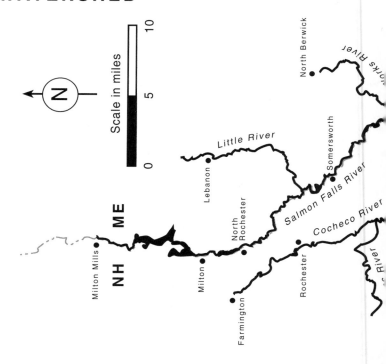

Scale in miles

0   5   10

N

Little River

North Berwick

orks River

Lebanon

Somersworth

Salmon Falls River

North
Rochester

Cocheco River

ME

NH

Milton Mills

Milton

Rochester

River

Farmington

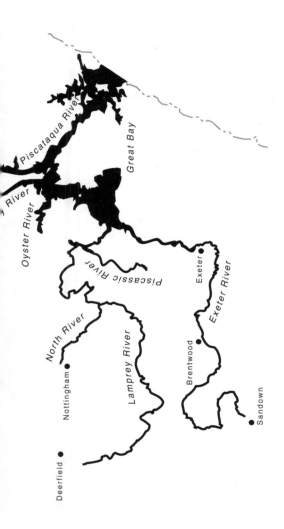

The Piscataqua Watershed is bypassed by many paddlers on their way north. The rivers generally are small, and since they do not rise from snowy heights as the Saco does to the north, they have a short runoff. During a peak of three weeks, however, they offer quickwater and Class I–II rapids in channels that are narrower and more intimate than those familiar to most paddlers.

The North and Little rivers offer by far the best Class II water in the spring, although portions of other rivers have shorter stretches of rapids worth exploring. The Cocheco from Farmington to Rochester and the last 5.0 miles on the Exeter to Fremont are the best of many quickwater stretches.

Summer paddling is quite limited. Portions of the Exeter, Lamprey, Salmon Falls, and Great Works rivers offer flatwater except in dry summers, but the tidewater portions of the Exeter and Salmon Falls, as well as the nearby York River in Maine, are always runnable.

The Piscataqua River itself is a tidal estuary, formed by the confluence of the Cocheco and Salmon Falls rivers, which continues the line dividing Maine and New Hampshire that the Salmon Falls River previously marked. It drains both these rivers and several others that flow into Great Bay. The upper part is wide, with moderate current. Below Dover Point, where Great Bay empties into the river, it is marked by one of the strongest tides on the eastern seaboard.

Cocheco River NH

The Cocheco River rises above Farmington, becoming runnable there as several smaller branches join forces. It is a pleasant paddle to Rochester.

Its course through Rochester to tidewater at Dover is marked by dams, waterfalls, and dangerous gorges. Therefore the lower section is not recommended.

Farmington ➤ Rochester	10.5 mi
Description:	Flatwater, quickwater, Class I
Date checked:	2001
Navigable:	High water (later March to early May)
Scenery:	Rural, urban
Maps:	USGS Alton 15, Berwick 15
Portage:	1.5 mi culverts 50 yd

Put in at the NH 153 bridge 0.5 mile south of the center of Farmington. Soon the river begins twisting and turning, with a moderate current. Watch out for fallen trees and overhanging bushes in this area. In 1.5 miles the river disappears into a pair of culverts. **Caution!** If the river is high, these culverts may be entirely underwater and hazardous because they create a strong suction. Take out with care and portage.

The next 5.0 miles are ideal for the beginning whitewater paddler, as they offer many sharp turns with a moderate current, plus a number of riffles and Class I rapids. The current slows down near a bridge (6.5 miles) connecting Chestnut Hill Road with NH 11. This is the recommended take-out, on the east side of the river (parking is available).

The remaining 4.0 miles are through an urban section of Rochester, and most are in the backwater of the first dam. If you are continuing through, be careful to take out at or above the NH 11/US 202 bridge (10.5 miles) because there is a dangerous waterfall 40 yards beyond this bridge.

Exeter River NH

The Exeter River was known in early times as the Squamscott River and is still so named on its lower, tidal section. It rises in Chester and flows 34.0 miles before reaching tidewater at Exeter, a trip the proverbial crow would make in only 15.0 miles. Because the river doubles back on itself so much, it does not pick up many feeder streams, so it remains narrow for its entire length.

Chester ➤ Sandown   4.0 mi

This section is no longer navigable. The river is a very small stream that has brush and trees all along the bank. When the water is high enough to run, it flows through the brush, creating dangerous strainers.

Sandown ➤ Fremont   12.5 mi
Description: Flatwater, quickwater, Class I
Date checked: 2000
Navigable: High water (late March to late April)

Scenery:	Rural
Maps:	USGS Haverhill 15, Mount Pawtuckaway 15
Portages:	1.0 mi e gorge at mill site
	1.25 mi e dam
	1.75 mi e mill site
	(12.25 mi R Fremont Dam 10 yd)

Much of the first 7.0 miles below Sandown is through marshes where perseverance, a map, and a compass all are helpful. There are also a few snowmobile bridges that may have to be lifted over.

The last 5.0 miles to Fremont are the finest on the river for scenery as well as being hazard-free, and constitute probably the best quickwater in the Piscataqua Watershed.

From Sandown, where the put-in is on NH 121A just north of town, the river flows gently for 0.25 mile to Lily Pond, which is 0.25 mile long and easier to paddle than the name implies. There is no dam at the outlet.

Below Lily Pond there are Class I rapids for 0.5 mile to an old mill site (1.0 mile) and a gorge that is unrunnable. The gorge can be inspected in advance from the bridge just below.

After another 0.25 mile a small backwater above a dam can be portaged on either side. Shortly below there is another gorge at an old mill site that has some interesting stonework remaining. There is another bridge just beyond.

Below the second bridge (1.75 miles) the river enters a large swamp where the route is difficult in low water. The old railroad grade is used as a snowmobile trail, and the river is spanned at the crossings by sagging bridges. In the next 3.0 miles it flows under two more road bridges, followed by 3.0 miles more of brushy meadow.

After passing under the seventh bridge (7.5 miles), the river becomes narrow and quick. There is some brush to be avoided and an occasional tree across the stream, but from here past 3 more bridges there are no impassable or dangerous sections all the way to the bridge at the center of Fremont.

Fremont ➤ Brentwood	5.5 mi
Description:	Flatwater, quickwater, Class II
Date checked:	2000
Navigable:	High water (late March to early May)
	Medium water (moderate summer rain fall)
Scenery:	Forested, towns
Map:	USGS Haverhill 15
Portage:	1.0 mi R second dam in Fremont 20 yd
	4.5 mi R West Brentwood Dam 20 yd
	(5.5 mi L waterfall 150 yd)

There are mile-long millponds on both ends of this run. The connecting 2.5 miles of quickwater are passable frequently during the summer. There may be trees down that have to be lifted over. The Class II rapids, all between the West Brentwood dam and NH 125, are short but exciting in high water.

From the bridge next to the general store in Fremont, the river gradually loses current until it becomes a millpond that extends for mile to a dam. Portage on the right. The next 2.5 miles are quickwater, with one short swampy section. There has been recent beaver activity, so a few lifts may be required. Just below a campground on the right bank there is a crude rock dam that is runnable in high water.

The last mile to West Brentwood is backwater from the dam (4.5 miles) with many cottages on both banks. **Caution!** The dam is about 0.25 mile after the NH 107 bridge. The dam is marked by a factory on the left. Take out on the grassy embankment on the right shore and walk along the road 100 yards to the bridge. Put in on the right at the bridge. This can be difficult at high water. Proceed 50 yards below the bridge to put in at a 50-yard Class II rapid. After a brief pause there is a second Class II rapid, also about 50 yards long.

Caution! Take out on the left above the NH 125 bridge: a Class III rapid begins directly under the bridge and leads immediately to a 10-foot waterfall under a second bridge 200 yards downstream.

Brentwood ➤ Exeter	12.0 mi
Description:	Flatwater, quickwater, Class I–II
Date checked:	2000
Navigable:	High water (late march to early May)
	Medium water (moderate summer rain fall)
Scenery:	Forested, settled
Maps:	USGS Haverill 15, Exeter
Portages:	5.0 mi R Pickpocket Dam—cross bridge put in L 50 yd

The backwater from Pickpocket Dam dominates the middle of this section, both by slowing the flow of water and by making the course far from obvious. Above this, however, there are 2.0 miles of pleasant quickwater through dense second-growth forest, and below the dam are several challenging Class II rapids that are runnable in high water.

Put in at least 50 yards below the waterfall after the NH 125 bridge. Easiest access is from the left bank past the general store. The first 100 yards are Class II, followed by quickwater and occasional Class I rapids to a bridge 2.0 miles below. Most of the next 3.0 miles are in the backwater behind Pickpocket Dam (5.0 miles). The course is hard to follow here. **Caution!** Portage the dam on the left side and carry all the way past the bridge below it. Put in near the bridge below.

The first 150 yards past Pickpocket Dam are Class II rapids, which can be run in fairly high water. Then there are intermittent Class I and Class II rapids to the NH 111 bridge (6.0 miles) a mile below the dam. A quarter-mile downstream, around a blind right turn, is a 75-yard Class II rapid that is especially difficult in high water.

The remaining 6.0 miles to Exeter have little current. The river passes under a railroad bridge 1.0 mile below NH 111, a back road bridge another mile farther, and the NH 108 bridge 0.75 mile beyond that. There are several blowdowns and beaver dams in this area, so be ready to climb over obstacles. The final 3.0 miles to Exeter involve sharp meandering and confusing junctions with side channels. Careful observation of the current by watching subsurface plants will get you through.

Caution! There is a 10-foot dam just below the first bridge in Exeter with no adequate access near it. Do not attempt to go under the bridge at high water; the banks are walled below the bridge, and takeout is impossible. There are two options: take out on the right bank anywhere from 5 to 50 yards above the bridge—depending on private property access, or take out 0.5 mile above the bridge at a public park on the left, adjacent to Phillips Exeter Academy playing fields. Remember to ask for and obtain permission if you do intend to cross private property lines.

One quarter-mile from the bridge, across Main Street, through the park, and by the library, the river is called the Squamscott, and it is tidal. With proper attention to the tide tables, a pleasant 5-mile paddle on an outgoing tide brings you to the N. H. Fish and Game boat access just after the NH 108 bridge on the right. Another 2.0 miles takes you to the head of Great Bay, which is marked by a deserted railroad trestle spanning the river.

Great Works River ME

This unassuming little river claims the distinction of having the first water-powered mill in the United States, in the section of South Berwick, Maine, called Great Works. Mills existed there for over three hundred years, until the 1940s, when the remaining few fell into disuse.

North Berwick ➤ South Berwick	11.5 mi
Description:	Flatwater, quickwater, Class I
Date checked:	2001
Navigable:	High water (late March to mid-May)
	Passable at most water levels for last 3.5 mi
Scenery:	Forested
Maps:	USGS Kennebunk 15, York 15, Dover 15

The first 5.0 miles to Emerys Bridge on Hooper Sands Road are narrow and winding, and the river shallows out early in the season. The next 3.0 miles to Junction Bridge, at the west end of Emerys Bridge Road, hold water a little longer. Both sections are prone to blowdowns.

The final 3.5-mile section from Junction Bridge to the village of Great Works is runnable except in very dry summers, and it is entirely flatwater. Take out at the Brattle Street bridge (11.5 miles), 0.25 mile below the ME 236 bridge.

Caution! Below the Brattle Street bridge there is a series of falls and rapids called Rocky Gorge. Stay well above it. Continuing to the Salmon Falls River, into which the Great Works River flows, is not feasible because Rocky Gorge requires a mile-long portage.

There is a dam on the Great Works River at the confluence with the Salmon Falls River.

Isinglass River NH

The Isinglass River flows from Bow Lake in Strafford to the Cocheco River in Rochester. At one time it provided water power for several mills in Barrington, but all that remains today is the small dam above the US 202 bridge. The banks are mostly wooded, and there are only a few houses within sight of the river. The river itself is quite clean, and there is an attractive waterfall near the end.

The first 2.0 miles can be paddled only in very high water. Check the old mill sluice above the US 202 bridge which can be seen from the bridge or reached by a short trail starting from the southwest corner of the bridge. If there is enough water here, the rapids above, which are considerably easier, will be runnable. Very high water in the river downstream tends to make Class I rapids easier and Class II rapids harder.

NH 126 ➤ Cocheco River	10.5 mi
Description:	Flatwater, quickwater, Class I–II
Date checked:	2000
Navigable:	High water (late March through April)

Scenery:	Forested, rural
Maps:	USGS Mount Pawtuckaway 15, Dover West, Berwick 15
Portage:	8.0 mi R waterfall 125 yd

There is good current for about 1.5 miles below the NH 126 bridge in Barrington. Then there are three short, easy Class II pitches as the river parallels US 202. Stay to the left of the island. Just above the US 202 bridge there is a quiet pool behind an old dam. **Caution!** The sluiceway is runnable, but it must be scouted, because there are some sharp boulders to avoid. When the water is very high, there are powerful currents that make it difficult to control a boat in the narrow channel.

The river below the US 202 bridges (2.0 miles) is mostly quickwater, with a few Class II rapids, for 2.5 miles to a small iron bridge beside a house on the right. In this section there are two pairs of bridge abutments that predate the Revolutionary War. Past the bridge the river is sluggish for 0.5 mile, below which there is another 0.5 mile of Class I and II whitewater. Halfway down the rapids at a sharp right turn, there is a Class II+ ledge—passable on the left—which stretches almost all the way down the river. The rapids end 50 yards below the Berrys Hill bridge (5.5 miles). The remaining 2.0 miles to NH 125 contain flatwater.

Below the NH 125 bridge (7.5 miles) there is a 0.5-mile slack current to a 25-foot waterfall. **Caution!** At a stone abutment on the right 20 yards above the first sign of rapids, take-out on the right and carry 125 yards along an old road. This is a good picnic and rest spot, because the falls shoot out between massive rocks and make an impressive sight. The next 0.25 mile is Class II–III—difficult in very high water, scratchy in moderately high water, and impassable in anything else. The rapids end with an S-turn between high banks, followed by a rock garden that is likely to add a few scratches to your boat. The next 1.5 miles to the Rochester Neck Road bridge are a pleasant quickwater run over a sandy bottom; catfish are often visible here.

One half-mile below the Rochester Neck Road bridge (10.0 miles), the Isinglass empties into the Cocheco River. It is 1.25 miles down the Cocheco to the next crossing, a bridge on County Farm Road (11.75 miles). This section is all flatwater except for the last 100 yards, where there is an easy Class II rapid.

Lamprey River NH

The Lamprey is one of the longest rivers in the Piscataqua Watershed, and it is probably the flattest. The section above Raymond offers Class I rapids for spring paddlers. Below town the river can be run for most of the year because there are few rapids. Packers Fall, Class II or III, depending on the water level, is runnable well into the summer by kayaks and canoes.

Deerfield ➤ Raymond	9.0 mi
Description:	Flatwater, quickwater, Class I–II
Date checked:	2000
Navigable:	High water (late March to early May)
Scenery:	Forested, settled
Map:	USGS Mount Pawtuckaway 15

Three-quarters of a mile above Raymond, a tributary named Cider Ferry enters on the right, flowing from Onway Lake. The name came from a barrel of cider that slipped and burst as it was being taken over the stream by some early settlers before there was a bridge.

Put in 2.0 miles south of Deerfield Center at the junction of NH 143 and 107. The Lamprey at this point is a narrow trout stream, with Class I–II rapids, shallow riffles, and quickwater. Beavers have made a strong resurgence on this part of the river, and you will surely encounter several of their dams. One and a half miles below, before the first bridge, are two ledges. The first is runnable on the left in very high water; the second must be lined or carried. From the first bridge to NH 27 is 2.5 miles, largely quickwater with a few Class I rapids, including a 100-yard stretch that ends right of NH 27.

From the NH 27 bridge (4.0 miles) the next 1.5 miles are flat and wide: follow a straight course here. Then there are more

Class I rapids in the next mile to the Langsford Road bridge (6.5 miles), with a Class II–III ledge just below. The rapids end in another 0.25 mile, and the final 2.25 miles to Raymond (8.0 miles) and the side-road bridge east of town are once again flat and wide. Take out at this bridge, since there is a gorge in the next mile.

Raymond ➤ NH 102/107 bridge   1.0 mi

Most of this distance is flatwater or quickwater. The gorge is within sight upstream from the bridge. It can be lined in low water, but it is difficult to portage.

NH 102/107 bridge ➤ West Epping   3.5 mi

Description:	Flatwater, quickwater, Class I
Date checked:	2000
Navigable:	Medium water
Scenery:	Forested, settled
Map:	USGS Mount Pawtuckaway 15
Portage:	(3.5 mi L dam)

Put in either at the bridge or, if the 50 yards of Class II rapids are too low, into Dead Pond. The pond is a pleasant paddle for 1.0 mile past some cottages. Then the river narrows again and drops over some easy rapids past a small bridge (1.25 miles) where there is an easy put-in but not much room for parking. This bridge is 1.0 mile down Prescott Road, which goes east off of NH 107. After another 0.75 mile of easy riffles, impassable at low water, the river passes the NH 101 bridge and then continues for a couple of miles to the backwater of the dam, which is below the next bridge.

West Epping ➤ Wadley Falls   12.0 mi

Description:	Quickwater, Class II
Date checked:	2000
Navigable:	High to medium water (spring)
Scenery:	Forested, town
Map:	USGS Mount Pawtuckaway 15
Portage:	(12.0 mi R dam at Wadley Falls)

Below the dam in West Epping is a short pool easily accessed from a portage along the right bank. Take out on right bank after passing under bridge, and follow road to park area. Class II ledges begin under the next bridge and continue for 0.5 mile, gradually becoming easier. The river passes a few rock dams, and the final ledge is underneath the first bridge in Epping (3.5 miles). All three bridges in Epping offer easy access and parking.

Below Epping (4.0 miles) the river meanders for 3.0 miles to the NH 87 bridge. After the bridge a long, smooth stretch twists, with numerous logjams, through old pastures and woods for another 5.0 miles past the mouth of the North River (10.75 miles) to the Wadley Falls dam (12.0 miles).

Wadley Falls ➤ Newmarket	10.5 mi
Description:	Flatwater, quickwater, Class I, III
Date checked:	2000
Navigable:	High water (late March to early May)
	Medium water (average summer rain fall)
Scenery:	Forested
Maps:	USGS Mount Pawtuckaway 15, Dover 15
Portage:	7.25 mi L Wiswall Falls Dam 50 yd

For a quiet retreat into the woods, the first 4.0 miles are superb. Paddlers continuing below the bridge on Lee Hook Road may have a scratchy time in moderately high water because the rapid starting under the bridge, and another shorter one a mile farther, need rather high water to run well.

One feature of the lower stretch is Packers Falls, which are not actually falls but rather one of the most challenging rapids in the Piscataqua Watershed. It is a roaring Class III run in early spring and is often well run into summer as a Class II drop. There are well-developed portage trails for those who want to run Packers Falls several times.

Below the dam at Wadley Falls there is a brief rapid, then 4.0 miles of quiet paddling past densely forested banks of hemlock and hardwoods to the Lee Hook Road bridge. Below the bridge are 200 yards of easy Class II rapids with large combers in high water. At the end of the rapid, there is a broken dam that cuts diagonally across the river; it can be run easily by following the current rather than the shore. A combination camp and trailer park extends for the next mile along the left bank to a short rapid on either side of an island (5.0 miles).

It is another 2.25 miles to the Wiswall Road bridge and Wiswall Falls Dam (7.25 miles). Below the dam there is a 200-yard Class II rapid, which, if unrunnable, can be carried on the left. Another 0.75 mile brings you to Packers Falls (8.0 miles).

Caution! Take out on the left at least 20 yards above the bridge and scout Packers Falls. This run is a difficult Class III in high water, and a moderate Class II, with some scratching at the bottom, in medium water. There are two more short Class II rapids just below Packers Falls, then 2.5 miles of flatwater to Newmarket, where the route through the flowage may be obscure. The Piscassic River (9.75 miles) enters on the right just above the dam (10.5 miles).

Little River ME

The paddling season is short but exciting on the Little River. Paddle it early in the morning or on an overcast day because it heads into the afternoon sun for most of its length.

Lebanon ➤ Salmon Falls River	11.25 mi
Description:	Flatwater, quickwater, Class I–II
Date checked:	2001
Navigable:	High water (late March to early May)
Scenery:	Forested
Map:	USGS Berwick 15

The usual put-in is below the broken dam beside an old mill in Lebanon. In high water the river can be run above the mill, either from Fall Road (1.0 mile upriver) or from ME 11/US 202 (3 miles above the mill). Determined explorers occasionally start even higher. The river above the mill is quite narrow, with Class I and II rapids.

From the mill there are two rapids, with one at a broken dam, in the first mile. In the next 1.0 mile, from the Lord Road bridge to the bridge on Little River Road, the river is smooth and winding. The next 4.25 miles to Stackpole Bridge pass through an area known as the Marshes, where the river maintains a good current around numerous tight turns and twists. Occasional breakthroughs create some confusion, but careful observation of the current will guide you through easily.

Whitewater enthusiasts frequently begin at Stackpole Bridge (6.25 miles), under which there is a small drop over a ledge. The next 2.0 miles are smooth and slow until the river reaches a small Class I rapid, followed soon after by 0.25 mile of Class I rapids up to Messenger Bridge, where Pine Hill Road and Little River Road meet.

Below Messenger Bridge (8.5 miles) there is another Class I rapid, then an easy Class II rapid. The river is narrow enough that you must pick either the right or left side, since there is no room for a middle route, and the only clear passage involves occasionally switching from a course down one side to a course down the other. Stop and scout frequently unless you like piling up onto ledges and into impassable rock gardens. One particularly interesting spot has a car-sized boulder perched on top of a ledge left of center; the usually runnable channels lead you within an arm's length of it.

The long rapid ends with a small ledge in a sharp right turn. The last 0.5 mile of this rapid, down a back-road bridge (9.5 miles), is very scratchy when the rapids above are marginally runnable. Flatwater follows. A half-mile above the Hubbard Road bridge (11.25 miles) there is a broken dam at the end of a sharp S-turn that can be run with caution or lined from the right bank.

The Little River empties into the Salmon Falls River (11.25 miles) just below the Hubbard Road bridge. Somersworth is 5.0 miles downstream (16.25 miles).

North River NH

The North River is a short tributary of the Lamprey River above Wadley Falls. Its paddling season is brief, but it definitely offers the best whitewater run in the Piscataqua Watershed, a 2.5-mile continuous Class II run above NH 152.

There is a lot of beaver activity, so be aware of downed trees on all sections of the river.

In very high water it can be run from the back-road bridge near the outlet to Pawtuckaway Pond or from NH 152 at a point 2.5 miles north of Nottingham. Both of these branches are somewhat overgrown but runnable, and both have quickwater and Class I rapids. The usual put-in is by the school in Nottingham.

Nottingham ➤ Wadley Falls	8.75 mi
Description:	Flatwater, quickwater, Class II
Date checked:	2001
Navigable:	High water (late March to early April)
Scenery:	Forested
Map:	USGS Epping 7.5
Portage:	4.0 mi R NH 152 bridge 30 yd

The first 1.5 miles are flat, with a fair current. About 100 yards above the Merellis Road bridge, Class II rapids begin. The most difficult rapid is 80 yards below the bridge. It is Class II–III and must be taken in the center. Class II rapids continue with only brief pauses for 2.5 miles to Harvey's Shingle Mill (long since abandoned) at the next bridge, NH 152.

Caution! Take out in the eddy on the right just above the NH 152 bridge (4.0 miles), because there is a Class IV rapid below the shingle mill. The drop has a rusted turbine in the middle of the drop. Put in on the left below the mill. The mile to Birch Hill Road bridge is swift-running, with Class I rapids. Beaver activity may create seasonal logjams on this section that may require lifting or portaging. Along this stretch there are some incredible stands of sycamore, which are uncommon in New Hampshire. In the next 1.5 miles to the NH 125 bridge (6.5 miles), the river flows with a moderate current past a stand of maple trees on the left. Take out at the bridge.

Below NH 125 there is 1.0 mile of flatwater to the Lamprey River (7.5 miles), with another 1.25 miles down that stream to the dam at Wadley Falls (8.75 miles).

Piscassic River NH

The Piscassic River is a large brook that flows eastward from Fremont and Epping to the Lamprey River just above Newmarket. The section above NH 87 is extremely difficult and is not recommended unless you enjoy hacking your way through thick alder and vine tangles. Below NH 87 the river is more open, and it has many narrow, tight turns in quickwater. There may be a number of downed trees.

Newfields ➤ Newmarket	5.75 mi
Description:	Flatwater, quickwater, Class I–II
Date checked:	2001
Navigable:	High water only (late March to mid-April)
Scenery:	Rural
Map:	USGS Dover 15
Portage:	0.25 mi R rapids 100 yds
	4.0 mi R rapids 100 yards
	5.0 mi L rapids 40 yds

Put in at the NH 87 bridge. Just below is an old mill site with some steep, narrow Class II rapids, which can be run solo or carried 100 yards on the right. In 0.5 miles you pass an old railroad bridge, and in another 1.5 miles a bridge (2.0 miles) on a back road. The river is swift and meandering here, with downed trees and bushes.

In the next mile there is good farm scenery, but beware of old wire fences across the river. This brings you to the bridge southeast of Four Corners. In 0.25 mile, there is another bridge (4.0 miles) where there is a Class II rapid that is sometimes runnable, even at reasonable water levels. In 1.0 mile there is another sharp Class II drop that cannot be seen ahead of time—it should be carried 40 yards on the left. The rapids should be portaged, as you will not want to risk a swim in rapids where barbed wire may run across the river. Shortly after that, the river reaches the NH 152 bridge. From there 0.75 mile remains to the high dam (5.75 miles) just west of Newmarket.

If you continue, it is 0.75 mile farther to the Lamprey River and another 0.75 mile to the dam at Lamprey River Falls (7.25 miles) in Newmarket.

Salmon Falls River ME, NH

The river flows south from Great East Lake and forms part of the boundary between Maine and New Hampshire.

Three sections of the river are not recommended. Above Milton Mills it is a very small stream with shallow rapids that are seldom deep enough to run. It is also a thick alder swamp where the channel is difficult to follow and frequently blocked by debris. Portions of the river immediately below Milton and from Berwick/Somersworth to South Berwick also are not recommended because of unrunnable rapids and dams.

Milton Mills, ME ➤ Milton, ME	9.0 mi
Description:	Lakes, flatwater, Class II
Date checked:	2001
Navigable:	High water (early spring)
Scenery:	Forested, settled
Maps:	USGS Newfield 15, Berwick 15
Portages:	1.0 mi L second dam in Milton Falls
	1.25 mi L third dam in Milton Falls

Below the first dam just north of town, bear right for almost 0.5 mile. The rapids, when runnable, are nearly continuous and very heavy. In 0.5 mile there is an old mill site with abutments and then a short stretch of rapids before a second mill site. Both should be lined, lifted over, or carried. The last 0.25 mile is mostly backwater behind the second dam (1.0 mile). Take out on the left immediately below the bridge. After this dam there is a short Class II rapid, then flatwater to the third dam. Land on the left well above the bridge.

A boat can be put in just below the third dam (1.25 miles). Paddle under the bridge and parts of the mill buildings. The first 0.25 mile is an alder tangle, but paddling improves as you proceed downstream. The river meanders extensively, and it is still somewhat impeded by fallen trees.

The river enters the extreme northern end of Northeast Pond (4.75 miles), from which it is 2.5 miles to the bridge (7.25 miles) between Northeast Pond and Townhouse Pond, and an additional 0.75 mile to the southeastern end where there is a good take-out. From the bridge it is 1.75 miles to the dam at Milton (9.0 miles).

North Rochester, ME ➤ Somersworth, NH	14.5 mi
Description:	Flatwater, quickwater, Class I–II
Date checked:	2001
Navigable:	High water (late March to early May)
	Passable at all water levels, below
	Little River
Scenery:	Rural, towns
Map:	USGS Berwick 15
Portages:	4.5 mi R East Rochester Dam 100 yd
	11.5 mi dam

The heavy use of the river for water power in the nineteenth century is evident by the dams (and factory buildings above the put-in) below the take-out and halfway down when the river passes through East Rochester. Quickwater enthusiasts will find a pleasant paddle above East Rochester but must be prepared to run over 50 yards of Class II rapids entering town. The next 2.0 miles to Step Falls, like the first 4.5 miles, are good only in high water. In contrast, the remaining 8.0 miles are flat and runnable all summer.

Put in behind the Spaulding plant just off NH 16. If your boat makes it over the first riffles 10 yards below the put-in bridge, you will have easy going all the way to East Rochester, even though the river seems shallow.

The river meanders through sandy areas of marginal farms and suburban sprawl, but it has a beauty of its own. The rapids are small and minor until you reach East Rochester, where a Class II rapid begins 40 yards above an abandoned iron bridge. The most difficult section is directly beneath the bridge, and it should be scouted. The US 202 bridge is immediately below this rapid. **Caution!** There is a 10-foot dam 100 yards below the bridge. Portage on the right.

Below the dam in East Rochester (4.5 miles), there are heavy Class II rapids for 75 yards, then primarily quickwater until Step Falls (6.5 miles), which is a series of ledges that are runnable under proper conditions. Below this point the river is almost without current for the remaining 8.0 miles to Berwick/Somersworth.

Five miles from East Rochester, the Little River enters on the left (9.5 miles). A bridge on Hubbard Road 400 yards up this stream offers access to the Salmon Falls River and is useful for summer paddling.

Two miles past the Little River there is an 8-foot dam. You can take out here, at the Rochester Street bridge (13.0 miles), or a Parson's Park (14.5 miles), 0.5 mile above the center of Berwick/Somersworth. **Caution!** There is no adequate take-out in town, and there is a dam 10 yards below the bridge connecting the twin towns of Berwick and Somersworth.

Somersworth, NH ➤ South Berwick, ME   5.25 mi

The next 5.25 miles are not recommended. First, there is the dam 0.5 mile below the last take-out suggested. Then there is a .075-mile section of the river behind the General Electric plant in Somersworth which contains unrunnable rapids and dams. Determined paddlers can put in below this obstacle, but they will have a 100-yard portage within the first mile. Below, the river is pleasant for 3.0 miles to Salmon Falls (19.75 miles), a 15-foot drop just above a railroad bridge.

Another portage is necessary here, because there are 150 yards of unrunnable rapids below Salmon Falls. Finally, there is 0.5 mile of flatwater to the ME/NH 4 bridge (21.25 miles), immediately below which there is a 10-foot dam.

Tidewater Paddling

An exception to the rule that water always flows downhill is found in the tidewater portion of coastal rivers. Tide introduces an entirely different dimension into canoeing.

The Atlantic Ocean has water even when all the interior rivers are dry and provides it to the lower parts of rivers in the

Piscataqua Watershed on an inflexible but precisely calculated schedule. Since the tide reverses every six and a quarter hours or so, return trips traveling with the tide both ways are possible, so there is no need to spot cars.

On the negative side, the tide must always be taken into account when you plan trips. The tide's rise and fall leaves a soft, slippery deposit of mud on the shores below the level of high tide, so landing anywhere, even at a prepared launching ramp, is difficult. Because sewage from towns upstream ends up in the harbor, the water is not clean enough for enjoyable swimming, which detracts from summer trips.

Tidewater paddlers should know something about the "the rules of the road" for navigation and about the markings on buoy. Although hand-driven craft may have the right of way, arguing the point is unprofitable. At low tide much of the upper tidal area is shallow, even for a canoe, so you may wish to follow the channel. The canoe's shallow draft gives it an advantage, so it is courteous to stick to the side of the channel, in file astern, and leave the center for deeper-draft boats.

The rivers of the coastal plain are the only ones in New Hampshire that reach the ocean within the state boundary. All the drops on the rivers that flow into Great Bay were once harnessed for power, so the head of tidewater is at a dam in all cases. The upper tidal portions seem little different from the nontidal portions, except for a different kind of grass, a preponderance of oaks and pines, and the exposed flats at low tide. Although there are some developed areas and motorboats, much of the shore is still wooded and looks as it did centuries ago, except that the trees are now smaller.

Descriptions for the following rivers start from the dam at head of tidewater. The approximate tide correction that should be added to the Portsmouth tide time is given for this point from both high and low tide. Note that the time the tidal current reverses does not necessarily correspond to the time of high or low tide. At Dover Point, for instance, the current will still be running in well past the time of high tide.

The river descriptions are arranged clockwise, starting at the southwest.

Maps

All of these rivers are on the USGS Dover 15-minute quadrangle except for the upper part of the Swamscott River, which is on the Exeter quadrangle, and the lower part of the Piscataqua, which is on the York, Maine, quadrangle. Also consider using navigation maps.

Tide Information

Tide charts for the whole eastern seaboard are computed and printed months in advance; copies may be available in libraries, where you would look under "Tides." Local tables covering a short period are often available free from marinas and banks. Daily tide information is published in local newspapers and broadcast on some radio and television station.

Exeter/Squamscott River NH

Exeter ➤ Great Bay   6.5 mi
Tide correction: +2 hr

The Exeter River changes its name to the Squamscott River when it passes the last cascade in Exeter and becomes tidal. Put in from a road on the left bank 0.5 mile downstream of the second bridge in Exeter. The shores are high marsh grass and almost entirely undeveloped. The "Oxbow" is an island of grass marked by a clump of trees. It can be rounded only at fairly high tide, which flows in from both directions. A marina is downstream from the last bridge.

When approaching the Squamscott River from Great Bay, you can recognize the railroad bridge at the mouth all the way from Adams Point. The dark wood of the two spans of bridge pilings makes a checkerboard against the island and the white-rock fill of the causeways at each end.

Lamprey River NH

Newmarket ➤ Great Bay   1.5 mi
Tide correction: +1.75 hr

A state boat-launching ramp is located on the right bank in Newmarket. The Lamprey has the shortest tidal section of any of the big rivers, coming in near the Squamscott River at the southwest end of Great Bay.

Oyster River NH

Durham ➤ Great Bay   2.75 mi
Tide correction: +1.25 hr

Put in from the left bank in Durham, downstream from the NH 108 bridge. Many boats are anchored nearby. At low tide even a canoe or kayak will need to follow the channel, which meanders back and forth across the mud flats and is marked by poles with yellow flags. Take out at Durham Point on the right at the mouth.

Bellamy River NH

Sawyer Mill ➤ Little Bay   4 mi
Tide correction: +1.25 hr

To put in on the Bellamy River, drive through the Sawyer's Mill parking area off NH 108. Bear left around the mill building, and continue past the old mill houses to a second mill and dam 0.5 mile downstream. Put in below the second dam from the left bank. The river is very small. Low tide exposes a short rapid. One mile downstream, a road on the left bank leads down to some houses. Near the mouth on the right bank is the Bellamy River Wildlife Management Area. Take out at the US 4 bridge.

Great Bay NH

Tide correction: +1.25 hr

Great Bay, a 3-by-6-mile triangular body of water, has many of the characteristics of a shallow lake of the same size, with the added complication of the tide. A navigable channel snakes back and forth like a river meandering across a floodplain. Your paddle will often touch bottom, even in the center. The prevailing wind is from the southwest, and when a heavy wind opposes the tide, the water is rough and makes for a challenging paddle.

Dover Point NH

Tide correction: +1.5 hr

Dover Point, central to the tidewater of the area, is a neck of land extending southward between the Piscataqua River and Little Bay, which leads from Great Bay. The point is traversed by US 4, which crosses to the south shore on a pair of high bridges. Hilton Park, on the tip, is accessible from both lanes. It has rest rooms (open only in summer). A picnic area with fireplaces, on the west side, and a launching ramp with parking, on the east side, are connected by an underpass. This park is a good starting point, lunch spot, or end point for these tidewater trips.

From the Dover Point launching ramp, to the left (north) is "upstream" on the Piscataqua River, which is formed by the confluence of the Cocheco and Salmon Falls rivers 4.0 miles above. To the right (southeast) the Piscataqua flows to the Atlantic Ocean, 8.0 miles away. The channel underneath the bridges leads west to Little Bay and from there to Great Bay.

Underneath the bridges, the three northernmost spans are blocked by rocks at low tide. The tidal current flows at up to 8 knots, with considerable turbulence and eddies at most stages, and is strongest at half-tide. Canoes and kayaks will find it necessary to pass this point with the tide. Ahead is Little Bay, with Goat Island in the center. Go right, under the low US 4 bridge, to reach the Bellamy River; bear left for Great Bay. The Oyster River is on the right just as the bay starts to widen.

To reach the Lamprey River follow the western shore. The checkerboard light and dark at the southwest end of the bay is the railroad trestle at the mouth of the Squamscott River. Great Bay itself is interesting to explore.

The paddler can leave the launching area at Hilton Point on the incoming tide nearly two hours past the tide in Portsmouth, explore around in the bay and any of the rivers, and return on the outgoing tide. Or for variety, go down one river with the outgoing tide and up another with the returning tide (spotting cars, of course).

Cocheco River NH

Dover ➤ Piscataqua River   3.0 mi
Tide correction: +1.5 hr

The dam and mill over the Cocheco River adjacent to NH 108 are worth stopping to see. At high water a rainbow appears in the spray. Put in below the mill from a side road on the left bank or at one of the various marinas. The river leaves the road immediately, with only occasional farms along the shore. In two places it cuts a narrow gorge through steep cliffs. The junction with the Salmon Falls River forms the Piscataqua River. Take out at the Eliot Bridge, NH 101, 0.75 mile up the Salmon Falls River.

Salmon Falls River ME, NH

Portland Road bridge ➤ Piscataqua River   4.0 mi
Tide correction: +1.5 hr

Put in from the left bank below the mill at the second dam below Salmon Falls. Blueback herring are often found here. Past the first mile of farmland, the dam on Great Works River is on the left. In another 0.5 mile the lawns of Hamilton House extend to the river. Downstream there are wooded cliffs, with an historical trail along the shore. At the picnic area downstream to the left of Eliot Bridge you can listen to the clatter of cars crossing. The confluence with the Cocheco forms the Piscataqua River. Take out at the Eliot Bridge, NH 101.

Piscataqua River

Confluence ➤ Atlantic Ocean   12.0 mi
Tide correction: Dover point, +1.25 hr

The Piscataqua is a large river from the start, and an adverse wind can cause much trouble. Always check the weather forecast and use caution. Dover Point is 4.0 miles down the right. Below Dover Point there are docks for ocean-going ships, tankers, and pleasure boats of all sizes. This trip will be enjoyable for people who don't mind a lot of traffic.

Huge eddies swirl around pilings and buoys, and in addition to the wind and the tide, wakes from large boats come from all directions, raising a tremendous chop. Keep well out of the channel and avoid big boats. This is no place for a novice. However, experienced paddlers, fortified with favorable wind and tide, can have an interesting trip that differs from paddling inland rivers.

Since the wind is most often from the south and strongest in the afternoon, the best plan is to start from Hilton Park, going down on a noon low tide and returning in the afternoon with the wind and tidal current behind. On the right below Dover point, oil company piers have pilings that must be avoided by hugging the shore. The river narrows and races past rocky cliffs and under the high I-95 bridge (4.25 miles). Two more bridges carry US 1.

Immediately below the lower bridge is Four Tree Island Park (5.5 miles), which has covered picnic tables, grills, and rest rooms. The launching ramp is under the bridge to the right.

Farther down the Piscataqua River there are many docks, and a prison rises conspicuously. Just at the point, on the right, stand a Coast Guard station and Fort Constitution (no public facilities).

For a better canoe or kayak trip, take the more-intimate right-hand route at Four Tree Island and go down among the islands. Strawbery Banke is on the right. The large white building on the left by the bridge is Wentworth-by-the-Sea. Fort Stark is on the point at the left.

If the wind is onshore and the tidal current running in, it is fairly safe and a lot of fun to ride the swells just inside the breakwater. Keep clear of the channel. Take out at the Four Tree Recreation Area in Portsmouth, New Hampshire.

Chapter 7
Saco Watershed

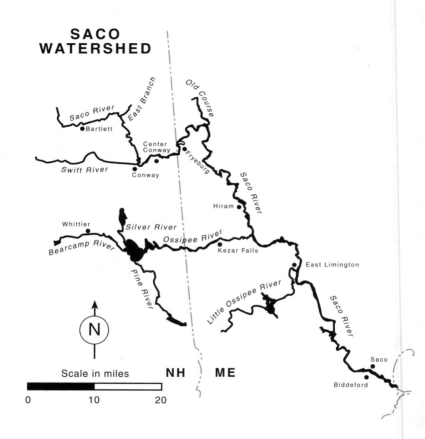

SACO
WATERSHED

Saco River

East Branch

Old Course

Bartlett

Center
Conway

Fryeburg

Swift River

Conway

Saco River

Hiram

Whittier

Silver River

Ossipee River

Bearcamp River

Kezar Falls

East Limington

Pine River

Little Ossipee River

Saco River

N

Saco

Scale in miles   NH   ME

Biddeford

0   10   20

Clean water, a mountain setting, and relative proximity to population centers have always made the Saco River and its tributaries some of New England's most popular rivers for paddling.

The headwaters, with their spring whitewater runs, lie mostly in New Hampshire; below the Maine line the river becomes more placid, flows more smoothly, and is marked by a number of dams. This book includes only the Saco River and tributaries that lie in New Hampshire. The Saco River downstream from Fryeburg, Maine, which includes the parts usually run in the summer, is described in the companion volume, the AMC River Guide: Maine, *3d edition.*

For whitewater thrills the upper Saco and the Swift rivers rate among the best and most difficult in New England. Nice runs with easier rapids can be found on sections of the Bearcamp and Ossipee rivers, and on the Saco below Bartlett. The Pine River offers the most secluded setting but is not an easy run. It is occasionally choked with alder and blocked by fallen trees, and much of it is impassable in low water. Only the last few miles of the Bearcamp, Ossipee, and Pine rivers can be run in low water.

Saco River NH, ME

The Saco River begins at Saco Lake at the north end of Crawford Notch and drains the southern slopes of the Presidential Range through the Mount Washington Valley. From Conway it winds generally southeast into Maine and reaches the Atlantic Ocean south of Portland, Maine.

In its upper reaches, the Saco River drops steeply, providing excitement for expert paddlers. As it approaches Bartlett, the difficulty diminishes and paddling becomes less demanding. Below North Conway there are fewer rapids and more sections of quickwater.

For detailed information, see AMC's *Classic Northeastern Whitewater Guide.*

Davis Path ➤ Sawyer's Rock	4.5 mi
Description:	Class III–IV
Date checked:	2001
Navigable:	High or medium water (mid-April to mid-May)
Scenery:	Forested
Map:	USGS Crawford Notch 15

This section, commonly known as the Upper Saco, is one of the most-exciting whitewater runs in central New England. In addition to its continuous rapids, the river passes through beautiful White Mountain scenery. Since the Saco drains the steep-sided Crawford Notch region, runoff takes place rapidly, and warm, sunny days or spring rains can lead to a rapid rise in the level of the river.

From the Davis Path footbridge, 0.5 mile above Notchland, there is a short stretch of easy rapids leading to a very difficult Class IV gorge at the mouth of Nancy Brook. The gorge is extremely narrow, less than a boat-length wide, with turbulence off the walls.

Since the portage around the gorge is very difficult, most people prefer the put-in off US 302 about 1.0 mile south of Notchland. Pull off the road into a dirt parking area, then cross the railroad tracks, and carry or line down a steep bank to the river.

At the put-in, the rapids are solid Class IV at any water level. The first mile is particularly shallow and twisty and requires constant maneuvering except in very high water. Class III rapids continue to the entrance of the Sawyer River (2.75 miles), where there is a Class III drop and a small beach on the right that makes a good resting or lunch spot. Another 0.75 mile of rapids leads to a railroad bridge (3.5 miles), followed shortly by a Class III drop in a sharp left turn. At this point US 302 is visible high on the right bank. In the next broad right turn lies a Class IV stretch with large waves.

Sawyer's Rock Rapids (4.5 miles) is run most easily on the left. Watch for hydraulics and haystacks below.

Sawyer's Rock ➤ Bartlett	2.75 mi
Description:	Class II–III
Date checked:	2001
Navigable:	High water (late April to early May)
Scenery:	Forested
Map:	USGS Crawford Notch 15

This section is usually run in conjunction with the one above or below and ranks between them in difficulty.

There is 0.5 mile of Class II rapids to another railroad bridge (4.75 miles) with a wavy ledge underneath. The large hydraulic found there can be skirted on the left side. This hydraulic is a keeper and should be avoided at all costs. One hundred yards below the railroad bridge is a right turn with large rocks on the outside—many inexperienced boaters have left their boats on these rocks.

Another Class III rapid lies about 1.0 mile farther. From above this rapid only swift, shallow rapids to a blind left turn are visible. Most boaters should scout the passage between the large rocks in the turn and ledge-and-waves combinations below. The Saco then passes through shallow riffles to the iron bridge in Bartlett (7.25 miles), where there is parking and access on the left bank.

Bartlett ➤ Humphrey's Ledge	8.25 mi
Description:	Class I–II
Date checked:	2001
Navigable:	High water (early May)
Scenery:	Forested
Map:	USGS Crawford Notch 15

The Saco from Bartlett to North Conway is a popular whitewater run of medium difficulty. The current is swift, and there are intermittent Class II rapids, some of which have heavy waves in high water. The riverbed is wide most of the way, with houses along the banks.

The Saco's current is strong enough to undercut its sand-and-gravel banks and to topple the trees growing on them. Sometimes the water is high enough to remove the debris, but frequently it is not. Therefore, low-lying tree trunks are an ever-present hazard, especially at the outside of the turns where the main current flows under them.

In the first 8.25 miles to Humphrey's Ledge, the current is swift, with frequent Class I and II rapids. **Caution!** Be alert for fallen trees that block the main current at the outside of the turns. After about 0.5 mile the river divides. The old, open channel goes to the right, and a new, narrower one continues straight into the forest. The latter was scoured out during the flood of July 1973, and it is more easily blocked by fallen trees than is the old route. There is a difficult Class II rapid that begins about 0.25 mile above the US 302 bridge (4.5 miles).

There are more rapids below US 302, with a Class II rapid in 0.5 mile just above the Rocky Branch, which enters on the left. Beyond the railroad bridge (6.0 miles) easier intermittent rapids continue to the Ellis River, which enters on the left just before a railroad embankment. In 0.75 mile the West Side Road follows along the right bank beneath Humphrey's Ledge.

Humphrey's Ledge ➤ North Conway	3.5 mi
Description:	Quickwater, Class II
Date checked:	2001
Navigable:	High to medium water (May)
Scenery:	Forested, rural
Map:	USGS North Conway 15

Below Humphrey's Ledge the river is smooth, but in high water the current is still very fast. In 2.0 miles be prepared for an S-curve at Lucy's Rock. To either side of the large rock in the center the channel is relatively unobstructed, but there may be trees and other debris on the left at the outside of the turn. The river flows quietly again to the North Conway bridge, whose easternmost span crosses the main river.

North Conway ➤ Conway	8.0 mi
Description:	Quickwater, Class I
Date checked:	2001
Navigable:	Medium water (May)
Scenery:	Forested, rural, settled
Map:	USGS North Conway 15

This section is easier than the ones above and below, and it contains no notable difficulties. However, it is wide and shallow, so it is not usually passable in summer without considerable wading.

The AMC Moose Campground is 2.0 miles down on the right and difficult to spot from the river. There is a railroad bridge at 4.5 miles.

There is a possible take-out on the left before the turn above the Swift River where the rapids start. However, at most water stages the wavy rapid provides an exciting finish to the trip. Take out on the left below the covered bridge.

Conway ➤ Center Conway   2.75 mi

Description:	Quickwater, Class I–III
Date checked:	2001
Navigable:	Medium water (May, sometimes passable in wet summers)
Scenery:	Forested, towns
Maps:	USGS North Conway 15, Ossipee Lake 15

Class II rapids start within sight of the covered bridge. A trip beginning here can also start on the Swift River, at the bridge 0.25 mile above the confluence, which is immediately above the covered bridge and enters in the middle of the rapid.

Below the NH 16 bridge (0.25 mile) there is another easy Class II rapid, and around another corner there is a short but difficult Class III rapid that can kick up 4-foot waves when the water is high. After a brief respite, a long rapid starts and is heavy at the beginning but less so as it continues until it eases off under the US 302 bridge (2.5 miles). Good access can be had on the left at the old covered-bridge site.

Center Conway, NH ➤ Swans Falls, ME   10.0 mi

Description:	Quickwater, Class II
Date checked:	2001
Navigable:	Spring, summer, fall
Scenery:	Forested, settled
Maps:	USGS North Conway 15, Ossipee Lake 15
Portage:	(10.0 mi R Swans Falls 300 yd)

This start is usually possible in summer. Shortly after the put-in in Conway Center there is a ledge, followed by some Class II rapids that can be bony in the summer. The riffles end by the Saco Bound put-in (3.25 miles).

Quickwater continues to Weston's Bridge in Fryeburg (6.75 miles). The river meanders slowly to the dam at Swans Falls, where there is an access, a portage trail, parking, and the AMC Swans Falls campground.

In the summer the Town of Fryeburg sets up docks and rafts just downstream of Weston's Bridge. Keep to the extreme right to avoid swimmers.

For the remainder of the Saco River see the companion volume, *AMC River Guide: Maine*, 3d edition. The most popular summer quickwater run is from Fryeburg to Hiram.

Saco River (East Branch) NH

Benchmark 784 ➤ Lower Bartlett   3.0 mi

This small stream is recommended only for closed boats. In high water it can be run down to the Saco River near Humphrey's Ledge in late April or early May. The rapids are continuous, and many are Class IV. They should be scouted carefully because precise and quick maneuvering is necessary. Fallen trees may present more than the usual hazard since it is hard to get out of the river once you have put in.

Scouting is possible on the north bank of the river from a paved road that leaves NH 16A in Lower Bartlett. The suggested put-in is at the first wooden bridge above the highway near Benchmark 784 on the USGS North Conway 15 map.

This table indicates river mileage from the Saco's headwaters at various points along the river. The information was generated by AMC's cartographers with the mapping software used to create AMC's river maps of the Androscoggin and the Saco.

0.0	Saco Lake dam, headwaters
8.6	Davis Path Trailhead, Bemis bridge
15.3	River Street bridge, Bartlett
27.2	First Bridge, River Road, North Conway

35.8	NH 16/Davis Park, Conway
38.0	Smith-Eastman Recreation Area, Conway
47.9	Swans Falls dam
51.7	ME 5 Canal Bridge, Fryeburg Center
58.9	US 302, Walkers Bridge, Fryeburg
67.7	ME 160 bridge, East Brownfield
82.2	ME 5 bridge, Hiram
84.9	Great Falls dam, Hiram
88.7	ME 117 bridge, Cornish Station
97.6	ME 11 bridge, Steep Falls
102.5	ME 25 bridge, East Limington
108.1	Bonny Eagle dam
109.7	West Buxton dam
114.9	Bar Mills dam/Route 4A bridge
116.2	ME 117 bridge, Salmon Falls
118.2	Skelton Dam, Union Falls
122.7	ME 5 bridge, Biddeford/Saco
127.7	Rotary Park boat access
129.4	West Channel Dam, Cataract Dam Complex, Saco/Biddeford
134.5	Mouth of river at Atlantic Ocean

Swift River NH

The beautiful Swift River rises in the west end of Albany Intervale and flows eastward to meet the Saco River in Conway. Most of the river can be paddled, and there are many challenging rapids to be negotiated. From Rocky Gorge to Darby Field, the Swift is suitable only for covered boats or those smaller open boats with thigh braces and maximum flotation.

Because of the large, high-altitude drainage, the Swift River tends to hold water fairly well and is normally runnable from mid-April to the end of May. The Kancamagus Highway runs through the Swift River Valley, providing convenient access at many points.

For additional and detailed information, see AMC's *Classic Northeastern Whitewater Guide.*

Pine Bend Brook ➤ Rocky Gorge   8.5 mi

Description: Quickwater, Class III
Date checked: 2001
Navigable: High to medium water
Scenery: Wild, forested
Maps: USGS Crawford Notch 15, Mountain Chocorua 15
Portage: (8.5 mi R Rocky Gorge 200 yd)

The rapids in this section are all or nothing! The quickwater is very wild and attractive, but access at either end is difficult unless you run the rapids.

Put in at the bridge over Pine Bend Brook from the Kancamagus Highway. The river starts with steep ledges and fast turns, and some scouting and perhaps lining or carrying is in order. After about 2.0 miles the rapids end, and the river enters a complicated beaver swamp, followed by about 2.0 miles of quickwater away from the road with mountain views.

The quickwater continues beyond Bear Notch Road (5.25 miles) for nearly 3.0 miles. The rapids start again abruptly 0.25 mile above the first road access and continue for 0.5 mile. The most difficult drop is the double ledge visible from the Kancamagus Highway. Take out on the right above Rocky Gorge.

Rocky Gorge ➤ Lower Falls   2.5 mi

Description: Class III
Date checked: 2001
Navigable: High to medium water (mid-April to mid-May)
Scenery: Forested
Maps: USGS Crawford Notch 15, North Conway 15, Ossipee Lake 15
Portage: 2.5 mi R Lower Falls 200 yd

This stretch is commonly referred to as the Upper Swift. It contains continuous, difficult rapids to challenge paddlers seeking whitewater sport. Expert open boaters will be able to navigate this stretch.

A put-in is possible over a smooth ledge right by the bridge at Rocky Gorge. Class III rapids begin just below the gorge and continue for about 1.0 mile. Then there are a couple of rapids that are more difficult: first through some large boulders in a left bend, and then two ledges after a right turn. These two ledges, sometimes known as the Washboard, are right next to the Kancamagus Highway. Rapids continue at a Class III pace, reaching Class IV in a bouldery stretch just above Lower Falls.

You should take out when you spot the picnic area on the right shore. Lower Falls is another 10-foot fall over ledges; although it is more gradual than Upper Falls, it is very dangerous. It has occasionally been run on the far left, but unless you are an expert paddler it should be portaged. The picnic and parking areas here have been used to take out or to put in for the stretch below.

Lower Falls ➤ Darby Field	6.0 mi
Description:	Class IV
Date checked:	2001
Navigable:	High to medium water (mid-April into May)
Scenery:	Forested
Map:	USGS Ossipee Lake 15

This section is one of the most-difficult uninterrupted runs in all of New England. The stretch from the gorge, 2.0 miles below Lower Falls, is often referred to as the Lower Swift. It provides excellent sport for very skilled paddlers, but it is not recommended for inexperienced paddlers. When the water is high, a damaged boat and a long, exhausting, and dangerous swim could result from any tip-over.

The pool below Lower Falls makes a good put-in for this run. However, there is little chance to warm up for the rapid below the falls, which is a rocky, turbulent Class IV. Easier Class III rapids follow to the covered bridge on Dugway Road (0.5 mile). Another 1.5 miles of shallow Class III rapids follow; this section can be very scratchy in medium water.

The next major rapids are at the Gorge (2.0 miles), where the river drops very steeply and the road is high on the right bank. The gorge is 1.0 mile below the covered bridge. Upstream from the Gorge the road is very close to the river. Scout the Gorge from the road.

Rapids continue below the Gorge, with a Class IV drop 0.25 mile farther along. More Class III–IV rapids continue to a left turn just above the Staircase (2.75 miles), where you should pull out and scout on the left. The Staircase is a short, steep, 50-yard drop over large boulders. It is Class IV at medium levels and Class V in high water. For those who do not wish to run these rapids, it is possible to carry or line down to the left of a rock island on the left.

Below the Staircase (2.75 miles) difficult rapids continue for another 0.5 mile to the site of an annual slalom race. The race course is set up in a Class IV section where the Swift drops, around many large boulders. More rapids follow, with Class IV and slightly easier rapids very close together. The last of the difficult rapids is at a spot where the Swift approaches the road, splits around a rock the size of a small house, and drops 2 feet into a hole (5.5 miles). This last hole is formed by a V-shaped ledge whose apex extends upstream. This is the largest, widest hydraulic on the river, and it can hold a boat even at medium water.

The last 0.5 mile to the sign is a Class III with shallow rapids. The sign is painted differently every year; you can also recognize the spot by the river's sharp turn away from the road and a side road leaving the Kancamagus Highway. Take out on the right.

Darby Field ➤ Conway		2.75 mi
Description:	Quickwater, Class II–III	
Date checked:	2001	
Navigable:	High to medium water (mid-April into May)	
Scenery:	Forested	
Map:	USGS Ossipee Lake 15	

This section of the Swift River is away from roads for much of the run. There is more hazard from fallen trees here than in the more difficult rapids above.

From a put-in near the Darby Field sign, there are continuous rapids for about 0.75 mile. These rapids are scratchy Class III, with many sharp turns required. The rapids moderate to Class II and later to snaky quickwater. The river continues its twisting until a bridge on West Side Road and a covered bridge, at which point there is another Class II–III rapid (2.5 miles). The Swift River enters the Saco River at a covered bridge over the latter in Conway, where there is another rapid.

Take out at the NH bridge just below the covered bridge over the Saco (2.75 miles). Cars can reach the river by following a dirt road behind the shopping center.

Ossipee River NH, ME

The Ossipee River flows east for 17.5 miles from Lake Ossipee across the Maine border and into the Saco River near Cornish, Maine. It has a dependable flow in the spring, but by summer the water is too low to run the lower section.

Ossipee Lake ➤ Kezar Falls	10.75 mi
Description:	Quickwater, Class I–II
Date checked:	2001
Navigable:	High and medium water (spring)
	Low water, passable, some lining required at rapids
Scenery:	Forested, rural, towns
Maps:	USGS Ossipee Lake 15, Kezar Falls
Portages:	10.5 mi first dam at Kezar Falls across island
	10.75 mi R second dam at Kezar Falls 30 yd

Quickwater characterizes this section, although there is one very nice rapid just above the NH 153 bridge in Effingham Falls. There are several more short rapids before Kezar Falls, but for most of the distance the river is smooth. Anyone seeking a paddle in remote surroundings will not find it here: vacation cottages line the banks near the beginning, and below East Freedom there are more cottages and houses, with a main highway close by on the left bank for much of the distance.

The dam at the outlet of Ossipee Lake is at the end of a side road 0.5 mile west of the junction of NH 25 and 153 in Effingham Falls. Put in below the gatehouse and run down the sluiceway to a pool of slackwater. A section of Class II–III rapids follows for another 0.25 mile; these are the most difficult rapids of this river. They lead up to the NH 153 bridge (0.5 mile).

Then there are 1.5 miles of quickwater past the NH 25 bridge (2.0 miles) to East Freedom, where 0.25 mile of Class II rapids leads under a bridge (4.5 miles) to the Maine border. The remaining distance to Kezar Falls is mostly quickwater, with two short Class II rapids, one before and one after the ME 160 bridge in Porter (7.75 miles).

In Kezar Falls, go to the right of the island and take out at a small bridge (10.5 miles). If you are continuing downstream, carry across the island to the foot of the main dam and continue 0.25 mile through the town to the second dam (10.75 miles). Take out on the right, carry across the canal, and put in below the dam.

Kezar Falls ➤ Saco River		6.75 mi
Description:	Quickwater, Class I–II	
Date checked:	2001	
Navigable:	High water, recommended (early spring)	
	Medium water (late spring)	
Scenery:	Forested, rural	
Maps:	USGS Kezar Falls, Cornish	

Below the second flood dam in Kezar Falls, the Ossipee River takes on a different character. It is a very scenic run past forests and farms almost all the way to the Saco River, with quickwater or rapids for the entire distance.

When the water level is up, the run from Kezar Falls to the ME 5/117 bridge over the Saco can be made in a little over an hour, but if you continue down the Saco for another 14.0 miles to the ME 25 bridge, you can make a long, scenic trip of mixed flatwater and rapids. Note, however, that Limington Rips, which begin just above the bridge, are very severe rapids in high water.

One half-mile east of the ME 25 bridge in Kezar Falls, turn north onto Garner Avenue and take the first right to reach the dam and power station.

Below the dam there are nice Class I and II rapids for 1.0 mile to Which Way Rips, where the river abruptly divides around an island. Quickwater and Class I rapids continue to the first bridge (3.5 miles), with more quickwater to the second 5.5 miles). Below the second bridge and past a few cottages, there are some easy Class II rapids that lead almost to the Saco River (6.75 miles) only 0.5 mile above the ME 5/117 bridge east of Cornish (7.25 miles).

Silver River NH

The Silver River, also called the West Branch on some maps, flows from Silver Lake in Madison to the north end of Ossipee Lake. It provides a secluded two- to three-hour run in high water. It has a good flow in the spring and also in the fall, when the level of Silver Lake is drawn down.

The first 2.5 miles to Ossipee Lake Road are the most pleasant because the current is faster and the banks of the river are more open. The lower portion is entirely wooded, and there are a few trees blocking the stream.

Silver Lake ➤ Ossipee Lake	6.0 mi
Description:	Flatwater, quickwater
Date checked:	2001
Navigable:	High water, recommended (spring and mid-fall)
	Medium water, some wading required (late spring and early summer)
	Dam controlled (annual fall drawdown of Silver Lake)

Scenery:	Forested
Map:	USGS Ossipee Lake 15

The dam on Silver Lake is next to Silver Lake Road, which leaves NH 41 on the right just over 2.0 miles north of West Ossipee. A marina at Westward Shore on Ossipee Lake (west of the mouth of the river) can be reached by turning east off NH 16 onto Nichols Road, which is 2.0 miles south of West Ossipee.

The quickwater at the beginning slackens somewhat as the stream enters a broad, open valley. Soon you reach the first of a score of beaver dams that dot the entire length of the river. Many of them can be run in high water. The banks become wooded again as you pass a sawmill on the right shortly before the Ossipee Lake Road bridge (2.5 miles). In the remaining 3.5 miles the river winds more, and there are a few obstructions. Take out at the campground 0.5 mile south on Ossipee Lake.

Bearcamp River NH

The Bearcamp River flows eastward into Ossipee Lake, draining a large portion of the valley between the Sandwich and Ossipee ranges. Since much of the drainage area is mountainous, the runoff from rain and melting snow takes place quickly. The upper section is an easy paddle through meadowland, the middle section provides some fine whitewater in the early spring, and the last 9.0 miles are usually passable whenever the river is free of ice.

The countryside is relatively unsettled, and there are occasional views of the Sandwich Range to the north and the Ossipee Mountains to the south.

Bearcamp Pond ➤ Bennett Corners	2.75 mi
Description:	Quickwater
Date checked:	2001
Navigable:	High water (April)
Scenery:	Forested, rural
Map:	USGS Mount Chocorua 15

This is the most scenic portion of the river. For much of the distance the river flows through meadows. Watch out for fallen trees.

Bearcamp Pond Road leaves NH 25 on the north side 0.5 mile east of the NH 25 and 113 junction at Bennett Corners. In less than a mile it crosses the river just below the pond.

The Bearcamp winds through meadows for 1.75 miles to the Cold River, which enters on the left and approximately doubles the flow. After another mile of meandering between tree-linked banks, you reach the NH 113 bridge at Bennett Corners (2.75 miles).

Bennett Corners ➤ Whittier   3.75 mi
Description: Quickwater, Class II, III, IV
Date checked: 2001
Navigable: High water (April)
Scenery: Rural, towns
Map: USGS Mount Chocorua 15
Portage: 1.75 mi L old dam at South Tamworth
                       20 yd

This popular whitewater section is good training ground for intermediate paddlers if the water is not too high. Most of the bard rapids are visible from the road, so you can judge the difficulty before you begin.

Below the NH 113 bridge at Bennett Corner, there is 0.5 mile of smoothwater with a slow current that ends up at a rocky rapid 100 yards long and rated Class II–III. A wood road on the left bank can be used as a portage if necessary. Soon there are two shorter, easier Class II rapids, followed by more smoothwater to South Tamworth. The road comes near the river (1.0 mile), and anyone who has had difficulty with the run up to this point should consider taking out.

A long rapid begins behind the post office, and ends below the next bridge (1.5 miles) with a difficult Class III–IV ledge. One popular route involves hugging the right bank above the bridge, then moving quickly left underneath, either running the ledge on the left or stopping in the eddy just past the bridge. There is a wooded road on the left bank for portage.

Caution! Just around the next corner to the right is Bearcamp Gorge, a narrow Class III–IV chute that consists of 30 yards of turbulence between low ledges. It should be scouted. A 4–5-foot drop now exists at the end of the gorge, with a huge rock on the left at the bottom.

The dam at South Tamworth can be inspected by walking upstream from a log yard off NH 25. It consists of a number of concrete piers supporting old timbers, a definite hazard to boaters. Portage to the left. Below the dam, the rapids are continuous; the next difficult pitch is a series of ledges just above a former bridge (2.5 miles). There are more easy rapids, followed by a sharp Class III rapid containing a moderate hydraulic. Easy rapids continue past the NH 113 bridge in Whittier (3.75 miles). In another 0.5 mile, just past a cemetery, there is a good place to take out at old NH 25, about 0.75 mile below the convenience store, where you can also park vehicles.

Whittier ➤ Ossipee Lake	10.5 mi
Description:	Flatwater, quickwater, Class I
Date checked:	2001
Navigable:	Passable at most levels
Scenery:	Forested, rural, settled
Maps:	USGS Mount Chocorua 15, Ossipee Lake 15

Except at the beginning, this section is passable for most of the paddling season. The bottom is sandy for many miles as the Bearcamp winds through woods and farmland.

There are many cottages and a large campground along the river in the 3.0 miles from NH 25 to NH 16, but the rest is forested.

Below the NH 113 bridge in Whittier, Class II rapids continue for 0.5 mile, after which there is about 1.0 mile of occasional riffles that are shallow in low water. To avoid these, start 1.5 miles east of Whittier on NH 25 where the road comes close to the river. After that there are only a few shallow sections, all short. Pass under a covered bridge (4.25 miles), NH 25 (5.25 miles), and NH 16 (8.25 miles). Under NH 16 there is a convenient take-out point on the right.

Pine River NH

The Pine River is a small stream of moderate length that flows into Ossipee Lake from the south. Although it is crossed by two highways and three side roads, only short portions of them follow the river's secluded banks. For most of its length it flows in narrow valleys, alder swamps, or wide meadows. Few streams in New Hampshire offer the river traveler such clean water and unspoiled scenery.

The river is narrow and occasionally choked with alders. When it flows through woodland, it easily can be blocked by fallen trees. For years there were many such obstacles, which made passage down the river difficult and frustrating. The trees are cut out from time to time.

You should nonetheless allow more time to run this river than your experience on others might indicate that you need.

Because of the gentle gradient and gravel bottom, parts of the Pine River provide year-round paddling, and even the steepest sections are passable in medium water. Each fall the Water Division (603-271-3406) draws down the level of Pine River Pond, and usually beginning in mid-October there is enough water in the whole river for one and a half weeks or more.

Pine River Pond ➤ Granite Road	5.0 mi
Description:	Quickwater, Class II
Date checked:	2001
Navigable:	High water (April)
	Medium water, recommended (May and midfall)
	Dam controlled (annual fall drawdown)
Scenery:	Forested
Map:	USGS Wolfeboro 15

The Pine River begins as a small stream confined between two low, glacial ridges. In this section particularly, there are many places where alders choke the stream, and in other sections low limbs and overhanging trees are hazardous in the fast-moving current of high water. In less than medium water levels, some walking may be required.

If the stream looks passable in the first few yards, there is sufficient water for the entire trip to Ossipee Lake. In the fall, when the level of Pine River Pond is being drawn down, the effect will be less noticeable below Granite Road.

In Wakefield a road east from NH 16 near the Ossipee/Wakefield town line leads in about 1.0 mile to the Pine River just below the pond. For about 1.0 mile it flows through woods before it enters an alder swamp, where there are several beaver dams. Then the current picks up again. Just after a pumping station a short portage may be necessary where the river passes under a road in three culverts. NH 16 (3 miles) is a short distance beyond, near a railroad crossing and the entrance to a gravel pit.

This section between the two NH 16 bridges begins with some quickwater through some woods. Then the current slackens where the river is backed up by beaver dams in an alder swamp, but it picks up in the woods beyond.

From the second NH 16 bridge there is good current as the river flows through another alder swamp and over some beaver dams. It flows through attractive woods for a short distance above the Granite Road bridge (5.0 miles).

Granite Road ➤ Ossipee Lake		15.0 mi
Description:	Flatwater, quickwater	
Date checked:	1983	
Navigable:	High and medium water (April, May, and midfall)	
	Passable at most water levels, below Elm Street	
	Dam controlled (annual fall drawdown of Pine River Pond)	
Scenery:	Wild, forested	
Maps:	USGS Wolfeboro 15, Ossipee Lake 15	

Put in at Granite Road. Halfway between Granite Road and Elm Street there is a 2.0-mile section of quickwater where the river flows through a very attractive wooded valley. Pine and hemlock grow along the banks between ridges that rise steeply from the flat bottomlands.

Below the Elm Street bridge the river is flat as it wanders through a wide valley of conifers and swamp maple. Occasionally you pass old campsites. From the mouth of the river at the south end of Ossipee Lake, there is a nice view of the Sandwich Range and the Moats.

Granite Road leads from NH 16 at a crossroads about 1.5 miles south of the junction of NH 16 and 28 in Ossipee. In the first 3.0 miles the river wanders through an alder swamp, where the flatwater is interrupted by an occasional beaver dam. Then there are 2.0 miles of quickwater, after which the river meanders through an open meadow where there are views of Green Mountain to the northeast.

The river enters the woods again about 0.5 mile above the Elm Street bridge (8.0 miles). For the rest of the way the current is weaker. The river passes under NH 25 (14.0 miles), and a mile beyond that it empties into the lake (15.0 miles).

A road from NH 25, a short distance east of NH 16, leads past the Pine River and along the southwest shore of Ossipee Lake.

Chapter 8
Androscoggin Watershed

CANADA

MAINE

Memphremagog

Upper
Connecticut

Androscoggin

Champlain

Saco

Merrimack

Piscataqua

Hudson

NEW
YORK

MASSACHUSETTS

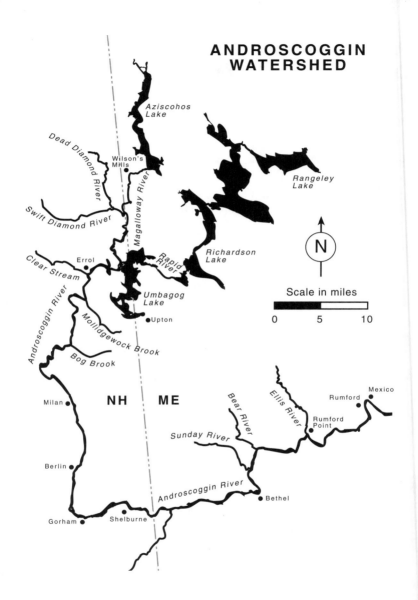

ANDROSCOGGIN WATERSHED

The Androscoggin rises in the Rangeley Lakes in Maine, but the rapids that make it so well known are in New Hampshire. Several other fine, near-wilderness rivers meet the Androscoggin in New Hampshire, offering a selection of excellent paddling opportunities.

Androscoggin River NH, ME

During the first half of the last century, the Androscoggin was one of the most polluted rivers in the United States. The Federal Water Pollution Control Act of 1972, better known as the Clean Water Act, has led the way to a much cleaner river. As the river's water quality has continued to improve, recreational use of the river has grown dramatically. A few sections have rapids that need to be respected, and, as always, water levels affect difficulty. The river's novice-friendly nature, ease of access, and beautiful scenery make the waterway a great paddling river.

All of the big lakes in the upper drainage area of the Androscoggin River—Rangely, Mooselookmeguntic, Richardson, Umbagog, and Aziscohos—have been made even bigger by dams, so the volume of ponded water and periodic releases, makes high water in the Androscoggin rapids very dependable in the summer.

The Androscoggin River begins north of Errol at the confluence of the Magalloway River and the outlet of Umbagog Lake. This is no longer a clearly defined spot because the dam at Errol floods many miles up both branches. The lakes in the headwaters form a vast storage area of impounded water to run the mills and power stations on the Androscoggin. This makes summer paddling possible.

Lake Umbagog ➤ Berlin	34.5 mi
Description:	Flatwater, quickwater, Class I, II
Date checked:	2000
Navigable:	Spring, summer, fall; controlled release
Scenery:	Forested, rural
Maps:	Errol 15, Milan 15, Berlin
Portages:	3.75 mi L Errol Dam
	21.75 mi R Pontook Dam
	(34.5 mi Berlin Dam)
Campsites:	4.5 mi R Errol Bridge private $ car
	8.0 mi R Mollidgewock private $ car

Below Lake Umbagog, the river is wide with extensive marshes on both sides. In 3.0 miles, it reaches NH 16 where there is a launching ramp; 0.75 mile beyond this ramp is the Errol Dam (3.25 miles), which is portaged on the left.

Below Erroll dam, there is a whitewater run all through the summer. Although the run is neither long nor difficult, it is popular because in July and August there are few alternatives in New England. The valley is attractive, though not wild because a main road follows the river closely almost all the way.

The section from Errol Dam to just below the NH 26 bridge, 0.75 mile long, consists of a short rapid, a pool, and another 0.5 mile of easier Class II rapids. Due to the slackwater below where Clear Stream enters on the right (which is immediately after the rapids) and the proximity of the road, these rapids are not as dangerous as the size and difficulty of the river normally would indicate. If you plan to run this section by itself, the best way to reach it is to park your car beside the pool above Errol, run the rapids, and take out on river right either by the bridge or at the end of the rapids.

Below Clear Stream (4.75 miles), there are 3.25 miles of flatwater to Mollidgewock Brook (8.0 miles). Downstream there are 3.0 miles of Class II rapids separated by pools, with mixed smoothwater and riffles for the remaining distance to Pontook Reservoir. There is an access point at the Dummer/Cambridge town line along NH 16. It is a section of old NH 16, and is just along the river. There is a bridge (12.75 miles) just above Seven Islands, with a nice wave. Bog Brook (18.25 miles), which enters on the left, is the next landmark. Portage at Pontook Dam (21.75 miles) on the right.

Caution! At the dam there is a strong, consistent, and dangerous reversal. This hydraulic is more dangerous than it looks; two people have drowned here. Heed the warning signs: put in at the canoe landing 50 yards below the dam, and do not go upstream to play in the reversal! Since the new dam has been in operation, the water level below the dam has been too low to create rapids. The river needs to flow at 1,200 cfs to create

Class II rapids. There are pre-arranged water releases on summer weekends, which provide enough water for boating. Call 603-449-2903 for release information. There is a public boat launch at the Paul O. Boffinger Conservation area, on the right side of the river, one mile below the Pontook rapids. This area has parking, restrooms, and interpretive signs.

The remaining 10.5 miles have a good current but no rapids. The bridge in Milan can be used as an access point, although the bank is very steep. Park on the left side of the river. The Nansen Wayside Park is also a good access point, with an easy paddle down to Berlin from here. There is a bridge in Milan (27.75 miles). In Berlin, you should take out at the playground (34.5 miles) located on the left below the first bridge, or continue down to the new boat launch and float installed in the summer of 2000 by the Northern Forest Heritage Park. It is on river right, but close to the Berlin Dam, so paddle cautiously.

Berlin ➤ Shelburne Dam   11.5 mi

Description:	Flatwater, quickwater, Class I
Date checked:	2000
Navigable:	Spring, summer, fall; controlled release (not recommended, dams)
Scenery:	Urban, forested
Maps:	Berlin, Shelburne
Portages:	7 dams

The river valley is attractive, with views of the Presidential Range to the southwest and lower mountains to the east. A recommended paddle would be to put in in Gorham and paddle down to the Shelburne Dam. No portages are necessary along this section, and the views of the Presidential Range in this section are wonderful. The river has been cleaned up substantially. You will hardly be able to discern the difference in water quality in this section from the first section. The seven dams above Gorham may each be portaged individually, or in series.

Shelburne Dam, NH ➤ Bethel, ME   17.75 mi

Description:	Flatwater, quickwater, Class I
Date checked:	2000
Navigable:	Spring, summer, fall; controlled release
Scenery:	Forested, rural
Maps:	Shelburne, Gilead, Bethel; DL 10

The water in this section is less polluted than in the past and the river valley is scenic, with views of the Presidential Range to the southwest and lower mountains to the east. The river can sometimes have an odor, but not everyone can detect it.

Put in below the dam at the bridge on which the Appalachian Trail crosses the river. Two log cribs dominate the view upstream over the dam. There is a good current with pleasant riffles for many miles, as the river continually separates around numerous islands.

There is a bridge at 2.75 miles. Above the next bridge near Gilead (8.75 miles) is the most difficult rapid in this section, dropping past rocky outcroppings. There is a boat launch on river right above this bridge. At 14.0 miles is the Newt's Landing Access site, owned and maintained by the Mahoosuc Land Trust. It is on the south bank and easily recognized by the log steps leading up from the river. Parking and river information are available here. The current continues slower to Bethel and the US 2 bridge.

See the *AMC River Guide: Maine* and the *AMC Androscoggin River* map for description of the Androscoggin in Maine.

Magalloway River ME, NH

The Magalloway River rises in the most northwestern part of Maine and flows south to join the Androscoggin River on the west shore of Umbagog Lake.

Aziscohos power plant, ME ➤ Wilson's Mills, ME   2.5 mi

Description:	Class III–IV
Date checked:	2001
Navigable:	Spring, summer, fall
	Dam controlled

| Scenery: | Forested |
| Map: | USGS Oquossoc 15, Errol 15 |

A quarter-mile below Aziscohos Dam, a side road from ME 16 reaches the river at the Aziscohos hydroelectric plant. A trail from the plant leads 75 yards downstream to the put-in just below an unrunnable 10-foot drop. The next 2.5 miles to Wilson's Mills is technical Class III–IV and is runnable at levels greater than 300 cubic feet per second. A scouting trail runs the entire length of the rapids on the right. Take out on the right just below the ME 16 bridge in Wilson's Mills.

Wilson's Mills, ME ➤ Lake Umbagog, NH   16.25 mi

Description:	Flatwater
Date checked:	2001
Navigable:	Spring, summer, fall
	Dam controlled
Scenery:	Forested, rural
Map:	USGS Errol 15

Put in for the flatwater trip at a gravel parking area on the right just below the ME 16 bridge in Wilson's Mills. Below the put-in the river meanders for 2.0 miles, then passes the Aziscohos Valley Camping Area and flows under a covered bridge. For the next 4.25 miles the river follows the road, meanders, and then meets the Diamond River. Three-quarters of a mile farther is a take-out on the left just below another ME 16 bridge. Below this point the Magalloway continues 9.25 miles to Umbagog Lake, where it joins the Androscoggin River.

Diamond River NH

The Diamond River is formed by the union of the Swift and Dead Diamond rivers, and it flows through an impressive gorge into the Magalloway River. Dartmouth College owns most of the lower watershed of the Diamond and its branches. A good gravel road leaves NH 16 just east of Wentworth Location and passes through the gorge, with roads up the Swift and Dead Diamond rivers. The gate below the gorge is closed year-round. Vehicle permits are issued only to members of the Dartmouth community, although foot and bicycle traffic is allowed. Remember to ask for and obtain permission before crossing property lines. Contact Outdoor Programs, Dartmouth College, Hanover, NH 03755 for further information (www.dartmouth.edu).

Confluence ➤ Magalloway River		2.0 mi
Description:	Class III–V	
Date checked:	2001	
Navigable:	High water	
Scenery:	Forested, rural	
Map:	USGS Errol 15	

Take out on the left 100 yards below the confluence at Peaks Camp and carry 0.5–1.0 mile down the road to a suitable put-in. The first 0.25 mile is no worse than Class III, but the next 0.25 mile contains some drops that, if they are runnable, are Class V, and they are nearly impossible to carry or line because of the cliffs on both banks.

After 0.5 mile along the road, the rapids diminish, and you can put in again whenever you decide that the road is close enough to the river. There is a good take-out just below the bridge (1.0 mile) adjacent to the road gate. After another mile of easier river, you reach the Magalloway River (2.0 miles).

Swift Diamond River NH

This small stream rises in the Diamond ponds in Stewartstown and flows east to join the Dead Diamond. Although famous for fishing, it is passable by canoe only for about two weeks during spring runoff, which is in early May, when access is likely to be poor. The upper end can be reached by a road that follows Corser Brook north from NH 26 about 4.0 miles west of Errol. The lower end can be reached by a branch road from the Dartmouth road along Diamond River. Both roads are likely to be closed or unusable during mud season.

Swift Diamond Farm ➤ Diamond River		9.5 mi
Description:	Class II–III	
Date checked:	2001	

Navigable:	High water only (May)
Scenery:	Wild
Map:	USGS Errol 15

Put in at a suitable point where the road approaches the river near Swift Diamond Farm. Pass under the access road in 1.0 mile. The run is mainly Class II, with a few harder spots that may be unrunnable depending on the water level. Line the remains of Dixie Dam (2.5 miles) and scout the two short drops below. Ellingwood Falls (6.5 miles) consists of three narrow flumes that are difficult but runnable. There are 2.0 more miles of easy rapids, then 1.0 mile of difficult rapids, including a drop that is probably unrunnable, to the junction with the Dead Diamond River (9.5 miles). Take out 100 yards below on the left.

Dead Diamond River NH

This stream flows south from the most remote part of New Hampshire, the southeast corner of Pittsburgh. The runnable portion lies almost entirely in the area known as the Second College Grant. The river is paralleled by a private Dartmouth College road that is not open to the public, so paddling is infrequent. Remeber to ask for and obtain permission before crossing property lines.

Hell Gate ➤ Diamond River		12.0 mi
Description:	Flatwater, quickwater, Class I	
Date checked:	2001	
Navigable:	High water (May)	
Scenery:	Forested	
Map:	USGS Errol 15	

The usual put-in is at Hell Gate Camps, although the river above is runnable. The river meanders, with moderate current; the only difficult spot is at Half Mile Falls (5.0 miles). The current starts to pick up just below the bridge at the Management Center (11.75 miles). Take out at Peaks Camp, 100 yards below the junction with the Swift Diamond River (12.0 miles).

Umbagog Lake NH, ME

Umbagog Lake is the largest "wild" lake in New Hampshire. Settlement is largely concentrated at the south end, where there is access from NH 26. The north end can be approached from the Magalloway or Androscoggin rivers, which come in from the west side. The northwest side is low and swampy. There are campsites at the Umbagog Lake Campground (Errol, NH; 603-482-7795). Reserve sites and pay a fee at the base camp located where NH 16 skirts the southern tip of the lake. Camping at Cedar Stump Campground, at the mouth of the Rapid River, is run by Saco Bound/Northern Waters (603-447-2177) in Errol, which can also arrange shuttle service for the Rapid River.

The lake offers clean warm water, fine scenery, excellent campsites, and wildlife, including loons, moose, and a pair of nesting eagles in its northern basin. Winds are mostly from the northwest and can easily kick up waves of 3 feet or more. An interesting side trip includes a paddle into Cedar Stump at the base of the Rapid River. Leave canoes at Cedar Stump and walk the well-worn trail along the Rapid. The trail is muddy and crosses over masses of tree roots before turning left and going uphill to meet a jeep trail running along the river.

The Rapid is a spectacular Class IV river with a setting appealing enough to attract boaters from all over the country. A popular picnic spot is Smooth Ledge, about 1.5 miles upstream from Cedar Stump.

Clear Stream NH

This mountain stream drains the eastern side of Dixville Notch. It is barely a canoe-length wide throughout. Though seldom visible, NH 26 is nearby.

Off NH 26 ➤ Androscoggin River		6.5 mi
Description:	Quickwater, Class I	
Date checked:	1983	
Navigable:	High water (early May)	
Scenery:	Forested, rural	
Map:	USGS Errol 15	

Put in from a side road to a farm on the right off NH 26 about 5.5 miles west of Errol. Above this point are more difficult rapids that require high water to run. Below here, the rapids are Class I, with perhaps one or two Class II rapids. In 1.25 miles the river reaches the NH 26 bridge. Halfway to Errol the river begins to meander and the rapids spread out, although the current continues. Fallen trees may partially or entirely block the channel. It is possible to take out at the NH 26 bridge in Errol (6.25 miles), but it is probably more convenient to paddle 0.25 mile, mostly deadwater, to the Androscoggin River and then continue 200 yards upstream to the take-out below the rapids just downstream of the NH 26 bridge.

Mollidgewock Brook NH, ME

Mollidgewock Brook flows from Mollidgewock Pond in Upton, Maine, northwest to the Androscoggin River opposite the Mollidgewock Campground. The paddleable portion is a small stream obstructed with alders and beaver dams. It can be ascended, possibly for 3.0 miles, from the Androscoggin; the distance varies directly with your desire to continue. It may be possible to reach the river at various points from a private road on the east side of the Androscoggin River.

This is also a good after-supper trip for people staying at the campground. See USGS Milan 15.

Bog Brook NH

Bog Brook is a small stream that flows west from the north slope of Cambridge Black Mountain to the Androscoggin River near the Cambridge/Dummer town line. It is similar to but smaller than Mollidgewock Brook and can be ascended about 1.5 miles from the Androscoggin. Nature lovers who wish to paddle only Bog Brook will find the mouth within sight of a pull-off on NH 16. See USGS Milan 15.

Appendix

Safety Code of American Whitewater
(formerly the American Whitewater Affiliation)

The following code, adopted in 1959 and revised in 1998, is reprinted with permission of American Whitewater, P.O. Box 636, Margaretville, NY 12455.

I. Personal Preparedness and Responsibility

1. Be a competent swimmer, with the ability to handle yourself underwater.

2. Wear a life jacket. A snugly-fitting vest-type life preserver offers back and shoulder protection as well as the flotation needed to swim safely in whitewater.

3. Wear a solid, correctly fitted helmet when upsets are likely. This is essential in kayaks or covered canoes, and recommended for open canoeists using thigh straps and rafters running steep drops.

4. Do not boat out of control. Your skills should be sufficient to stop or reach shore before reaching danger. Do not enter a rapid unless you are reasonably sure that you can run it safely or swim it without injury.

5. Whitewater rivers contain many hazards which are not always easily recognized. The following are the most frequent killers.

A. **_HIGH WATER_** The river's speed and power increase tremendously as the flow increases, raising the difficulty of most rapids. Rescue becomes progressively harder as the water rises, adding to the danger. Floating debris and strainers make even an easy rapid quite hazardous. It is often misleading to judge the river level at the put in, since a small rise in a wide, shallow place will be multiplied many times where the river narrows. Use reliable gauge information whenever possible, and be aware that sun on snowpack, hard rain, and upstream dam releases may greatly increase the flow.

B. **COLD** Cold drains your strength and robs you of the ability to make sound decisions on matters affecting your survival. Cold water immersion, because of the initial shock and the rapid heat loss which follows, is especially dangerous. Dress appropriately for bad weather or sudden immersion in the water. When the water temperature is less than 50 degrees F., a wetsuit or drysuit is essential for protection if you swim. Next best is wool or pile clothing under a waterproof shell. In this case, you should also carry waterproof matches and a change of clothing in a waterproof bag. If, after prolonged exposure, a person experiences uncontrollable shaking, loss of coordination, or difficulty speaking, he or she is hypothermic, and needs your assistance.

C. **STRAINERS** Brush, fallen trees, bridge pilings, undercut rocks, or anything else which allows river current to sweep through can pin boats and boaters against the obstacle. Water pressure on anything trapped this way can be overwhelming. Rescue is often extremely difficult. Pinning may occur in fast current, with little or no whitewater to warn of the danger.

D. **DAMS, WEIRS, LEDGES, REVERSALS, HOLES, AND HYDRAULICS** When water drops over a obstacle, it curls back on itself, forming a strong upstream current which may be capable of holding a boat or swimmer. Some holes make for excellent sport. Others are proven killers. Paddlers who cannot recognize the difference should avoid all but the smallest holes. Hydraulics around man-made dams must be treated with utmost respect regardless of their height or the level of the river. Despite their seemingly benign appearance, they can create an almost escape-proof trap. The swimmers only exit from the "drowning machine" is to dive below the surface when the downstream current is flowing beneath the reversal.

E. **BROACHING** When a boat is pushed sideways against a rock by strong current, it may collapse and wrap. This is especially dangerous to kayak and decked-canoe paddlers; these boats will collapse and the combination of indestructible hulls and tight outfitting may create a deadly trap. Even without entrapment, releasing pinned boats can be extremely time-consuming and dangerous. To avoid pinning, throw your weight downstream towards the rock. This allows the current to slide harmlessly underneath the hull.

6. Boating alone is discouraged. The minimum party is three people or two craft.

7. Have a frank knowledge of your boating ability, and don't attempt rivers or rapids which lie beyond that ability.

   Develop the paddling skills and teamwork required to match the river you plan to boat. Most good paddlers develop skills gradually, and attempts to advance too quickly will compromise your safety and enjoyment.

   Be in good physical and mental condition, consistent with the difficulties which may be expected. Make adjustments for loss of skills due to age, health, fitness. Any health limitations must be explained to your fellow paddlers prior to starting the trip.

8. Be practiced in self-rescue, including escape from an overturned craft. The Eskimo roll is strongly recommended for decked boaters who run rapids Class IV or greater, or who paddle in cold environmental conditions.

9. Be trained in rescue skills, CPR, and first aid with special emphasis on the recognizing and treating hypothermia. It may save your friend's life.

10. Carry equipment needed for unexpected emergencies, including footwear which will protect your feet when walking out, a throw rope, knife, whistle, and waterproof matches. If you wear eyeglasses, tie them on and carry a spare pair on long trips. Bring cloth repair tape on short runs, and a full repair kit on isolated rivers. Do not wear bulky jackets, ponchos, heavy boots, or anything else which could reduce your ability to survive a swim.

11. Despite the mutually supportive group structure described in this code, individual paddlers are ultimately responsible for their own safety, and must assume sole responsibility for the following decisions:

   A. The decision to participate on any trip. This includes an evaluation of the expected difficulty of the rapids under the conditions existing at the time of the put-in.

B. The selection of appropriate equipment, including a boat design suited to their skills and the appropriate rescue and survival gear.

C. The decision to scout any rapid, and to run or portage according to their best judgment. Other members of the group may offer advice, but paddlers should resist pressure from anyone to paddle beyond their skills. It is also their responsibility to decide whether to pass up any walk-out or take-out opportunity.

D. All trip participants should consistently evaluate their own and their group's safety, voicing their concerns when appropriate and following what they believe to be the best course of action. Paddlers are encouraged to speak with anyone whose actions on the water are dangerous, whether they are a part of your group or not.

II. Boat and Equipment Preparedness

1. Test new and different equipment under familiar conditions before relying on it for difficult runs. This is especially true when adopting a new boat design or outfitting system. Low volume craft may present additional hazards to inexperienced or poorly conditioned paddlers.

2. Be sure your boat and gear are in good repair before starting a trip. The more isolated and difficult the run, the more rigorous this inspection should be.

3. Install flotation bags in non-inflatable craft, securely fixed in each end, designed to displace as much water as possible. Inflatable boats should have multiple air chambers and be test-inflated before launching.

4. Have strong, properly sized paddles or oars for controlling your craft. Carry sufficient spares for the length and difficulty of the trip.

5. Outfit your boat safely. The ability to exit your boat quickly is an essential component of safety in rapids. It is your responsi-

bility to see that there is absolutely nothing to cause entrapment when coming free of an upset craft. This includes:

A. Spray covers which won't release reliably or which release prematurely.

B. Boat outfitting too tight to allow a fast exit, especially in low-volume kayaks or decked canoes. This includes low-hung thwarts in canoes lacking adequate clearance for your feet and kayak footbraces which fail or allow your feet to become wedged under them.

C. Inadequately supported decks which collapse on a paddler's legs when a decked boat is pinned by water pressure. Inadequate clearance with the deck because of your size or build.

D. Loose ropes which cause entanglement. Beware of any length of loose line attached to a whitewater boat. All items must be tied tightly and excess line eliminated; painters, throw lines, and safety rope systems must be completely and effectively stored. Do not knot the end of a rope, as it can get caught in cracks between rocks.

6. Provide ropes which permit you to hold on to your craft so that it may be rescued. The following methods are recommended:

A. Kayaks and covered canoes should have grab loops of 1/4-inch (or more) rope or equivalent webbing sized to admit a normal-sized hand. Stern painters are permissible if properly secured.

B. Open canoes should have securely anchored bow and stern painters consisting of 8 to 10 feet of 1/4-inch (or more) line. These must be secured in such a way that they are readily accessible, but cannot come loose accidentally. Grab loops are acceptable, but are more difficult to reach after an upset.

C. Rafts and dories may have taut perimeter lines threaded through the loops provided. Footholds should be designed so that a paddler's feet cannot be forced through them, causing entrapment. Flip lines should be carefully and reliably stowed.

7. Know your craft's carrying capacity, and how added loads affect boat handling in whitewater. Most rafts have a minimum crew size which can be added to on day trips or in easy rapids. Carrying more than two paddlers in an open canoe when running rapids is not recommended.

8. Car-top racks must be strong and attach positively to the vehicle. Lash your boat to each crossbar, then tie the ends of the boat directly to the bumpers for added security. This arrangement should survive all but the most violent vehicle accident.

III. Group Preparedness and Responsibility

1. Organization. A river trip should be regarded as a common adventure by all participants, except on instructional or commercially guided trips as defined below. Participants share the responsibility for the conduct of the trip, and each participant is individually responsible for judging his or her own capabilities and for his or her own safety as the trip progresses. Participants are encouraged (but are not obligated) to offer advice and guidance for the independent consideration and judgment of others.

2. River Conditions. The group should have a reasonable knowledge of the difficulty of the run. Participants should evaluate this information and adjust their plans accordingly. If the run is exploratory or no one is familiar with the river, maps and guidebooks, if available, should be examined. The group should secure accurate flow information; the more difficult the run, the more important this will be. Be aware of possible changes in river level and how this will affect the difficulty of the run. If the trip involves tidal stretches, secure appropriate information on tides.

3. Group equipment should be suited to the difficulty of the river. The group should always have a throw line available, and one line per boat is recommended on difficult runs. The list may include: carabiners, prussick loops, first-aid kit, flashlight, folding saw, fire starter, guidebooks, maps, food, extra cloth-

ing, and any other rescue or survival items suggested by conditions. Each item is not required on every run, and this list is not meant to be a substitute for good judgment.

4. Keep the group compact, but maintain sufficient spacing to avoid collisions. If the group is large, consider dividing into smaller groups or using the "buddy system" as an additional safeguard. Space yourselves closely enough to permit good communication, but not so close as to interfere with one another in rapids.

A. A point paddler sets the pace. When in front, do not get in over your head. Never run drops when you cannot see a clear route to the bottom or, for advanced paddlers, a sure route to the next eddy. When in doubt, stop and scout.

B. Keep track of all group members. Each boat keeps the one behind it in sight, stopping if necessary. Know how many people are in your group and take head counts regularly. No one should paddle ahead or walk out without first informing the group. Paddlers requiring additional support should stay at the center of a group, and not allow themselves to lag behind in the more difficult rapids. If the group is large and contains a wide range of abilities, a Sweep Boat may be designated to bring up the rear.

C. Courtesy. On heavily used rivers, do not cut in front of a boater running a drop. Always look upstream before leaving eddies to run or play. Never enter a crowded drop or eddy when no room for you exists. Passing other groups in a rapid may be hazardous: it's often safer to wait upstream until the group ahead has passed.

5. Float plan. If the trip is into a wilderness area or for an extended period, plans should be filed with a responsible person who will contact the authorities if you are overdue. It may be wise to establish checkpoints along the way where civilization could be contacted if necessary. Knowing the location of possible help and preplanning escape routes can speed rescue.

6. Drugs. The use of alcohol or mind-altering drugs before or

during river trips is not recommended. It dulls reflexes, reduces decision-making ability, and may interfere with important survival reflexes.

7. Instructional or Commercially Guided Trips. In contrast to the common adventure-trip format, in these trip formats, a boating instructor or commercial guide assumes some of the responsibilities normally exercised by the group as a whole, as appropriate under the circumstances. These formats recognize that instructional or commercially guided trips may involve participants who lack significant experience in whitewater. However, as a participant acquires experience in whitewater, he or she takes on increasing responsibility for his or her own safety, in accordance with what he or she knows or should know as a result of that increased experience. Also, as in all trip formats, every participant must realize and assume the risks associated with the serious hazards of whitewater rivers. It is advisable for instructors and commercial guides or their employers to acquire trip or personal liability insurance:

A. An "instructional trip" is characterized by a clear teacher/pupil relationship, where the primary purpose of the trip is to teach boating skills, and which is conducted for a fee.

B. A "commercially guided trip" is characterized by a licensed, professional guide conducting trips for a fee.

IV. Guidelines for River Rescue

1. Recover from an upset with an Eskimo roll whenever possible. Evacuate your boat immediately if there is imminent danger of being trapped against rocks, brush, or any other kind of strainer.

2. If you swim, hold on to your boat. It has much flotation and is easy for rescuers to spot. Get to the upstream end so that you cannot be crushed between a rock and your boat by the force of the current. Persons with good balance may be able to climb on top of a swamped kayak or flipped raft and paddle to shore.

3. Release your craft if this will improve your chances, especially

if the water is cold or dangerous rapids lie ahead. Actively attempt self-rescue whenever possible by swimming for safety. Be prepared to assist others who may come to your aid.

A. When swimming in shallow or obstructed rapids, lie on your back with feet held high and pointed downstream. Do not attempt to stand in fast-moving water; if your foot wedges on the bottom, fast water will push you under and keep you there. Get to slow or very shallow water before attempting to stand or walk. Look ahead! Avoid possible pinning situations including undercut rocks, strainers, downed trees, holes, and other dangers by swimming away from them.

B. If the rapids are deep and powerful, roll over onto your stomach and swim aggressively for shore. Watch for eddies and slackwater and use them to get out of the current. Strong swimmers can effect a powerful upstream ferry and get to shore fast. If the shores are obstructed with strainers or undercut rocks, however, it is safer to "ride the rapid out" until a safer escape can be found.

4. If others spill and swim, go after the boaters first. Rescue boats and equipment only if this can be done safely. While participants are encouraged (but not obligated) to assist one another to the best of their ability, they should do so only if they can, in their judgment, do so safely. The first duty of a rescuer is not to compound the problem by becoming another victim.

5. The use of rescue lines requires training; uninformed use may cause injury. Never tie yourself into either end of a line without a reliable quick-release system. Have a knife handy to deal with unexpected entanglement. Learn to place set lines effectively, to throw accurately, to belay effectively, and to properly handle a rope thrown to you.

6. When reviving a drowning victim, be aware that cold water may greatly extend survival time underwater. Victims of hypothermia may have depressed vital signs so they look and feel dead. Don't give up; continue CPR for as long as possible without compromising safety.

V. Universal River Signals

These signals may be substituted with an alternate set of signals agreed upon by the group.

STOP: Potential hazard ahead. Wait for "all clear" signal before proceeding, or scout ahead. Form a horizontal bar with your outstretched arms. Those seeing the signal should pass it back to others in the party.

HELP/EMERGENCY: Assist the signaler as quickly as possible. Give three long blasts on a police whistle while waving a paddle, helmet, or life vest over your head. If a whistle is not available, use the visual signal alone. A whistle is best carried on a lanyard attached to your life vest.

ALL CLEAR: Come ahead (in the absence of other directions proceed down the center). Form a vertical bar with your paddle or one arm held high above your head. Paddle blade should be turned flat for maximum visibility. To signal direction or a preferred course through a rapid around obstruction, lower the previously vertical "all clear" by 45 degrees toward the side of the river with the preferred route. Never point toward the obstacle you wish to avoid.

I'M OK: I'm OK and not hurt. While holding the elbow outward toward the side, repeatedly pat the top of your head.

VI. International Scale of River Difficulty

This is the American version of a rating system used to compare river difficulty throughout the world. This system is not exact; rivers do not always fit easily into one category, and regional or individual interpretations may cause misunderstandings. It is no substitute for a guidebook or accurate first-hand descriptions of a run.

Paddlers attempting difficult runs in an unfamiliar area should act cautiously until they get a feel for the way the scale is interpreted locally. River difficulty may change each year due to fluctuations in water level, downed trees, recent floods, geological disturbances, or bad weather. Stay alert for unexpected problems!

As river difficulty increases, the danger to swimming paddlers becomes more severe. As rapids become longer and more continuous, the challenge increases. There is a difference between running an occasional Class IV rapid and dealing with an entire river of this category. Allow an extra margin of safety between skills and river ratings when the water is cold or if the river itself is remote and inaccessible.

The Six Difficulty Classes

Class I: Easy. Fast-moving water with riffles and small waves. Few obstructions, all obvious and easily missed with little training. Risk to swimmers is slight; self-rescue is easy.

Class II: Novice. Straightforward rapids with wide, clear channels which are evident without scouting. Occasional maneuvering may be required, but rocks and medium-sized waves are easily missed by trained paddlers. Swimmers are seldom injured and group assistance, while helpful, is seldom needed. Rapids that are at the upper end of this difficulty range are designated "Class II+".

Class III: Intermediate. Rapids with moderate, irregular waves which may be difficult to avoid and which can swamp an open canoe. Complex maneuvers in fast current and good boat control in tight passages or around ledges are often required; large waves or strainers may be present but are easily avoided. Strong eddies and powerful current effects can be found, particularly on large-volume rivers. Scouting is advisable for inexperienced parties. Injuries while swimming are rare; self-rescue is usually easy but group assistance may be required to avoid long swims. Rapids that are at the lower or upper end of this difficulty range are designated "Class III-" or "Class III+" respectively.

Class IV: Advanced. Intense, powerful but predictable rapids requiring precise boat handling in turbulent water. Depending on the character of the river, it may feature large, unavoidable waves and holes or constricted passages demanding fast maneuvers under pressure. A fast, reliable eddy turn may be needed to initiate maneuvers, scout rapids, or rest.

Rapids may require "must" moves above dangerous hazards. Scouting may be necessary the first time down. Risk of injury to swimmers is moderate to high, and water conditions may make self-rescue difficult. Group assistance for rescue is often essential but requires practiced skills. A strong Eskimo roll is highly recommended. Rapids that are at the lower or upper end of this difficulty range are designated "Class IV-" or "Class IV+" respectively.

Class V: Expert. Extremely long, obstructed, or very violent rapids which expose a paddler to added risk. Drops may contain large, unavoidable waves and holes or steep, congested chutes with complex, demanding routes. Rapids may continue for long distances between pools, demanding a high level of fitness. What eddies exist may be small, turbulent, or difficult to reach. At the high end of the scale, several of these factors may be combined. Scouting is recommended but may be difficult. Swims are dangerous, and rescue is often difficult even for experts. A very reliable Eskimo roll, proper equipment, extensive experience, and practiced rescue skills are essential. Because of the large range of difficulty that exists beyond Class IV, Class 5 is an open-ended, multiple-level scale designated by Class 5.0, 5.1, 5.2, etc. Each of these levels is an order of magnitude more difficult than the last. Example: increasing difficulty from Class 5.0 to Class 5.1 is a similar order of magnitude as increasing from Class IV to Class 5.0.

Class VI: Extreme and Exploratory. These runs have almost never been attempted and often exemplify the extremes of difficulty, unpredictability, and danger. The consequences of errors are very severe and rescue may be impossible. For teams of experts only, at favorable water levels, after close personal inspection and taking all precautions. After a Class VI rapids has been run many times, its rating may be changed to an appropriate Class V rating.

AMC and the Relicensing of Hydroelectric Dams

AMC has been both a regional and national leader in the relicensing of hydroelectric dams. The waters of our rivers are publicly owned. Hydroelectric dams may be granted a license to dam and divert water to generate power for thirty to fifty years. In effect, the dam owner is a tenant, and the public is the landlord.

Thanks, in part, to efforts by the AMC, a federal law passed in 1986 requires that during the licensing process the Federal Energy Regulatory Commission (FERC) must now consider a river's environmental and recreational value on an equal basis with its value as a power source when it issues the terms of a new hydro-dam license.

Dams frequently reduce water quality, block fish movement, flood out boating opportunities, and at times turn flows on and off like a faucet spigot. When hydro dams were licensed over a half-century ago they had to meet few standards. Many of these original licenses are or will soon come due for renewal for new thirty- to fifty-year licenses. The AMC works hard to achieve updated license conditions during these renewals. This includes mitigation for dams' impacts on river's recreational opportunities and ecosystems as well as a better balance of priorities.

The AMC has been a successful leader in achieving considerable gains in river protection both through the relicensing process and by negotiating settlement agreements with willing dam owners. The AMC helped pioneer major relicensing settlements on the Kennebec, Androscoggin, Rapid, Connecticut, and Deerfield Rivers to name a few. Today more than 40,000 acres of protected river shorefront, improved flows in several hundred miles of river, and guaranteed water releases for whitewater boating, plus over $20 million in river enhancement funds have resulted from the AMC's work.

Ken Kimball

Index

About the AMC

Since 1876, the Appalachian Mountain Club has helped people experience the majesty and solitude of the Northeast outdoors. We offer outdoor skills workshops, guided trips, and lodging options for all levels of outdoor adventuring. Our programs include trail maintenance, air and water quality research,  and conservation advocacy work to preserve the special outdoor places we love and enjoy for future generations.

Join the Club!

Take a hike, ride a bike, paddle a canoe. We believe that people who enjoy climbing mountains, splashing in streams, and walking on trails have more fun and take better care of the outdoors. Join the fun today. Call 617-523-0636 or visit www.outdoors.org for membership information. AMC members receive discounts on workshops, lodging, and books.

Outdoor Adventures

From beginner backpacking to advanced backcountry skiing to guided hiking and paddling trips, we teach outdoor skills workshops to suit your interest and experience. Our outdoor education centers guarantee year-round adventures. View our entire listing of workshops online at www.outdoors.org.

Huts, Lodges, and Visitor Centers

With accommodations throughout the Northeast, you don't have to travel to the ends of the earth to experience unique wilderness lodging. Accessible by car or on foot, our lodges and huts are perfect for families, couples, groups, and individuals. For reservations call 800-262-4455.

Books and Maps

We can lead you to the best hiking, biking, skiing, and paddling destinations from Maine to North Carolina. With more than fifty books and maps published, we're your definitive resource for discovering wonderful outdoor places. To receive a free catalog call 800-262-4455 or visit our online store at www.outdoors.org.

Contact Us

Appalachian Mountain Club
5 Joy Street
Boston, MA 02108-1490
617-523-0636
www.outdoors.org

Leave No Trace

The Appalachian Mountain Club is a national educational partner of Leave No Trace, Inc., a nonprofit organization dedicated to promoting and inspiring responsible outdoor recreation through education, research, and partnerships. The Leave No Trace Program seeks to develop wildland ethics—ways in which  people think and act in the outdoors to minimize their impacts on the areas they visit and to protect our natural resources for future enjoyment. Leave No Tracè unites four federal land management agencies—the U.S. Forest Service, National Park Service, Bureau of Land Management, and U.S. Fish and Wildlife Service—with manufacturers, outdoor retailers, user groups, educators, organizations like the AMC and the National Outdoor Leadership School (NOLS), and individuals.

The Leave No Trace ethic is guided by these seven principles:

- Plan ahead and prepare.
- Travel and camp on durable surfaces.
- Dispose of waste properly.
- Leave what you find.
- Minimize campfire impacts.
- Respect wildlife.
- Be considerate of other visitors.

The AMC has joined NOLS—a recognized leader in wilderness education and a founding partner of Leave No Trace—as the sole national providers of the Leave No Trace Master Educator course through 2004. The AMC offers this five-day course, designed especially for outdoor professionals and land managers, as well as the shorter two-day Leave No Trace Trainer course, at locations throughout the northeastern United States.

For Leave No Trace information and materials, contact:

Leave No Trace, Inc.
P.O. Box 997
Boulder, CO 80306
800-332-4100
www.LNT.org

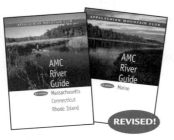
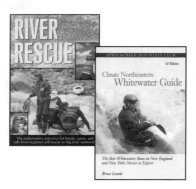